Rebellious

Women Who Broke the Rules and Changed Their World

Dr. Sam Collins

Dedication

*To my husband Robert who found a way to love
a rebellious woman.*

Contents

Preface 1

Chapter One
The Promise - Dr. Sam Collins, USA 9

Chapter Two
Girls are like Goats - Sister Zeph, Pakistan 40

Chapter Three
Hamilah - Zareen Ahmed, UK 58

Chapter Four
Free to be Fearless - Lilly Lewis, UK..................................77

Chapter Five
Job of a Lifetime 104

Chapter Six
Kadama - Awah Francisca Mbuli, Cameroon....................121

Chapter Seven
Shooting Stars - Destiny Ayo Vaughan, Ireland.................149

Chapter Eight
Ray of Sunshine - Pip Hare, UK 169

Chapter Nine
Step by Step - Nasreen Sheikh, Nepal...............................189

Chapter Ten
Crossing the Bridge - Ibtissam Al-Farah, Yemen...............208

Chapter Eleven
Spandex Gate - Jen Coken, USA 227

Chapter Twelve
Twelve Miles - Sarah Kitakule, Uganda.............................242

Chapter Thirteen
Bad Mother - Karen Sherman, USA...................................255

Chapter Fourteen
Motherboards - Eileen Brewer, Iraq 277

Chapter Fifteen

Choose Life - Aletta Raju, South Africa 295

Chapter Sixteen

Amazing Grace 307

Meet the Rebellious Women.. 326

PREFACE

Deep into the Covid-19 pandemic, I attended a virtual conference where Gloria Steinem was interviewed. The moderator asked her a question that went something like: "What do women need to do right now?"

In her beautiful genius, Gloria simply said, "Women need to be less grateful and more rebellious."

In that moment, as I madly wrote it down, something ignited in me. I wanted to do something about it. I wanted to be more rebellious myself. I wanted to take part in the rebellion that is happening right now across the globe.

So, what is it about being rebellious that I hope to convey in this book?

As a child, and throughout my adult life, I have always challenged authority. When I was six years old, my mum wanted to buy me a pair of rain boots. She selected the blue ones for practicality. I chose the bright red ones. I took them to bed with me every night, so they were always in my sights. They were my rebel boots, and I was brave and powerful when I wore them.

I don't know that I would have used the word 'rebellious' to describe myself, but I suppose I am. I've been told I am irritating, difficult, and hard to live with. I'm not one to scream and shout, necessarily. I'm not even one to get out and march, I'll admit. Yet, I cannot help challenging authority when it is clearly in the wrong—I can't stop myself. And parents, teachers, bosses, CEOs, and government leaders have never scared me.

I remember my dad saying to me at an early age, whenever I was confronted with doubts or tempted to compare my power to someone else's power: "They are no better than you, Sam. You have a voice. Always remember that they are no better than you."

This is the foundation of true rebellion.

Surely enough, I still find myself in situations often challenging the norms and encouraging others to do so, especially women. Women's leadership and equality is my passion and my work for the past 21 years. I founded an organization called Aspire and I speak, write, and lead events and conferences for women around the world.

When I looked up the definition of rebellious, here's what I found: People who are rebellious are people who like to break rules. They resist authority, control, or convention that they oppose in authority or dominance.

Rebellion, of course, is a collective resistance, often to an established institutional system. It is an act of defiance, a countercultural act against a system that has either stopped serving people equally or realized that it never did serve people equally.

Whether the system takes the form of expectations of women in the home, family, or culture; whether the system is how women as managers and leaders are expected to be or not to be; whether it is our government systems or our business systems that impact climate change, equality, poverty, homelessness, race, gender identity, and sexuality; whether the system is our organizations that are even today run as traditional, patriarchal, male dominant organisms.

These organisms, when they are not growing and evolving the way organisms are supposed to do by increasing efficiency and service to the harmony of all life, rebellion is the natural and normal catalyst to change.

Everything is being challenged today. Isn't that exciting? Many of us are clamoring to find our place. How are we part of this? What should we do? What does this look like for us? What is the risk involved to ourselves and to future generations on this planet?

In some ways, this book is Part Two to my first book, Radio Heaven, where I left the readers in the jubilant place of having finally found my adopted daughter Grace in the Democratic Republic of Congo, but not how we got her home. So many people have come up to me at my Aspire events and conferences who ask me the same question: What happened next?

I always smile and say that Grace did finally come to us and she's doing great. Until now, I've never told the whole story or shared what really happened, because it was terrible, and heart breaking, and it took such a long time.

We often gloss over things, don't we? Did she arrive? How is she? Yeah, she's fine, she's great. Come here, look at my phone. Here's a picture of her. Isn't she beautiful? Blah, blah, blah. I may have made it sound easy, but there were many times when I didn't believe it would happen. And there were times—many times—when I nearly gave up.

When people would say to me, are you going to write another book? I would say, "No, one book is enough! I'm not a writer." Besides, if I ever did write another book, I would joke about calling it Radio Hell or perhaps Radio Silence!

So, for the first time, I'm sharing the story of how Grace came to us, the toll it took on me, on my family, on my health, and on my marriage. I found myself dropped into the middle of an actual rebellion in Congo with a gun to my head, believing my life was over.

As there is in many of our lives, there was a dominant man, the president of Congo at that time, who made a hell out of Grace's life and my life and the lives of so many of his fellow citizens. It was up to me to challenge the norm, to challenge his authority. Doing something every single day that would bring this adopted daughter of ours to her new home.

And I'm not alone.

Dr. Sam Collins 3

Quiet, untold, rebellion is happening right now everywhere. Often, we don't speak of it before it arrives, we only speak of the final successes. Then, we measure the triumph only by how many people hear about it. We don't speak much of the journeys and the difficulty of that path that got us there.

For hundreds of years now, thousands in some places, women who are rebellious have been ridiculed, vilified, imprisoned, or institutionalized, burned at the stake, and killed. Women that break rules, speak out and go against the norm are laughed at in the least, and murdered at the worst.

Recently, the bias against women has become underground, hasn't it? They now call it unconscious bias. As if unconscious behavior is an unwritten pass on bad behavior. We're told to settle down. Don't be emotional. Don't be so aggressive. Have more presence. Where's your assertiveness?

We're told to be grateful, to "look how far we've come." Twenty percent of women hold senior levels now—used to be ten—aren't we doing well?

We're encouraged to focus on other things. Focus on motherhood first, focus on your career and job first, then you can follow your true passions. Retirement, time to settle down, time to quiet down, time to wind down, time to die. Yet rebelliousness is growing. Women are saying no. We've had enough. We are sick of conforming to a model of perfection which is impossible to attain. We are refusing to believe that it is our fault, that we need to change who we are.

This time, the book is not only about me, but about the rebellious women I know—my rebellious friends that I have met through my organization, Aspire. From the UK to the USA, to Pakistan, to Ireland, Nepal and across the globe. My friends, whom I admire deeply, are rebelling in different ways, in different forms, in different countries with different causes, every day.

I didn't want this to be an academic case-study book of these women. I wanted to be able to truly reflect who they are, what they do. So these stories are told by me in their voices and written by me in the first person. I want you to be able to hear their voices, feel their fear and their joy, and understand their path. I want you to be able to extract their advice, the tools, the tips, the understanding, the inspiration, and the motivation to follow through on your rebellion. All the stories are completely and utterly true and often quite unbelievable. No Hollywood fluff, no composite stories, no "based upon actual events."

In some of the stories, the names have been changed to protect the storyteller. These are not famous women. I'm sure you would not have heard of many of these women before. To have a platform to share their stories is my privilege, it's an honor. It's also terrifying because I wanted to make sure I got it right, to reflect them well. I am sharing their Radio Hell and their Radio Silence.

Some of their stories might not be easy to read. I am addressing many gender equality subjects that are increasingly taboo. Some of it is shocking to know that it is still happening now. From human trafficking to sexual abuse, to religious persecution, to motherhood, feminism, and being in prison.

My advice is to read each chapter and then have a break. Breathe and think about the story you have read before you move to the next one. At the end of their stories, I offer my own reflections and a call to action for you.

I'm a born Brit, a Londoner who has been living in the US since 2006. My ancestors are from Belarus, Romania, and Ireland and I have traveled to most places. I consider myself a global citizen. I've chosen to write and spell this book in American English. Although, I still can't bring myself to do it for certain words—so the word "mom" is usually rendered in the UK version "mum."

Dr. Sam Collins 5

More importantly, I wanted to explore what makes rebellious women persevere. What makes a woman rebel when everyone and everything around them tells them not to? What makes a nine year old girl from India escape her village? What makes a 40-something sail around the world on her own? How did they follow through? How did they keep going? What's happening to them now? How do they feel about it? What's their advice? Would they do it again? What were the turning points?

This book is about the moments when we make a life changing decision. Like the woman who was in a psychiatric hospital and about to go to prison. She woke up in her bed one day and felt... Love... for the first time, she felt something bigger than herself and decided to completely turn her life around.

All these women believed that they were at odds with others, they felt different somehow. And it was often a curse to them. They all said in one way or another that others thought they were foolish and irrational, including those closest to them. For all of them, it's taken time — in many cases, a long time — to achieve the things that they wanted to achieve. It wasn't the instant quick fix the self-help industry would have us believe.

Despite their adversity, these women are happy and content with their lives. They are grateful for their rebellious experiences and are thriving as a result. They each share their own unique formula for rebellion and demonstrate a powerful link between self-care, personal confidence, and joy in their lives. They did not suffer their way through their rebellions.

Ultimately, their rebellion saved them. And in many cases, saved many others consequently.

I want you to know that you're not alone in your rebelliousness. That there are many of us out there who are as rebellious as you.

I hope this book gives you a big dose of rebelliousness. I hope it reminds you of who you are and that you are part of a wonderful community of rebellious women around the world. That being difficult is a badge of honor. That whether you are thinking about something new, or doing something different, or you're in the middle of it and stuck, or scared, or procrastinating, or coming towards the end of a particular path and know it's time to reinvent—know this: rebelliousness is your friend.

Here's your opportunity to question, to do something different, to break the rules, to make a difference, to change yourself and the world.

Rebellious

Women Who Broke the Rules and Changed Their World

CHAPTER ONE

The Promise

In the Words of

Dr. Sam Collins, Founder, Aspire, USA

It was January 2015 and I was sitting alone in Addis Ababa Airport, Ethiopia waiting for my connecting flight to Kinshasa, when I opened Facebook.

Why is everyone praying for me?

I had flown from Los Angeles with a quick stop over in London to look for a venue for my next Aspire conference and then on to see my darling Grace in the Democratic Republic of Congo for her sixth birthday.

My stomach lurched. I was hoping this visit would be different than the last one...

On September 25, 2013, two weeks after we had found our adopted daughter Grace, the President of the Democratic Republic of Congo had unceremoniously put an indefinite suspension on all international adoptions. Always the optimists, Robert, my husband, and I proceeded with the adoption. We had already been through the Congolese courts and held our legal adoption papers, but even with adoption papers, the Congolese government refused to grant exit visas for any children to fly out of the country. Grace, and 400 other children like her, could not leave the DRC, even though they had legally adoptive parents all over the globe wanting nothing more than to give them a home.

I remember in my early research, an adoptive mother telling me international adoption was "not for the faint of heart." I had chuckled back at her, assuring her that I was a tough person. Little did I know, this journey would test me to my absolute limit.

Grace seemed fairly settled in her orphanage. Robert had visited her, and we were beginning to build a bond. Updates were scarce and we were in a holding pattern. One day, our adoption agency informed us Grace was no longer at her original orphanage. It had been closed overnight and the kids had been 'rehomed' into another orphanage. No reason was given, and the kids had been scattered across Kinshasa.

For weeks, and then months, there were none of the usual updates we'd come to rely on. No photographs, no Skype calls, only a handful of emails saying she was doing fine, whatever that meant.

Sometimes it is easier to accept a difficult situation. To cope and survive and do what we believe is our best. Time ticks by and we tell ourselves that this is all we can do, all we can control. Yet, my intuition that all was not right was kicking into full gear.

The only way you will know what's happening is to go.

Yes, but ... what about the money, the time, not to mention the anguish? Protect yourself.

Ever practical, I tagged a weeklong trip to DRC onto an Aspire-UK business trip and off I went.

When I landed in Addis Ababa in Ethiopia, the last pit stop on the way to DRC, my concern was eclipsed by my excitement over seeing Grace again and the adventure of visiting Africa.

I arrived at the new orphanage, and I knew at once why my intuition had kicked in so strongly. Initially, I was pleased, the outside building seemed better and sturdier than the former place. It was well kept and painted in bright colors. Looks can be deceiving.

I went in and found Grace, and at least 20 other children, sitting in a dark room watching a small television in the corner of the room. The thick, rank smell of urine filled the air in that cramped space. The children were quiet and zoned out—not a good sign for 20 kids together. I squinted to adjust to the light. Where was she? Something was very wrong here.

I felt scared. I desperately looked for her and tried to maintain my composure. It was a depressing mess. I saw a girl I thought I recognized. Honestly, I was maybe 60 percent sure it was Grace. I smiled, hugged her, and walked out into the light. She was thin and weak looking and had been trapped in that room for much too long of a time. She barely recognized me. In fact, she seemed oddly surprised to see me, even though I had been told repeatedly by the orphanage staff how much she was looking forward to my visit.

I had a wave of guilt. Why did I not come sooner?

Before coming, I had promised one of the other adoptive mothers I would check on her child and send news while I was there. I couldn't find the little girl in that room or anywhere around the orphanage. I asked various staff about her. Eventually, they told me she was sick and at a local medical clinic. I was told that she was doing fine. But I had promised a fellow mother I would check on her daughter and that is exactly what I had to do.

I asked if I might visit her and was given directions to the medical clinic. At that moment, perhaps my focus should have been exclusively on Grace, my skinny little girl, the one screaming at me with her eyes, "Please don't leave me here!" Yet, something told me I had to investigate what was happening with the other child.

I grabbed Grace by the hand, and we walked the road to the clinic together. It was hot and noisy and, of course, everyone stared at us. When we arrived, I recognized how generous it was to call it a medical clinic, more of a shed on the side of the road. We walked inside and I asked the receptionist about my friend's little girl, saying Grace was her friend and wished to visit. The receptionist told me she didn't know if she was there, and we could wait while she looked for her.

We waited for three hours. Grace was getting hungry, I was already tired, and I wondered if we had done enough or if we were wasting our precious time together. I told myself to give up and take Grace back to the mission where I was staying, clean her up, have some food, share some hugs. I had done what I could.

Since we didn't seem to be creating a fuss, the receptionist took a break. This was my window of opportunity. I stood up, left Grace happily playing on my phone, and went to look for the girl myself.

Turning a corner behind the reception desk at the entrance, I was confronted with a bucket on the floor, filled with what looked like blood and body parts. There was so much blood covering the floor. I am not the best with blood, and I felt my airplane meal coming back up. Had I stepped into a weird horror movie? I was scared. I had no idea what was going on there. I didn't think I wanted to know more. I was conscious that it was none of my business and I was not meant to be there anyway, but I kept going.

As I looked around, I could not find the little girl anywhere. In fact, I could not see anyone at all. Eerily empty beds with IV drips hanging, blowing in the hot breeze coming in through the open windows. It looked like everyone had left in a hurry. The girl was gone, and I didn't want to stay any longer than necessary. I hurried back to reception, once again taking Grace by the hand, and walking quickly back down the road to the orphanage.

Magically, the girl in our absence had somehow reappeared back at the orphanage, looking as weak and frail as Grace and the rest of the children. When I asked, she said she had been at the medical clinic and that they had "taken her blood." What could they be doing with these kids? I gave her a bag of treats and toys that I had reserved for Grace and vowed that I would make sure she got out of there one day (she did, by the way)!

I tried my best to settle the girl in as comfortably as possible so she could rest, but all my instincts were now telling me to leave. I took Grace outside and told her we would be leaving together so she should collect her things and bring whatever she wanted. She didn't want to bring anything. Nothing. Not even the many things we had sent her over the last months, which I rightly assumed she no longer had in her possession to bring.

On the way out, I recognized a new washing machine on the porch still in its packaging. All the well-meaning adoptive parents had raised funds back in the USA and sent that machine for the children to have clean clothing. I asked someone why it was not being used and they said it was to be sold.

We left. I carried Grace as she didn't have the strength to walk very far, and she loved the close contact. As her legally adoptive mother I was allowed to take her out of the orphanage and she could stay with me for the duration of my visit, after which she should be returned to the orphanage. With no exit visas being issued there was no way to take her back to the US with me. She had the visa to enter the US, but she could not get out of DRC.

We had been through so much already. Extensive paperwork, home checks by social workers, interviews, medical checks, financial checks—the works, all for the US government. Then, that same paperwork and checks were required by the Congolese government on top of a lengthy court process with a legal representative in the Congo. They call it, "pregnancy by paperwork." Everything had been done. We were her legal parents. All she needed was an exit visa to leave the Congo and they had been suspended.

I knew there was no way I wanted her to return to that orphanage—but what was I going to do now?

I was concerned about her health. After a clean-up and a good meal, as Robert and I had done on other visits, I took Grace for a health check up with a Congolese friend who worked at the hospital in Kinshasa. He was an old PhD student of one of the dads at school back home.

Grace seemed so somber, so world weary, and she didn't speak any English, so it was difficult to know what she was feeling. I have always struggled with languages so I could not speak her dialect. Thankfully, we had a very kind translator named Felix.

While sitting in the hospital waiting room, I asked Felix to inquire how she had liked the new orphanage. A long conversation started between them. He looked very concerned the entire time Grace was talking and was clearly not giving me the whole translation. I asked him how she was, he said she was "okay."

"She's not okay," I said. I looked at him sternly and demanded the truth.

"She doesn't like this orphanage," he said. Taking a few moments as if to assess his loyalties, he said, "she says, every night, two older girls are kicking her around, as if she was a ball. Kicking her from one side of the room to the other. They laugh like it is a game."

I tried to retain my composure. As Grace spoke to Felix, her voice barely a whisper, I saw a flash of flame, a light behind her eyes. I witnessed her rebellious spirit arising in her right in front of me. And it was wonderful. I could feel and see my beautiful girl. She might not have been able to stop this abuse, but she would retain her spirit.

"Apparently, these girls are older and have lived at the orphanage their entire lives," Felix explained. "They are too old to be adopted and they now work at the orphanage. When they heard Grace was going to be adopted and go to America, they became jealous."

I was out of my depth. What could I do? Would I need to move here to be with her until this government suspension passed? Would it ever pass?

God, I hate this.

I felt wretched. I was at the end of my rope. Completely and utterly without hope. There was a moment when time stopped, I was without any control with no ideas or plans. Suddenly, a lifeline appeared. Felix slowly said he would speak to his wife—maybe they could take her in temporarily so she would not have to go back to the orphanage. We would have to arrange an official transfer into foster care with all the necessary legal paperwork.

Yes! Yes! Yes! This could be it! Come on, Grace, let's go!

The hospital doctor explained that Grace was recovering from a bad bout of tonsillitis and had a nasty urinary tract infection. She had received no medication or care for either but everything else was fine. I was encouraged by our adoption agency representative to lower my standards and be grateful it wasn't anything more serious.

At last, we all focused on moving Grace into foster care with Felix and his family. While the transfer was not easy, Grace lived with Felix and his family for the next 2 years.

I promised her I would come back.

Those years seemed like an eternity. Robert and I went back and forth to see her the best we could combined with the occasional Skype call when the internet was working in Felix's house. Life went by, my biological sons Jake and Charlie became seven and five and Grace's sixth birthday was coming up. I decided to go and see her to celebrate.

I hoped this time would be a happy visit with lots of fun and getting to know each other, and not another challenging, frightening legal extraction from one home to another.

Thankfully, there was a strong internet signal at the airport in Ethiopia. I opened Facebook on my computer to kill some time between connecting flights. The adoptive parents had set up a Facebook group and we were all very supportive when someone was going for a visit. As I scrolled through my messages and post replies, it began to dawn on me that all the parents were sending me prayers and messages of concern.

I haven't even arrived yet. What the hell is happening?

I quickly realized there was civil unrest cooking in the DRC, political problems with the citizens and the government and the army. People were rioting in the streets. There had been violence against the President, and judging by the tone of the messages, things were escalating.

The first thing I did was call Robert—my love, my go-to, my rock—to discuss the situation. He had already heard about it while I had been flying, of course, and had already contacted the US Embassy as well as our friend who worked at the hospital in Kinshasa who had told him it would be fine, that by the time I arrived the army would have dealt with it.

We were reassured that this had happened before and that this type of unrest wasn't so unusual in DR Congo. Robert trusted our friend, and I trusted Robert. After all, I told myself, I had come all this way, and I would not miss Grace's birthday if I could help it. Everything will be fine!

But as I ran to the plane, I heard a familiar voice in my head... Turn around and go home. Turn around and go home. I ignored it. My heart said proceed. I affirmed that my will and my love for Grace was stronger than any voice of doubt in my head. In fact, I would make this happen. So, although it didn't feel right, I went ahead anyway.

Hey, this is how I operate. And when I arrive at Kinshasa Airport, Grace will be waiting for me. She will run to me. We'll hug tightly. I'll shower her with gifts. We will have a birthday cake with the candles I brought. It will be beautiful!

I could already see it all happening. And no person, no political unrest, nothing was going to stop me. Sometimes, we get our will and our intuition confused. I was forcing the situation, then justifying it all in my mind.

After a pensive 4-hour flight, the plane landed, and I disembarked into the intense heat and now familiar smells of Kinshasa airport. I went through customs, which was always slightly nerve wracking as there had been many stories of adoptive parents being turned away at the border for no reason.

I made my way to the solitary baggage carousel, pumping out bag after bag, hundreds of people crowding around to find their luggage. It was so loud, and I had to adjust to being stared at. A lone white woman with bright red hair was an unusual sight.

"Get your bags," said a helpful woman, shoving me to the front. "There is no line. Force your way!"

At last, I saw my bags—one for me and one for Grace that was crammed full of new clothes, toys, medicine, food, and fun things for us to do over the week of my visit. I grabbed them both and headed over to the arrival area to see my girl. No one was there to meet me.

No worries! Maybe they had been delayed. I found a quiet spot and plopped down on my bags. The bubble of reuniting with Grace at the airport was bursting, but never mind, she would be here soon, and all would be well. I justified it, ignoring the sinking feeling in the pit of my stomach.

After a little while, a man I didn't know arrived, making a beeline toward me. He held a piece of card with my name on it. I supposed being the only white woman had given me away, or my reputation had finally preceded me—who knew?

The man didn't speak much English but managed to tell me there was trouble in the city and Felix had asked him to pick me up instead of bringing Grace to the airport. He explained he would drive me to the Catholic Mission where we normally stayed, and that Grace and Felix were already waiting for me there.

Okay! Relief swept over me. A change of plan. Grace will be at the mission, and I'll be there soon enough. Still no problem. I rationalized that, since there was trouble, this was a safer option. It was certainly understandable that they would not want to bring a child to the airport and expose her to any potential risk of violence along the way. Very smart!

We headed to his minivan in the parking lot and I climbed into the back. It was still day and the car had been baking out in the parking lot, clearly for some time. I began to sweat and I was thankful no one else was in the minivan with me to see it pouring out of me. I settled into my seat and the man closed the sliding door, walked around, and hopped into the driver's side. Immediately, he reclined his seat the whole way back, laying himself flat with a long sigh.

"What are you doing?" I said, confused.

"Trouble," he said. "Safer here."

It was so hot in that minivan, stifling. I had one small bottle of water and a purple fleece jacket that had kept me warm on the air-conditioned flight, now a totally unnecessary accessory. I told myself to settle down, drink my water, and wait it out as advised. The wisdom of this idea was reinforced as I looked out of the window and saw that many other cars with passengers were also staying put. Everyone was hanging back in the relative safety of the airport.

And there we remained, sweating and sighing, for four hours. God! I am so frustrated. I was losing time and it was getting later and later. It was Grace's birthday and all my plans to make it special were slowly dissolving in the back of this toaster oven of a minivan. What would Grace think? I had no control over this situation. I hate having no control.

I checked my phone. I tried to call Felix but the phones were down. That was worrying. That meant I couldn't call Robert to tell him I had arrived and was stuck in the hottest parking lot on earth. I also knew he would be worried about not hearing from me.

Suddenly, there was activity. Someone came by to let my driver know that a DRC Army General was scheduled to fly into the airport. People started to reason that the General would naturally have security. He would be well protected. A plan began to emerge when the General and his entourage left the airport, all the cars in the parking lot would follow along behind him.

And now, somehow, the toaster oven was filling up with people. I didn't have a clue where they had all come from. An eclectic group of locals and a ton of bags, some chickens in a cage, a priest, and a nun—DRC doesn't have tourists.

Soon the General had apparently arrived and was making his way out of the airport. I saw a fancy car and some open air trucks with armed guards with their guns in the air following him. Masses of vehicles began pouring out of the parking lot, ours included. The convoy drove out of the airport—and I'm not kidding—straight into the middle of a riot.

Hordes of angry young men were running all over the street throwing things, pouring gasoline on cars, and lighting them on fire. Trucks were veering crazily, young men piled into the back of them firing guns into the air, or at other people. The anger over General Whoever's presence had created an explosion of violence, the likes of which I had never witnessed, became even more real upon realizing a few of them were following our minivan.

Following the General had made us more vulnerable. Okay, bad plan. Very bad plan. A heated conversation erupted in our vehicle. I could barely understand what was being said, of course, but the gist of it was whether I should get down on the ground and cover my head because, apparently, I was conspicuous.

One person, gesticulating wildly, said, "It is an insult! She is a guest in our country!"

Others argued in unison, "No! Her life is at risk, and she is putting our lives at risk!"

Ridiculously, I wanted to be polite and not offend anyone. I felt so meek but I decided to be brave and take matters into my own hands. I got down on the floor of the minivan, which was burning hot, and covered my head with my purple fleece jacket. That was the end of that conversation.

As it is the ultimate modern distraction, I got on my phone to check any messages. La, la, la, all is well. On the floor of the minivan, in the imaginary safety of my sweaty, purple cocoon, I felt panic rising. I felt a fear that was deeply unfamiliar. I was almost certainly about to die. I was so frightened. What have I done? I'm in a war zone, for Christ's sake. How stupid, how naïve can I be? I want to go home! I want Robert! I want my mum!

Instinct kicked in and I began to get practical. If I am about to die, then I must write something. An appropriate goodbye. I opened the Notes application on my phone. I figured since neither a text nor a call would go through right now, if something happened to me and my phone was found, my sister Emma would conduct a forensic study of my phone and would find this note in my phone and tell Robert. The minivan rocked as it drove through the urban warzone, and my hands shook as adrenaline pumped through my body, I managed to type something out:

Robert, sorry about all this. You are going to need to look after Jake and Charlie now and sorry about Grace. I did my best but some things just don't go how you think. I do love you so much and I'm okay. You can do it without me, you can. Love you all. Jake and Charlie, grow up well and be good people.

Not my best work but it would have to do. I kept my head buried in my jacket for what seemed like an eternity. I could hear noise all around us outside the car, a 'pop-pop-pop' kind of noise. It was gunfire, of course, but it sounded so pathetic. Like kids toys or hundreds of faraway Christmas crackers being pulled. It wasn't at all like the gunfire in movies or television, and yet, it was killing and injuring people on these desperate streets. It was totally and utterly surreal. Hello, I am a girl from sleepy Farnborough in Hampshire, England. I am not designed for this!

The noises faded in and out as the car bumped and swerved. At that moment, the gunfire seemed to diminish. I peeked out from under my jacket. My face appeared in the window of the minivan. We were traveling quickly with a truck racing erratically right alongside us. In the back were three or four young men, all firing guns ahead of them—at the General, I supposed.

I turned my head to look at the truck, and at the same time one of the gun-wielding young men turned his head and his gun, facing me. We locked eyes. He wasn't firing at that moment, the barrel of his rifle pointed directly at my nose only a few feet away, a thin sheet of window glass between us. I looked at him, at the gun, and back at him, and for a short moment I felt—peaceful.

So this is what staring death in the face feels like.

The young man looked at me quizzically as if I wasn't real. As if to say, who is this red-headed white woman, and why is she here? And as crazy as this sounds, I smiled at him.

I had no fear. I was extremely calm. I had no blame or judgment. I could see and feel all that was happening around me. I imagined it must be like this when people say that they see their life flash before their eyes right before they're about to die. Maybe this is what they mean? If this was it, then so be it. I felt at peace with whatever my destiny held.

In a flash, the young man turned his gaze and his gun back forward. The truck sped away and the young man disappeared down the road ahead of us. As I looked out of the minivan, the fear poured back in. Of course, I was in shock and didn't know it. I felt strangely disconnected and viewed everything from a distance. I needed to survive. I was so very frightened. I was numb.

I had escaped death. Outside the scene was bleak. Cars were overturned, some were on fire, a rancid smelling smoke hung in the air punctuated by black billows from the tire fires. People were screaming. It was so loud. People were trampling over others. It was a horror scene.

We continued to drive fast through the chaos. After a while, the streets became clear of people and calmer. My fellow passengers started to settle down. One by one, they left the minivan at their drop off points. We said goodbye, never to see one another again.

At last, I arrived at Procure Saint-Anne, the Catholic mission where Robert and I had stayed when we had individually come to visit Grace. It was now late in the evening. My adrenaline was still pumping from the ride over. I felt nauseous and exhausted as I walked slowly up the steps. I wobbled through the entranceway, and inside the reception area were Grace and Felix.

As happy and relieved as I was to see her, I noted that she looked exhausted. I didn't know if she even knew it was her birthday. I didn't know if she even knew what a birthday was, or who I was, and if she did know who I was, she didn't look very excited to see me. It was after 9 o'clock at night. Goodness only knows how long they had been waiting. My perfect dream visit washed out of me completely. I had tried so hard. I was here. I made it. I wanted a band to start playing and fireworks to begin. Grace looked at me with distaste. All I wanted to do was say, have you any idea what it took for me to get here?

I fought back the tears. And as mothers often do, I managed my biggest smile and my best hug and wished her a happy birthday. Admittedly, it all felt a bit fake, but we needed some kind of birthday celebration, and some kind of cake, and that was my plan. I will, God help me, stick to my plan.

We all walked together to a shop to see if we could find something for a celebration. Grace picked out some chocolate wafer cookies and we walked back to the Mission. Felix said goodbye and we went upstairs to the room for presents and cookies, and perhaps, one of the least fun birthday parties in history.

My next job was to try to get hold of Robert. He must have been beside himself with worry wondering where I was. I tried my phone, no signal. I tried the mission phone, no outgoing calls. I opened my laptop; no email, no Twitter. As a last ditch, I tried Facebook and by a small stroke of good luck, was able to get a weak signal and some news.

What I didn't know at the time was that the President of DRC had shut down all social media within the country; a move calculated to stop the spread of political propaganda and unrest. Somehow Facebook and Skype were working intermittently.

I managed to get a message to Robert, who was so relieved to hear from me. Robert told me the situation in Kinshasa was escalating, and the rioting was getting worse. It was rumored that the President was threatening to cut off food supplies into the city. I wasn't safe and I would need to leave right away. He had already been working on getting me out immediately and arranging flights. I was to expect a call from the U.K. Embassy and then, from the U.S. Embassy, who would explain my options.

Are you kidding me? I've come all this way, survived a riot, finally got to see Grace, barely celebrated her birthday, and now you want me to come home?

Everything he was saying made sense, of course. And I was feeling like a scared child myself.

Why do I always put myself in these kinds of situations? How on earth am I going to get out of this one?

By then, Grace was exhausted so I put her to bed and she fell fast asleep. I walked downstairs from the room to see if I could find something to eat in the bar and dining area. There were some others in the hall, and I recognized one, a reporter, so I sat and tried to eat a little bit and watched the news play out a synopsis of the riot on television. Then a debate started out around the table about what we all should do.

"Yeah, this reminds me of when we had to escape Rwanda during the genocide," said one man from the United Nations, a little too casually.

The reporter, whom I had met some months before, had covered child rape and labor violations in the Congolese mining industry. He said, "Right now, like right now, we should all be crossing the river into Brazzaville!"

The Congo River has notoriously dangerous rapids. And to cross late at night into a different country with a child in tow? I didn't think so. Still, others debated whether the road back to the airport would be safe, you know, the one where I had barely escaped with my life. For a moment, I thought I had fallen into the scene of a bad war movie. What struck me was how jovial everyone appeared. They talked almost as if they were discussing a trip to the park—and why not with a picnic, while we were at it?

I didn't stay long and maybe for the first time ever, I could not eat. When I arrived back at the room, the phone rang almost immediately. It was the British Embassy. I was advised that I should leave. Okay, genius.

"I know I should, but how?" I said.

And the phone went dead.

I tried to think of someone, anyone that I knew, or anyone who knew of anyone who could help me. I remembered a friend and former client in the U.K., another Gillian with a 'G' like my mum. She knew a U.S. Senator personally. Maybe she would help? I managed to get hold of her in the U.K. and she immediately reached out to her friend in the States who immediately messaged me back.

Wow! Women helping women when they need it! How quickly we respond.

While the senator also advised that I leave, she couldn't do much from there. She suggested a few common-sense protocols I could follow. I felt a little better that people knew where I was. I felt less alone. I could hear gunfire outside my windows, and in my imagination, it was rolling closer and closer. Perhaps I would die here, alone in this scary Catholic mission, starved to death, without social media. What a way to go!

Then a small miracle. Robert managed to reach me on Skype, which kept freezing and unfreezing. He said he had been working on getting me a flight out of Kinshasa within 24-hours, and ... Skype disconnected. I looked over and saw Grace sleeping peacefully under her mosquito net across the room, knowing nothing of what was happening.

I decided it was time to try to contact my dad. I knew Robert would have already been in touch with him by now. I managed to connect to him on Skype, and it was a conversation I would never forget. While working for IBM, I knew my dad had spent some time in Northern Ireland during the conflict there, during some of the riots. What I didn't know was how well he had been trained.

"Sam," he said, flatly, "we are not going to get emotional here. We are not even father and daughter here. I am your emergency advisor."

"Yes, Dad," I said, doing my best to listen. And maybe, slightly, to not laugh.

"You need to evacuate this country and here is how you're going to do it: First, you need to make sure Grace is safe and back with her foster family."

"Alright, Dad."

"She cannot come with you. You may never see her again."

"I understand, Dad."

"You will leave at dawn."

"At dawn? Why?"

"Because everyone is either asleep or waking up and drinking their coffee. Riots rarely happen at dawn."

"Okay, Dad."

"Now, go downstairs and find someone who can arrange a car for you with a driver who has protection. They need to come for you at dawn. They will be paid by me, by wire, when you are safely at the airport and your flight has taken off."

I was blown away. Was my dear retired old dad, living in sleepy Somerset in England, some kind of deep-cover MI-5 secret agent or something?

It seemed like a good plan, and my dad had given me even more comfort that things would turn out fine. Go-time was six hours away. So I returned downstairs again to check the television.

The bar was now buzzing with activity. I even found someone else I knew who could arrange a car to get me to the airport. I didn't have a flight, but I was confident my Robert would sort that all out for me, even if I had to wait hours at the airport once I managed to get there. I went back to the room.

The dark of night crept slowly forward. I couldn't eat. I couldn't sleep. I felt nauseous. I looked at Grace, hugged her while she slept, wondering if this was the last time I would see her. I felt quite matter of fact about it. I had reached my limit. I had not signed up for near death. Perhaps she would do better without me? Perhaps, also, the critics who say white people who adopt children of color from Africa should leave them alone are right? What a fool I am.

The electricity kept going in and out, the lights occasionally dimming brown. Mosquitoes buzzed outside the net over our bed. I had never felt so nauseous and tired in my life. My lullaby of gunfire eventually faded out. I wanted to grab Grace and leave so badly. I wanted to run into the arms of my mum, who died when I was 21. Sorry, Mum. I went the wrong way somehow. I've ended up somewhere bad. I don't like it here. I want to go home. Can you come and get me?

My computer buzzed with a message from Robert. He had managed to find flights to get me out. He had been working on it for hours. Oh, my God, I have a flight number! Some small piece of evidence that I would not die today. All I had to do was get back to the airport.

I was able to get hold of Felix, who seemed to understand that I had to leave. We arranged to meet to drop Grace off with him on the way to the airport at dawn. And so the journey home began as the dark of night gave way to dawn. I hadn't unpacked so I was ready when the car arrived with a driver. And, believe me, no one would mess with this guy. My escape had all been arranged around me, thanks to my support network.

Grace had no idea what was going on when she awoke in the car. I'd been with her for only a few short hours. When we arrived at the rendezvous point with Felix, she got out of the car, started crying and completely snubbed me—the woman who keeps coming and going, but mostly going. She walked right across the road to meet her foster mother, turning back to look at me only once with one huge, tragic tear falling down her face. "Why do you keep coming here? Who are you? I want to trust you but I don't get it!" I took a breath and told the driver to go. This wasn't the day Grace would come home with me. Maybe that day would never come. Perhaps this was not meant to be.

I arrived at the airport and we drove into the parking lot. Within 24-hours I had flown in, been smuggled through a riot, thrown the worst birthday party ever, and left as hastily as I had arrived. After several hours of sitting in the same parking lot, I boarded a plane back to Ethiopia. On the plane, I tossed down a well-deserved beer, wondering if I would ever see Grace again. Honestly, at that point, part of me didn't care. It was too hard. It was time to go home, crawl under my bed covers and perhaps never, ever come out.

Back at home in the comfort of my home office I was making plans to interview potential speakers for an upcoming Aspire conference in London. I put out a call for speakers on social media. I always love that part. I love going through the hundreds of responses, which I shortlist based on my intuition. I then speak to each woman I've shortlisted on the phone.

I had been back from DRC for months, and I was certain I was suffering from PTSD. I found it hard to sleep. The riot repeated in my mind, replaying every detail. The guilt I felt about leaving Grace was overwhelming. I was a failure, and I had given up. I knew that I couldn't face going back. I hated myself, so I overworked and ate too much.

I walked through the Santa Monica mountains whenever I could. I would listen to sad songs and cry for Grace. I vowed to her in my mind. I promise, I am coming for you. Wait for me.

We had managed a few Skype calls with Grace, and we were getting regular updates from her foster family. We got a few photos with fake smiles that made her seem so sad, yet also somehow settled. I remember thinking that she had her life and I had mine. Maybe it was time to get on with it. We had all been on hold for so long. Taking no vacations, arranging no family get-togethers. Our total focus on Grace had deprived my other children in many ways. It had now been over two and a half years of waiting and wondering. It was futile. I was confused and completely doubted the silly visualization I'd had at the work retreat where I had seen her in my mind so clearly.

Robert and I settled into another idea, resigned ourselves, that the visa-suspension might never be lifted and so we would sponsor Grace until she became an adult and could leave the DRC of her own free will. It is what it is, I told myself to somehow justify the permanent ache in my heart.

Not many of the other adopting families were campaigning the DRC government anymore, as nothing had worked so far. Even President Obama had apparently tried unsuccessfully to contact their President over the adoption issue.

Some families moved to the DRC, renting apartments to be with their adopted children to guarantee their safety. With Jake and Charlie, that was impossible. Other families had found, shall we say, less conventional ways of extracting their children from the country. We had heard all sorts of stories, ranging from hiring human traffickers to driving across dangerous, contested borders. None of which we could stomach, much less risk.

I found solace in my work. It was when I was deep into interviewing speakers for the next Aspire conference that a woman named Nancy came up next on my list. When we talked, she told me how she had started her own business, a law firm in a city that was extremely male-dominated. I wasn't particularly impressed at that point because lots of us had established ground among male-dominated industries and locales. I probed deeper.

"Tell me more," I said. "What kind of law do you practice?"

Nancy explained how she had started out working for a not-for-profit that helped children, and today her firm specialized in child law, also supporting families with foreign adoptions.

"Where are you from?" My interest was piqued.

"Well, I'm originally from Canada," Nancy said. "But now I live and practice in a city called Kinshasa, in the Democratic Republic of Congo."

Radio Heaven, you sure took your time on this one!

Adrenaline pumping, I explained a little about Grace's situation. Nancy was compassionate and said, without promising anything, she might be able to help. We decided on the spot to send over the adoption paperwork for her team to review. We said goodbye and I slammed the phone down.

"You won't believe this!" I screamed, running down the hallway to Robert.

As promised, our new angel reviewed the paperwork. She discussed everything with her team who began looking at all the legal options and strategies. When that was complete we received a call. They believed that they could help Grace. They wanted to meet her as soon as possible.

There was hope.

When they did meet her, Nancy informed us that, in her view, Grace was undernourished and very likely suffering from depression. She and her team worked to get the appropriate visas. After five weeks, and very close to the expiration of her American entry visa, they informed us she would be able to leave. So that I wouldn't have to return to the DRC, which was still extremely volatile, we agreed to meet in Dubai. I would take her home from there, just the two of us.

As the day drew nearer, I decided to spend some of our savings on business-class tickets for the two of us. I wanted to celebrate and travel home in style. I envisioned us lounging back in business-class, clinking our glasses together, one with champagne and one with her favorite Orange Fanta. I could see her little face in my mind as she marveled at the plane and the faces of the other passengers staring at us as we laughed together.

I booked the flights, told only our close friends in our neighborhood what was happening, and started preparing for the day to arrive.

When it arrived, of course, everything went wrong. Robert drove me to LAX. We were late getting into the car. The traffic was awful, and I thought I would miss the flight. We hadn't received final confirmation from Nancy verifying that everything was indeed fine, that she and Grace were on their way. I reasoned, it was a 16-hour flight and they would need to be in the air around the same time I was flying. I should get on with it and get going. Robert would check for updates and we would try to communicate on the plane.

During the car ride to the airport, I kept hearing that voice. Don't go. Don't go. You shouldn't go! Are you kidding me? This is it, it's been nearly three years waiting for her! I ignored it.

I rushed into LAX, rushed through security, rushed to the boarding gate, rushed down the gangway to my flight, and plopped into my seat. After takeoff, I tried calling Nancy from the airplane phone, not caring about the cost. I managed to get hold of her colleague who was not sure whether their plane had taken off or not. I had faith. I couldn't wait to bring Grace home. We're flying business class, for God's sake! I gleefully told the flight attendants I would be flying back tomorrow with my adopted daughter, and they were all thrilled for me. This was my moment! Robert and I had worked so hard to get here. We deserved this. Finally, after 16 hours in the air, I touched down in Dubai.

The first thing I did was call Robert who, as ever, had been amazing. We had decided to never travel together to mitigate risk, but he was always there to make sure I was ok. Had he heard anything? Did they leave all right from Kinshasa? When would they arrive in Dubai? When would I be able to meet them? Unbelievably, during my entire flight he hadn't heard one thing. Despite his desperate attempts to get information, there was none. That sinking feeling began to creep up around me again.

I somberly checked into a Dubai airport hotel. I sat on my computer in my room, waiting for word. Suddenly, a message came in from one of Nancy's colleagues. They had boarded the plane in Kinshasa, right on time!

Yay! And whew!

I waited hours to hear anything more. I started searching flight information online and found out something that snatched my breath: The plane was nowhere to be found. It seemed that while they had both boarded, the flight had never actually taken off. And when I called, no one knew where Nancy or Grace were!

Panic. Nancy's colleague said he would head to Kinshasa airport to try to find out what had happened to them. Then the story unfolded. Hours earlier, the plane had been raided to find anyone traveling illegally. Nancy and Grace were legally free to travel but others had not been, so everyone had been detained and taken to the police station for questioning. They had all been sequestered without being able to make a call to tell anyone where they were.

Fortunately, Nancy's colleague was able to get them released from the police station and back to her apartment. We had to decide what to do next, and quickly. Grace's U.S. visa was about to expire, and she was required to land in the States within the next 24 hours or we'd have to apply for a new one, which would take about five weeks. Was it even possible to find flights at such short notice?

If there was, I would find a way.

So there I sat, grounded at a Dubai airport hotel, hunched over my computer, desperately trying all combinations of flights to get her somewhere, anywhere in the States in the next 24 hours. It also needed to be somewhere I could get to at the same time, so my odds weren't looking good. The flight alone takes a minimum of 16 hours, and with connections, it's often well over 30 hours to reach Los Angeles from Kinshasa.

I desperately looked at every single possible place Grace could fly to get to me. From Casablanca to Nairobi to Luanda. My geography was improving rapidly. Overwhelmed and stressed, I kept going in my little hotel room in the middle of nowhere. I would not give up. Time flew past. I refused to stop. I became a travel agent expert. I found routes and cities I had never heard of. It was exciting, I could do this. The movie finale was coming!

Finally, hours later, I had to reluctantly—very reluctantly—admit defeat. Robert gently let me go on for much longer than was needed. I kept going even after there was no time left. I was expecting magic. It did not come.

There was no way to make it happen. I had tried everything and it had beat me.

I got up from my desk and went into the bathroom where my legs gave way. I fell to the floor and the tears started rolling. "F..u..c..k you!" I screamed. "Why? I can't take this! What is this, some kind of test? Why did you bring me all the way here for nothing?"

The room next-door - and perhaps the entire corridor of rooms - may have wondered what was happening.

I managed to eat a full room service binge, slept restlessly and then got ready to depart back to Los Angeles, empty handed. I was so angry on the flight home. I tried putting my bags in the overhead container when a flight attendant offered to help me.

"I don't need any more help today," I snapped.

I sat down resentful, tortured over the next 16 hours by the empty seat next to mine.

It is amazing to me how we humans bounce back. Without this resilience, we have no ability to go on. When I got home, Robert hugged me without words and we managed to recover our hope by focusing our energy on renewing Grace's US entry visa, which would take five to seven weeks.

Nancy took good care of Grace. Her hollow cheeks began filling in. She was looking a little healthier, and a lot less depressed. Of course, that made me delighted. I remember thinking, goodness knows how she will remember all of this! I couldn't wait to be able to communicate with her one day and try to see it all through her eyes.

Five weeks passed and Grace was issued another US entry visa. Nancy said that this time she would fly all the way to Los Angeles with her. They didn't want to put me through yet another transit ordeal. Nancy said they would tell me when Grace would be leaving and... that we should be ready for a party!

We were so ready. Grace's bedroom had been prepared for years. Jake had been saving and storing toys for her since he found out he was going to have a sister. Charlie couldn't wait to meet her.

Of course, I was excited, but once or twice bitten and I was also feeling a little cynical. By now, I had learned that you never know what might happen. And literally anything could happen. So until she was safe in my arms, I wanted to remain steady and ready for whatever was coming.

A few weeks later, the call came. Grace was leaving that day! While all her paperwork was completely in order, the window of opportunity was small, and Nancy didn't want to risk any last-minute issues. The pair would be traveling first to Brazzaville, then to Ethiopia, then Dublin and from there directly to Los Angeles. Nancy told us they would be in contact at every point along the journey, so we would know how everything was unfolding and that they were on schedule.

Early the next morning, Nancy messaged that they were on their way!

Robert and I eagerly awaited the next update. I kept refreshing the Skype screen, but no messages came at all that day. It started getting late in Los Angeles, so we went to bed with every single device we had—phone, iPad, open laptop—with the volume all the way up in case we heard a welcome 'ping' giving us the next update. I was restless. I had half-convinced myself they were being held in Addis Ababa to be sent back to DR Congo. I don't know why. There was no reason they should be. There was a certain comfort in this defeatism, I supposed. If my hopes were not raised, the disappointment of bad news would be lessened.

In the darkness of early morning—PING!—a message came through and all it said was "We are in Addis Ababa!"

They should be in Dublin by now! Damn—I knew it! They were being held and questioned and would be sent back to DR Congo. Of course, something had gone wrong. I felt the blood drain out of my body. A few seconds later...

PING!

"Hello, from Dublin!"

What? I was confused until I realized they had sent the first message from Ethiopia that probably had not actually gone through due to a poor Internet connection. Both messages went out simultaneously once they had reached Dublin. Dear God, are you kidding me?

Dublin was merely a fuel stop, so they were not expected to leave the plane. Yet for some reason, Nancy said, everybody was taken off the plane and everyone's paperwork was checked. More torture. Eventually they got back on the plane for the last leg of the flight.

Was I allowed to feel a little hopeful now? I began to feel a little back in my step as I went about my day, checking the flight status regularly. We were all getting excited. Everyone was going to get dressed up and we planned how we would take Grace to Santa Monica to see the ocean and have lunch as a family.

Then, a few hours before the flight was due to land, it disappeared from the trackers. I couldn't find it on any of the usual websites. I looked at LAX arrivals and the flight number was gone! Had the flight been turned around? Did it even leave Dublin? I called Ethiopian Airlines and they couldn't give me any straight answers. They insisted it was in the air and I should wait to see if it arrives.

Seriously?

I called my secret agent dad, who among other things, was also a Ham Radio expert who is somehow able to access information the rest of us can't.

"Sam, the flight is for sure in the air," he confirmed. "It's over the Canadian/U.S. border right now. I can't tell you if Grace is on it, but the flight is going to land in LAX in a couple of hours so you should get going to the airport."

So Robert, Jake, Charlie, myself—and a big bunch of balloons—set off for LAX, unsure whether Grace would arrive or not. We got to the airport and the flight number had reappeared on the arrivals listing. We watched the plane land. We stood waiting, watching arrivals from the lounge, seeing many people arrive from Ethiopia, but no Grace and no Nancy. We waited, and waited, and waited.

Is this happening again?

Then, around the corner came two familiar faces, Nancy with a big, beautiful smile holding hands with our little Grace, tired and tousled, but finally here!

I ran to her. Pushing my way through the crowd in a dramatic airport scene. This was my moment and people stopped to stare. Picture a white woman launching herself through a busy US airport crowd to hug a black child. Even in this day and age, people turned and looked quizzically.

So many years. So much effort. Tears streamed down my face and I wiped them away to try to give her some impression of composure. I bent down, not wanting to overwhelm her. I hugged her tightly and she looked at me very calmly. Almost as if to say, "Okay. I'm here, I'm hungry, I'm tired, and I'm still not sure who you are."

I felt total joy. It rushed through every cell of my body. Clearing away all the worry, the doubt, the cynicism, and the fear. I saw my mum's face in my mind's eye, and she said, "You did it, Sam! I am so proud!"

When Robert saw Nancy, he realized instantly they had met before. On Robert's first visit to DRC to see Grace, while staying at the mission, they had met at breakfast in the dining hall. When Nancy mentioned she worked for a not-for-profit and was looking to start her own business, Robert had suggested she look me up and Aspire! Robert is always my public relations man. So that is how she came to apply to be a speaker at the Aspire conference.

All roads, as they say, lead here.

We drove straight from the airport to Santa Monica beach. Grace was excited to see the ocean because she had never seen one before. She was not aware of the power of the waves, because she ran fast away from me up to the water's edge and right into one that swallowed her up, turned her over, and spat her around again. She was face down in the sand, completely soaked head to toe, her new dress covered in sand.

Oh, my God! I thought. She's been here two minutes and we've killed her!

Grace looked up, spat out a mouthful of sand and sea water, and burst out laughing.

That's my girl.

When we arrived home we had prepared Jake's favorite meal—chicken with macaroni and cheese. Grace took a big bite and promptly fell asleep with the fork still in her mouth. We brought her up to her new bed and she slept for 14 hours straight.

After nearly three years, Grace was finally home. Our family was complete. Nancy stayed a few days in LA and then went back to continue her crucial work in the DRC.

The journey to Grace was over, yet in many ways, was about to begin. I had learned the importance of listening to my heart and intuition and when I had ignored my inner voice and justified it in my mind, it had never led anywhere good.

I understood, at a deep level, the quote: "What doesn't kill you makes you stronger." And how a journey such as the one to Grace was not only about the child, but also about my ability to deal with immense pressure and stress with grace. Robert and I had demonstrated our integrity and resilience and showed our children that we must do what we say we are going to do and never, ever give up.

I realized the power of a support network, the enduring love of my husband, and the importance of asking for help. Now I understand the value of patience, that a journey sometimes takes longer than one anticipates. I had never given up and now I was proud of myself, extremely proud. I had received so much help along the way, ultimately, I am a woman and with that DNA and determination, I have a fierceness and rebellion that will change the world.

I could never have imagined that there would be so many obstacles. Incredible as my story may seem, it is indeed what happened. I am an everyday girl from a council estate in England, and if I can overcome these obstacles, you can too.

So whatever is going on for you, hang in there. You will persevere. You can do it.

You are on a journey that will take you somewhere amazing!

I promise.

CHAPTER TWO

Girls Are Like Goats

In the Words of
Sister Zeph,
Teacher, Women's Activist and Philanthropist, Pakistan

It was Christmas Eve 2006.

I awoke to the sound of gunfire.

I sat upright in my bed, struggling to get free of the haze of sleep. There were heavy footsteps, all around me, in the walls ... above my head? Was I still dreaming? Gunfire again, then yelling. Rage.

Footsteps rumbled on the roof above me.

In Pakistan, especially in the small villages, it is very easy to get on the rooftops. All the houses are flat at the top and built adjacent to one another. In many places, the brickwork of the walls is made in such a way that it is like a stairway, giving access to nearly every house in the village.

And then I heard my name.

"Stop what you are doing, Zeph!" They shouted between pops of gunfire. "You will stop teaching the girls!" They cursed and swore with terrible words that I will never repeat. They called me, my students, my family, some of the most demeaning things I had ever heard. Things I had never heard.

From the next room I heard a scream and crying. I leapt from my bed, my only thought was to make sure the baby was not hurt.

My father stood in the hallway rushing back to my mother, standing dazed in the doorway with one of my sisters at her side. Then I saw my youngest sister and her husband, who were visiting from the Philippines on that

Christmas Eve, holding their baby tightly. Their eyes wide with fear but still dazed from sleep. The baby, little more than a year old, wailed in all the confusion.

Instinctively, we ran together to the middle of the house. We held each other tightly and cried out.

As we huddled together underneath the chaos above, weeping, and frightened, we slowly began to realize nobody had been injured. As the shouts and violence continued, we still did not know if they were firing into the air or down into the house at us.

The men shouted, "You must leave here! You must stop! Will you not leave?" They fired more rounds. "You will be responsible for the death of the baby!"

Dear God, they can hear the baby!

I shuddered inside because part of me thought they were right, that I was responsible for this. I would be blamed for everything. I felt that I had to keep them all safe somehow, that it was my job, but there was nothing I could do. We were trapped like animals in a cage.

At that time in our little village, a cell mobile phone was unheard of, something only very rich people could afford. My brother-in-law who was visiting from the Philippines had brought one with him in case it was needed for business. I still remember feeling my tears, my heart full of fear of losing my family, my hands trembling. The weight of my fear, so heavy in my throat as I tried to suppress my tears to be strong in front of my family. He scrambled to power his phone on as we frantically told him how to dial the police.

The men continued cursing and yelling death threats until we could hear through their shouts, the distant sound of sirens growing closer and closer.

They finally fired a few final shots and gave us the final warning, "Leave now, Zeph, or you will pay!" Then they ran toward the back of the house and disappeared into the darkness.

When the police arrived it was still night and they did all the investigation they could, finding some bullets and spent shells in our courtyard, but none inside the house. The men who had fled would never be found, so nobody was detained. We already knew the investigation would not continue after this night. The only reason the police had moved even this quickly to get here was they knew a foreigner was staying in our home once my brother-in-law called. Otherwise, they might never have come into the village at all.

I should have known this would happen. The day before at our school, condoms were thrown into the front courtyard and on the roof of the girls bathroom. All this to harass us and try to make the villagers think the teachers and I, and even the students, were all prostitutes. Killing a woman who does this is a guaranteed way to get into heaven in this country. Even if you are caught for such a murder, you will be celebrated.

The police sat with us, staying until morning, with the same kind of questioning repeatedly. They repeatedly said that this must be the fault of an enemy, a neighbor with a grudge. Did we have any enemies in the village?

It is very common for people in our villages to make enemies of each other. They fight back and forth, throwing insults, sometimes exchanging violence. It is a futile way of living that always ends in more hate, more poverty. Nothing is ever resolved. I knew this was not the reason.

In our family, we have had arguments with our neighbors. My father is well known for his simplicity and for his kindness. My mother and my sisters have never, ever, had a fight with anyone. If we had an enemy, it was not known to us, and here, that kind of thing is always made known long before it comes to violence of this kind.

No, the men on the roof made it very clear they were sent here to give me a message: that I should stop doing my work of giving girls a free education and teaching them valuable skills. Because, they said, the girls we teach have started speaking.

"Started speaking" is an expression we have that means that a girl has begun to question her father and brothers aloud. It is thought that to express yourself as a woman means you are unruly and rebellious, bringing shame to your family in the eyes of the males who have authority over you. It means you will not make a good wife, and if that gets around, you will not be married, making you useless.

These girls have only started to question the status quo, to ask genuine questions about why they are not allowed to make decisions on their own, to express their opinions, or to exercise their minds.

The police stayed with us the rest of the night. At daybreak, they forced us to pack our belongings and leave the village. It was simply easier to make us go and tell us to stay away for a long time. We hired a car and set out to stay with my other sister in Rawalpindi, close to Islamabad, the capital of Pakistan.

As we drove away from the village where I grew up, where all my students had come to learn, I was heartbroken. I was so upset leaving the children behind. I felt like I was betraying them all. And the further we drove, the heavier the burden grew.

During the car ride, my family treated me like it was all my fault. That I was responsible for everything. I felt that deeply. I also felt responsible for my students. What would become of them now? It was so difficult to control my tears. I wanted to get to Rawalpindi and go someplace private where I could shout.

Something was lodged in my heart, wrapped tightly around it like a plastic sack. My mind was bursting, racing with so many thoughts. I was 22 years old. I had been teaching and managing my own school since I was 13. And while I was certainly controlling my feelings, I needed some huge, silent place to scream out loud, cry, and express the helplessness of being forced to stop, to give up my life's work.

As we drove, I thought about how the gunmen on the roof were not the first to target me for violence or to make me feel so trapped, so helpless.

I remember the day my mother gave birth to my youngest sister, the fourth daughter. It should have been a day to celebrate this beautiful new life coming into the world. In Pakistan, when a girl is born, there is no celebration. Nobody is joyous. There is no feast, nobody gives out sweets to friends and neighbors. There is no rejoicing together. Things are different in the cities now, as people are educated and accept their daughters as blessings. A huge improvement from 30 years ago.

One girl was bad enough, a burden upon the family. Four was an embarrassment, an extreme public shame. And even though men are responsible for the gender of a baby, the women receive the blame.

So when my uncle, my father's younger brother, heard the news, he took it upon himself to make a point. He burst into the birthing room and began beating my mother with his fists, cursing her, and calling her names. Now she was not only experiencing blood loss from giving birth, but also from his repeated blows to her head.

When I saw the blood and the fear on my mother's face, I cried out. My uncle turned and stomped toward me. He grabbed me by the arm and dragged me up the brick stairs to the roof of my house. I cried for help. Everyone was shouting. My uncle, blinded with rage, cursed me and my mother, cursed his brother, and before he was stopped, threatened to throw me from the roof to relieve the family of some of its burden.

I am not afraid anymore. This is why I am here. This is why I was born.

Once the car arrived at my sister's home, I went into the bathroom and let go of as much emotion as I could, as silently as I could. I faced the mirror and screamed without sound. It was not helpful. I needed to scream and cry out loud. I wanted to go on the roof and yell to the world. I wanted to know why.

Why do you treat girls so badly? Why do you want us to stay at home, keep our mouths shut, learn nothing, discuss nothing, be nothing? Is it like this everywhere in the world? Will it always be this way?

This kind of expression is looked down upon. It is not acceptable for a woman to show such feelings, and she would be taken even less seriously for showing it. So that pain stayed locked inside of me for a long time.

As I laid in a strange bed that night, I remembered my visions. I have always seen a very large school, on eight acres of land where we grow our own food and live in peace. A school where underprivileged children from all parts of Pakistan could come to be educated. Children from extremely poor families like mine, who have had no opportunities, who have had no chance to get an education.

These are the girls who have the highest chance of becoming victims of child marriage, child labor, or trafficking.

I could always see it so clearly. How could we advance the cause of education in Pakistan, which is ranked so low in the world for literacy? I could see teachers from all over the world coming to teach us. I could see them sending well-educated children back to their villages to share their knowledge with other children as they continued to grow. I could see the day where every girl, every woman would be empowered, able to make their own decisions and exercise their own authority over their lives and bodies.

They would have the skills to depend only upon themselves. They would be enabled to feed themselves and their children. They would have enough money to never feel trapped into dependence on men who insulted them over petty things or beat them on a whim. This is the Pakistan I envisioned.

I knew I had to go back. But I had some work to do first.

———————————— ❦ ————————————

There is another figure of speech in Pakistan: "Girls are like goats."

This means that the parents, fathers, brothers, and then husbands, have the authority to bring her anywhere and tell her to do anything. A girl has no choice, no right to her own opinions or decisions. It is a challenge.

People around me have always tried to interpret my challenges for me. Sometimes they'd tell me to give up, to move someplace else where things were easier, to think of myself. Sometimes they'd say, "This time, it's too big for you to handle."

They don't realize I love to face challenges. I don't know why, but somehow, I love them.

In 1997, when I was 13 years old, one of my teachers at school beat me for being mischievous. I made up my mind to leave that school. This was the first big challenge of my life and it was difficult because the abuse from the teachers was bad. Schools in many places throughout Pakistan are a breeding ground for sexism, child labor, physical abuse, and religious intolerance.

Even then I had studied about all religions and I knew Christianity and Islam are religions of peace. I realized that the inner workings of our society were not to be blamed as much on religion as on the culture. In fact, there are other places in the world where men and women and people of many religions live in peace together. I knew that to be true and I wanted it for Pakistan.

I had gone as far as I could go with that school. I decided that I would never go back and the treatment I endured would never happen to anyone else if I could help it. I would educate myself and teach others as I was doing it.

So my teaching career began at age 13. I started my own free school in my backyard. I began by inviting students by visiting families door-to-door in the village. I recruited them by telling their parents how important education was. Among poor people, opinions are divided about education. Some think education is harmful for a girl and if she is educated, she is more likely to start speaking and lower her chance of a marriage proposal. Others think that with a little education or learning of skills, she can be more useful to a husband and family, and therefore, can get a better marriage proposal.

My school was set up inside the yard of my parent's home. There was no cost to the parents, and because I was a young person recruiting other young people, the resistance was lower than usual.

Around 96 percent of the people of Pakistan are Muslim. The Christian minority, like myself and my family, make up about 1.6 percent of the population. Because of the religion and the culture, women and girls are not only a target for forced conversion to Islam, but Christians in general are more subject to discrimination and false accusations under Islamic "blasphemy laws" that are often abused simply to get someone into trouble with the authorities as a form of revenge.

Despite that, I decided to teach Muslim and Christian girls together. I believed that not only could we give ourselves a better formal education, we could also learn to become friends with each other. I wanted to be an example that we could create an atmosphere of peace, understanding, and support for each other.

As a girl, I loved all my friends so much. Part of me wanted nothing more than to wear a ponytail and play, to be carefree, to be young and have fun. Being a schoolgirl should be like that, I thought.

Once I started my school, all of that changed. Suddenly, I became a mother to so many children, especially the girls. I started feeling not only my own pain, but their pain. I quickly lost my childhood. I forgot my youth. I have also always known I was different from other girls.

I have always been dissatisfied with the treatment of girls, always unsettled by the culture. Growing up, I was stuck in a cage and to feel free, for all of us to feel free, that cage would need to be broken. The way to do that was education.

Soon after beginning my school, I wrote my first article on the equality of women and men. When I said I wanted to find a way to publish it in the Daily Jang, Pakistan's oldest newspaper, people said it would be impossible. They would never publish something written by a 13-year-old girl from an underprivileged family like mine.

Your parents are not educated! You have always lived in a village! You are poor and will never be anything else!

True, it was very difficult being poor and living in a village and such people are not held with esteem in my country. I found a way to approach the newspaper. I learned who to talk to and contacted them. I explained that my article was well-written, well-documented, and most of all, it was true, so it should be published. The newspaper miraculously agreed.

Even when I was a very young girl, my parents were often angry with me because of how I would express myself to them about injustices. In truth, it was because of them that I knew that women and men are equals as human beings. I had no trouble expressing that, as much as it would irritate my family, friends, and neighbors.

My father is rare among men in Pakistan. To this day, I have never heard him say to any of his daughters, "I wish you were a son!"

There are some men in my country who are good. My father is one of them. When my mother gave birth to his fourth daughter, he later said, "We are not going to give birth to any more children in our desire for a son."

He is not very well educated, but he always reads newspapers. He keeps himself updated about current affairs. Growing up, he always reminded us girls to watch BBC and CNN. He would remind us to read the English newspaper and then the Urdu newspaper so we could know and understand what was happening in the world. He also made us aware about different cultures around the world.

Men here are taught from a very young age that if their wife cannot give them a son they can go and marry another woman who will. There is a patriarchal society in Pakistan. Many men are not well educated. They do not have a bright future. They waste their time sitting beside roads and gawking at women who walk past. Because these men are not successful, they are afraid of women who get an education or who want to have a career. They satisfy themselves by keeping women weaker, creating an illusion that there is somebody who depends on them and their decisions.

Women have always been taught in our society that if you have a son, you will have respect in your family. By having a son, you give a gift to your husband, and in return he will love and respect you. When a woman has a son, she must teach that boy that he is everything. He is the decision-maker, the authority, and everything in the home belongs to him. His sisters, and eventually his wife, will depend on him. This is a centuries old mindset.

Not only do men blame women for giving birth to girls, but other women do as well. The husband's mother, the sisters-in-law; they always blame the mother. People are not ready to believe the scientific reality that the sex of a child is determined by a man. They do not accept it. Therefore, a man has a choice: if he doesn't have a son from one wife, he may try again with another. It is an expectation that the other woman will then give birth to a son.

I often look at my mother and think how brave she is! Having four daughters, she could not be otherwise. She had never been to school, and yet, she wanted my sisters and I to have an education. She, too, has never once said she regrets not having a son, even though it would mean a better quality of life.

I was born different. I was born a community leader. I was born to make a difference. I was born to tell other girls that we are not less than men. We are equal as human beings and we must realize it.

***

After the gunfire incident, my silent screams at the bathroom mirror, and time away from my village, I found my resolve to return.

"What do you mean you want to go back?" My father said, with disbelief on his face. My mother sat nearby with a blank expression on her face.

"I have to go back," I said, my eyes welling up with tears. "The students need me, the girls need me. They need this education."

Finally, my mother said, "And what happens when those men also come back, and instead, shoot into the house?"

"I guarantee you that they will not come back. Nobody will do that again, Ammi," I said. "Please, listen to me. I cannot sleep. We have been here for weeks and I cannot sleep. All I can think about is going back and doing this work."

When we had first come to Rawalpindi, my parents might have hoped I was going to get a job and settle down into some new life. I think they knew me better.

"I cannot live like this," I said, pointing around outside. "I came into the world for this cause. If these girls do not have an education, you know how it will be for them. I cannot stand idle when I know that I can be of help. We can be of help. And I need your help."

"What about your life? What if you die?" My father said. My mother pleaded with her eyes.

I sat quietly for one moment. "Each one of us has to die," I said. "We cannot decide how we are to die. We only have the authority to decide how to live. I have decided to live with dignity, and to teach that dignity to other girls."

They agreed with me fundamentally, but it would take some time and more convincing for them to agree to return to our village and resume the school.

After days of grieving, I had come to realize that to make the school everything it needed to be, to give the students everything they needed, I had to get a better education myself.

Even though I had already been teaching at the school for nearly 9 years by that time and I had achieved so much, my qualification was still under high school standard. So I was determined to earn my bachelor's degree. Eventually, I would also go on to earn a master's degree in political science, history, and education.

I also found a job at a multinational company as a receptionist. I worked, studied, and saved the money I earned so that I could return and make my school as secure as possible. Meanwhile, I continued praying and convincing my parents. After 6 months, we returned to the village and began planning to reopen the school.

When we drove back to the village, I was so excited. I expected that everyone in the village would be so happy. The students and their mothers would welcome me home and be so glad that the girls would be able to resume their education.

Instead, everybody was terrified.

At first, they thought I must be absolutely insane, that my family and I had lost our minds and wished to die by suicide. Why else would you put yourself in the way of certain violence, yet again? And if they join the movement with me, well, then they must also want to die.

I had to start over. Once again, I visited door-to-door. This time chaperoned by my mother and father with some conditions.

Before we set out on that first visit, my father said, "You will have to do it all yourself. We will go with you but we are not going to help you convince anyone."

So I did all the talking. Sometimes, people were hard to convince. When people fervently resisted, it was because it was all they had ever known. Even as a child I knew teaching children and empowering women was the way to help them find a better way. In Pakistan today, nothing is more important than empowering women and teaching boys and girls what is right.

I have somehow always known it, but many do not.

For some people, it is only a matter of telling them something new, and they see it is true very quickly. Sometimes it takes years for a family to realize education and skill training is important for their daughters. Other families simply never agree.

One of my students was killed by her father and brothers because they thought she was talking to a man on the phone. They killed her. In such a culture where people think their honor can evaporate for such a small reason and the life of another human being is no more valuable than a goat, men do not want to send girls anywhere they could possibly meet a man, even by accident.

You can only lead by example. So it is part of my job to reassure families that their girls will be protected at my school, and that no man is ever allowed in the school or skill center. If necessary, we pick them up and drop them off by car so they never have to walk on the road. We also teach our students self-defence techniques, so they are as prepared as possible.

I am 37 years old now and I have devoted my life to this cause. That's why I changed my name to Sister Zeph, a name which came to me in prayer. I'm a sister to everybody in my country, in the world. I have no plans to marry. Why? Because people trust me and they send their daughters to my school.

I am now a mother. I adopted Eva, my daughter, on March 18th, 2019, and my son, Zephaniah, on January 2nd, 2021. I must admit, however, that since my own two children have come into my life, I have experienced fear as a single mother that I was not expecting. I have never been scared for myself. But I often wonder if something happens to me, if I am not here, what will happen to my babies? Eva is two-and-a-half years old and Zephaniah is 11 months.

Along with that, however, I believe nothing will happen to me until another person is prepared to replace me and take over my mission. Therefore, I have faith because I know since the first day I came into this world, I came for a reason. How can I go?

While I must be careful, I also must stick with my mission because there are now a thousand people involved. If I show weakness, it weakens them. So I must be there and present. This is how I live with every fear.

Leaders often have to make sacrifices. I have to do everything in my capacity, to bring more children into the school so that we can all create something new together, a generation that will make a difference.

The girls want to stay in school if possible because they want freedom. We give them an opportunity to develop something to say and to ask any question in their minds. We invite them to give their opinion on any topic, so of course, they love school because they start growing mentally.

In my village they say that if a girl starts speaking and giving her opinion, she's not a good girl and she will not make a good wife, which is the ultimate goal for a girl. This is repeated to her over and over. Anytime she speaks, wears nice clothes, or puts on makeup, she is told she is not good and she will not receive a good marriage proposal. Be composed, keep yourself covered all the time, be quiet!

Not everybody is against me, and I know it. There are so many people who respect the work we do with girls, many of whom are unexpectedly receptive.

Not long ago, some Muslim women in my village said to me, "We are with you and we will stand by you. You are not alone." They called the landlord, the decision-making authority for the village, and told him, "Sister Zeph has done good to our daughters! They are educated and they can take care of themselves, something we could not do by ourselves. She helps us with our daughters, and we will always be thankful to her."

The only way we can start to change biased and deeply rooted views is education. Not only reading the books and passing the exams, but helping girls realize their true value and their core qualities as human beings.

Everyone must eventually accept reality. Women are equal to men, and they can do anything a man can do. Women have so much courage, and they have the guts to achieve any goal. Education and skills do not make you a worse wife or mother, but a better, more capable, and thoughtful human being.

Still, less than 50 percent of girls in Pakistan are allowed to go to school because they are forced into child labor, child marriage, or sex trafficking. We owe it to them to create a culture where all Pakistanis realize girls should go to school.

If I could say anything to the men and women of Pakistan, and to the rest of the world, it would be this: "Love each other."

When I choose to love somebody who hates me, in return I multiply love. If I hate them in return, the chain of love is broken. Love must never be stopped. You must love your work, love yourself, and love every living being around you.

Grassroots leaders like me must face so many challenges the rest of the world knows nothing about. But now I have received many awards and have had a documentary made about my life and work. I celebrate myself and my achievements.

So whenever you have a challenge, tell yourself to celebrate it!

Say to yourself, "Congratulations! This challenge has brought an opportunity for me to learn more, to do more, to make more connections, to make more friends."

Always keep in mind that to obtain success, we must accept our failures. Failure doesn't mean it is time to stop, it means try again. Approach the challenge in a different way. No matter how many times you fail, try a new approach until you achieve the vision you have seen in your mind.

Look fear in the eyes and make it afraid.

Rebellious Reflections

How does a 13-year-old girl survive in an environment that is oppressive to girls? Not only that, how does she thrive in it? Sister Zeph is truly fearless. It is remarkable how she can live without fear. She has a measure of courage that I have never seen. It comes from her inherent belief that she is on this earth to make a difference to girls' education. She believes that she will stay on this earth if necessary for her to do her part. She is protected somehow, immune from the tension around her.

We are fearless when we are connected to our purpose. We are here on this earth for a reason and we are guided and protected. Even when the most terrible, life-threatening things happen, there is a way through. You can stray from the established path in front of you. That is how a girl at age 13 decided to leave the broken school system in front of her, create a new solution, and went on to sustain it for over two decades.

Not only is Sister Zeph an advocate for girls' education in a culture that doesn't value women as it should, she also belongs to a minority religion within Pakistan. She has been persecuted for it. Her school, however, welcomes all religions.

Many people don't like her. Many don't like what she's doing. Her life is regularly threatened. She teaches us the possibility of prospering despite adversity.

As she evolves into her adult years and now has adopted children, she creates her legacy. Her battles continue. Her enemies grow stronger. But so do her allies.

If a 13 year old girl can do this, what can you do?

You can confront fear, move beyond it, and even use it as an instrument of change.

How will you think differently when fear comes your way now?

CHAPTER THREE

Halimah

In the Words of
Dr. Zareen Roohi Ahmed,
Founder and CEO, Gift Wellness, UK

We were sitting in the lounge in Lahore airport; my husband, my sister, and me. There were magazines on the table. I picked up Time Magazine and started reading about current affairs and political happenings.

The only thing in my mind was, what am I going to do with myself now?

As I flicked through the magazine, it came to an article about the Zaatari Syrian refugee camp, the world's largest at around 80,000 people, and about the circumstances of women there. There were reports from the UN and stats from different NGOs who were talking about the fear.

These women live in fear. They're scared to even go to the bathroom because chances are they'll be assaulted by a soldier or other men who are supposed to be looking after them in the refugee camps. There were stories of women having to make sexual exchanges or sell their daughters for a night to get food to feed their children and themselves.

There was a severe lack of hygiene and no access to sanitary products for menstruation. Women were having to fight over some token shipments of pads. In the end, they had to tear strips from the bottom of their dresses to fold up and use as pads. They might have found the opportunity to wash them somewhere. If not, they would find scraps of clothes in the rubbish heaps they could brush off and use. Unthinkable things.

I get these vibrations when something powerful hits me, a certain energy. I often feel it when I'm speaking at an event. It's not nerves. It's a reception of energy. I don't know where it comes from, but when I'm getting it, and I can feel my body shuddering inside, I know the vibration of energy. I get that when I'm passionate about something. The longer I read this Time Magazine story the more I started shaking.

Suddenly, I started to visualize those women, and there I was giving sanitary pads out to them.

I looked over at my husband and my sister and I said, "This is what I need to do. These women in refugee camps are struggling. I'm going to give them pads."

Ash and Tehsin looked at me. That "here we go again" look. They know when I say I'm going to do something, I will have a go.

When we first told people about our plans to build the school we'd recently completed in Pakistan, everyone thought we were going to build a tiny little school house somewhere. No one ever thought it would be on the level we had accomplished. But I had seen it.

What I do when I visualize something is to then work backwards. I trust the timeline. If I put a vision in my timeline a year from now, two years from now, and I look back from that point to the current moment, I will see all the things that need to happen for it to materialize. That's how it works.

"I'm going to create a business and I'm going to get pads for these women." At that point, I thought I was going to create a business and then with the money I made I would buy pads to give away. I didn't think I'd create my own social enterprise business and my own brand of pads and do it all myself.

I believe the best businesses are the ones where you're simply thinking about the end product, the result of your business or the result of your project; the positive impact that it's going to have on people.

The school wasn't a business, even though we had to plan things out financially and do all the things that you have to do in a business. The difference in a business is that you're doing it for profit and you're raising money by selling products. So we were selling a product, we were going to build a school, and people were giving their money for it. But it wasn't for profit, it was for love.

I think that's why it worked so well. The secret to business is to find something to sell that pulls at the heartstrings, that isn't something people buy for any other reason, that it really affects people viscerally.

So at first it was like, I'll sell any kind of widget, stuff, and with part of that money, I will buy pads and send them to these women. That's what I had in my head because at the time, I didn't consider myself to be a business person, nor did I yet realize the connection between the school project and a business. I wasn't even aware of the concept of a "social business" where I could make a profit and make a difference at the same time.

There was a turning point when the penny dropped, and I realized I needed to stop treating my business like a charity and start treating it like a social business. I wouldn't be able to do the charity side of it unless the business side was working.

And at last, I had my starting point.

Halimah would be proud.

———————————— ❧❧ ————————————

My daughter Halimah and I had made a pact. As soon as she graduated from college, we were going to do an adventurous project together. We loved The Body Shop business model. Anything that involved cottage industries or social entrepreneurship and had to do with the environment.

Whenever there was a disaster around the world, an earthquake or something, Halimah would be fundraising for it at school. She'd often bake something to sell.

"Halimah," I would say to her in the kitchen. "What are you doing, making us cupcakes?"

"No, I'm going to sell them in school and raise money for the earthquake victims."

Eventually, she got into her dream degree course, Third World Development, and International Relations at Nottingham Trent University in the UK, down the road from us. We got her a car and everything she needed.

Six weeks into her dream course, Halimah was abducted and murdered.

She disappeared suddenly. The night before we'd been in London at the ExCel Conference Center, and I was speaking as CEO of a national organization that was set up after the London 7/7 terrorist bombings. It was a global peace and unity event.

Halimah was there in the front row cheering me on, manning my stand, and looking after my volunteers and things. All weekend. We came back on Sunday night. I remember that car ride coming back because Halimah and my son, Faiz, were sitting in the back seat, both asleep.

Ash, my husband, was driving and I was sitting back exhausted in the passenger seat. I looked back and Halimah's head was on Faiz's shoulder, and his head rested on her head.

"Look at them," I said. "They worked so hard and had so much fun this weekend. I'm so proud of them."

We got home and before Halimah went off to bed she gave me a big hug and said, "I'm very proud of you."

"I'm proud of you, too," I said.

"I love you, Mum."

We hugged again and then said goodnight. That was the last face-to-face conversation I had with her. The next day I went to work and she had lectures in the afternoon and then was going to meet her friend on campus. She called me while I was in the office, a normal hurried call.

"Mum, can you pick up Faiz from school?" She said, "I'm meeting Rosie on campus and then I'm going out."

It happened on her way there.

The school was very close, and so were we. The next day I hadn't heard from her which was extremely unusual. She would text me dozens of times during the day. What should we do this evening? Should we go to town? What's for dinner? Sometimes she would pick me up from work and we'd go someplace together.

We went looking for her. We contacted the police on Monday night and they started checking the hospitals and all the go-to places. The next day was horrible. We'd been to the university that morning, putting up posters of her and asking people if they had seen her. We contacted everybody we knew who knew her. It was a nightmare.

My nephew in Leicester saw something on TV on the East Midlands news that said that they'd found two bodies, one was a girl. The address was only a few streets from where we were. We thought there was no way it could be Halimah, but we needed to rule it out.

We drove down there. It was evening, almost dark. We parked away from where the incident was because there was a house that was all cordoned off with police everywhere. The energy was tense around, forensics stuff happening, and crowds of people outside. Ash asked me to stay in the car.

"Stay here. Let me go first and see what's going on," he said. There was a parking lot across the road and he said, "I'll go in there. Her car won't be there. And then we'll know that it's nothing to do with Halimah." He left with my nephew across the road from the incident.

Only a few moments later, I saw him kind of staggering out of the parking lot. I got out of the car and walked towards him, and then from the corner of my eye, I saw Halimah's car in the car park. That was the worst moment.

The absolute worst moment.

My legs started to give way and Ash held me up. A police officer found us there and we said, "Our daughter is missing and that's her car over there."

They sat us in the police car. From her phone, they could see she'd been contacted by a man, an asylum seeker who knew a friend of hers and lived on his street. They went to school together. He'd contacted her friend and said he'd seen Halimah in town or something and wanted her number because he was a Muslim and she was a Muslim, and she would understand the problem that he was having. He'd asked if she could advise him on something?

Halimah was not going to say no to anybody in need, because that's who she was. So the friend had given over her name and number, and that morning he called her to his house. All she was planning to do was pop over for a minute on the way to school to see how she could be of help. She had left her phone, her bag, and everything in the car. She wasn't going to be there for long.

The autopsy revealed she'd most likely been dragged into the house. There was a struggle and she was hit on the head with something blunt and then she was suffocated with a cushion. Then the boy hung himself.

Oh my beautiful, kind, sweet, world-changing Halimah had gone through such terror. I played it over and over in my mind, every detail of what it must have been like for her. I tortured myself. Over and over.

The young man was mentally unwell and also a victim. He was an Iraqi boy, who had seen his family killed during the Iraq War. Ironic, because I was trying to create peace and address all the issues that came out of the Iraq War. That was my job.

He had been suffering badly from post-traumatic stress disorder, we later learned. One of the findings of the inquest was that he'd been stalking her for some time. They gathered evidence from both of their phones and learned of things he'd said to others.

We don't know how long this obsession existed. But he'd spoken to his mental health nurse about her and said that he was completely in love with her and besotted by her. He had been following Halimah, looking for an opportunity to speak to her. Eventually, he contacted one of Halimah's friends, someone he'd seen her with. This friend lived on his same street, which gave him the connection he wanted. Halimah trusted him because of that, because he knew one of her best friends from school who lived on his street.

When he finally got the opportunity, he said something to her and she had maybe refused him. He then dragged her into his house from the doorstep. There was a struggle. The inquest said that it was premeditated to a certain level, because that day he had finalized his will. He said some things to his brother, wrote a will, and had been to a solicitor. They believed he already knew what he would do if she refused him.

Almost straight after it happened, after the funeral, my husband and I started talking. What do we do now? We have to do the work that she said she was going to do. In her second year of college, she was looking forward to being in Ghana. She was going to spend the year building schools and working on water projects, digging wells, things like that.

She would get so excited talking about it.

All I could think about was what Halimah had said we were going to do together. How was I going to do that now that she was gone? But it was a case of, "Right. That's what I'm going to do. And if it kills me doing it on my own, then that's the way I'll go. I will do that work."

I had to have that kind of attitude, because it was either that or give up completely. I had to do something or I knew I would not get up the next morning. I could hear her saying, "Come on, Mum. You can do this."

I set up a charity almost straight away, The Halimah Trust, and our first project was to build a school in Pakistan where my parents are from. She would have liked that a lot.

———— ✥ ————

It took three years to build the Halimah School of Excellence.

We'd inaugurated Halimah's school a day before sitting in that airport lounge in Lahore, reading Time Magazine. I spent a week with all the girls and my heart was so full of love. Being held and holding hands with hundreds of girls for so many days. I was in an emotional space and I didn't want to leave. I cried on my way to the airport from Wazirabad, which is where the school was, and that last goodbye was like leaving my own daughters.

I felt like a mum to them. I felt Halimah there. I saw Halimah in all their faces. It was so powerful. I described it to my mum when I came back home. It was as if Halimah had gotten married and she was there with them and that was her family now. Whenever I go there now, I still can see her in all those girls. So it felt like I'd dropped her off there and I was leaving her there too.

I was desperate to hold on, to keep her with me. I knew she would be with me, it was something we all felt. I've got a little bit of video somewhere of them saying, "Think of us as your daughters now. We haven't got mothers and you haven't got a daughter, so you will be our mother and we'll be your daughters."

I feel a pull to them all the time. But I was sitting there and thinking, Okay, this part is done.

Tehsin, my sister, said, "What are you thinking now?

"I'm thinking about what I'm going to do when I get back," I said. "Workwise, the school project is set up, the fundraising is done. It was like my survival strategy, you know?"

"I know. You needed that. We all did."

"For the last three years that's what got me out of bed. And it kept me going and made me feel like I was doing something with Halimah—for her. So what am I going to do next?"

I never considered therapy. I was the one who was looking after everyone else. Therapy wasn't properly offered to us, either. I think a police officer gave us some leaflets at some point for victim support but that was about it.

I'd done Neuro-linguistic programming (NLP) to help with my thoughts and personal development and used those tools on myself. But I didn't properly cry out loud until six months later. I couldn't even cook for nine months.

Families were bringing food to us, or we were going to someone else's house to eat, or we were going out to eat or getting takeout. I couldn't bring myself to do it because we had a table for four people and there was one chair empty. I couldn't do it. I didn't want to. I hated going into the kitchen where my daughter and I had spent so much time together.

Six months had gone by and we were going to pick up something that we'd ordered from a restaurant. We drove down Normanton Road, the road where it had happened, which we hadn't driven down for a long time. In fact, I avoided it at all costs.

Ash parked the car and he went to the restaurant. I don't know what it was that triggered it, but I started crying and screaming, my heart was palpitating. I couldn't stop. I was screaming and crying so much that at one point, I couldn't get a sound out. Like having a nightmare where you want to scream for help but you can't utter a word. I don't know how much sound was coming out from me. All I knew was that I thought I was going to die. Then Ash came back to the car and found me like that, shaking and crying.

He quickly drove home and called my sister on the way and asked her to come up. He had to carry me out of the car and put me on the sofa. I couldn't move, I couldn't do anything. I was in that state for a couple of hours. Then I slept.

It's good that it came out eventually. But up until that point I was in work mode, crisis management mode.

As far as Ash was concerned, that was it, we'd done it. We had built a school. And now it was back to normal. It was never going to be back to normal for me. I knew I'd never work for anybody else again. No way. The kind of work that I was doing before, I had to be ready for the media and talking with ministers and having to fly off to another country at a moment's notice.

I couldn't see myself doing it. I was disinterested in politics at that point. I didn't know what I wanted. I hadn't earned anything for three years. I'd done some consultancy work, but nothing significant, nothing to earn a wage. I knew that whatever I was going to do, it had to have an element of charity in it. There was that fear because I had never worked for myself before. I had only ever worked in a job.

"The thing that me and Halimah discussed," I reminded myself, was that when she graduated we were going to set up an ethical business. That's what I want to do. But I didn't have any idea where to start."

I didn't think it was going to happen then either. I thought it would be down the road somewhere.

"For now, I will probably carry on doing some consultancy. To keep my hand in some kind of expertise.

I had a lot of fear. I was afraid of not having anything to do and going into a dark place. Because if you're not busy, or you're not doing something that is fulfilling your need to work and feel as if you're doing something good, something of benefit to others ideally, what's going to happen? I can't be idle, I can't do it. Even if I'm sitting in front of the TV, I must be doing something with my hands, whether it's sewing, making notes, doing some mind maps, or planning.

I must be a step ahead.

Mainly, I felt that if I wasn't busy I would fall into a hole of depression, of sadness that I wouldn't be able to climb out of. I still get that sometimes, but because I know there's so much to do, I never allow myself to stay in that place. I've got no excuse to go that way at all. I've got a lot to be grateful for.

I couldn't afford to be idle. I did not want to end up being a depressed person sitting around at home. That was my worst fear.

Halimah's school was the first thing I did. Once that was done, then it was about me. I was on the road to keeping the promise. I've done something to keep that promise to fulfill Hamilah's dream. Then, once the school was opened, I felt that fear again.

"Oh shit. What am I going to do now?"

Sitting in the airport lounge, my purpose was suddenly so clear. God had sent me that Time Magazine article about the refugee camp.

I was praying at that point. I prayed throughout that trip to be put on a path that will fulfill that promise to my daughter. I prayed that God would be satisfied with me, that I would have done enough to make a difference.

I've not reached my capacity in this life and I don't want any of my capability to be wasted. I know I have a lot of capability, strength, and intelligence. I always think of these sensibilities and sensitivities, where do they enable me to help people? I don't want any of that to be wasted.

If I'm sitting on my own, depressed in a house and not doing anything with it, to me it is sickening—a waste.

As soon as I read the article I was excited. But I was scared because I didn't want to get into something that I would fail at, I was digging myself into a hole that was beyond my capability. I'd never done anything like it before. I saw it so clearly. I saw myself giving pads to these women, and that's all I could see. I could feel their hand in mine, as vivid as I could feel Hamilah's hand.

In my mind, I was already doing it.

I immediately started making notes from the article. I got on the plane and I was so excited, so emotional. I was shaking. I picked up the magazine from the airport and tore the margins away and made notes on them.

I feared where this was going to lead. I think my husband was quite eager for me to start earning as the whole burden of income was on him during those three years. I had been earning more than him at the time Halimah passed away. So we had lost major income. Little did we know it would be a long time before I made a profit because, at first, I treated it like a charity.

When I came back, I started researching and realized I couldn't just sell anything, make money, and then go buy regular pads. I learned how toxic the regular pads in the shops are, and how unethically many are made. It made me realize how much I hated the pads I'd always used. They shouldn't make me as sick as they make me feel every month. That started me on the journey of developing my own business and unique and ethical brand.

I had to teach myself how to do everything; websites, design, marketing, everything. I'm still teaching myself. 18 months later, my first container of pads arrived, my own brand of pads, and then my social enterprise, Gift Wellness, was up and running.

The first thing I did before I sold a single item was contact a local charity taking a container of aid to Syria, to that same camp, the Zaatari camp I had read about in the magazine. I said, "Come and pick up a few pallets!" That felt so good to say that.

They didn't agree. "Oh, sister, you know, we'd love to but maybe in the next container because this one's nearly full now and we've got important stuff in it, like food, medicines, and clothes."

I said, "Brother, where are you? Let me come down, see your container, and let me see what you've got."

I got in my car and drove. I arrived and I sat him down. I explained to him why menstrual products were so important for him to take. "Imagine if your mother, your wife, your daughter, your sister was homeless all of a sudden," I said to him, "and they were going to get their period."

At first, it was like ... Oh, my God, the woman in the hijab said the P-word.

Five minutes later, he was in tears.

"I've never looked at it from that perspective," he said. Since then, every container that goes, he takes a load of my stock and other charities are doing the same.

He had to imagine how they would deal with bleeding each month. Bleeding without any sanitary pads. In fear every day. What would you do? These women only have the clothes on their backs. These are mothers and sisters and daughters of somebody—all of ours.

I'm proud that now my pads, the GIFT range, is currently the fastest growing brand of its kind in Europe and is a best seller in the store chain, Holland & Barrett.

Halimah leaving was a pivotal point in my life. It was a leveler. That event was a catalyst for a complete change in my whole world view. From that point on, I became who I was meant to be.

The thing is, I don't feel like I'm without her. She's more alive than she ever was right now because she is in everything that I'm doing.

I do talk to her and I do silly little things for her. It's my connection. Some are quite physical things, like when we were driving we used to hold hands, her fingers laced in my fingers. So when I'm driving and my handbag is on the passenger seat, I'll run the strap of my bag between my fingers and hold it as if I'm holding her hand.

It's one of those little survival strategies, I guess. I do it kind of automatically. Not all the time, but when I feel like holding a hand. Or when I'm coming home from somewhere, I'm still very aware that she's not at home. But because I completely submit to my faith, I also know that this is a temporary separation and that there was a reason for it.

To me, the reason is the work that I'm doing. If Halimah had been here, we would have done something fun together, we would have done something. I doubt if we would have had the Halimah School of Excellence, and the college next to it, serving over 850 girls from orphaned and needy backgrounds from all over Pakistan who are absolutely thriving and loving it.

Lives have been saved because of Halimah. God knows where the girls would have ended up. It is because of what happened. I have no doubt at all that this was the best plan for Halimah to fulfill her dreams. For the work was so very visceral to her. You could see it in her face. She wouldn't talk very much. She wouldn't get involved in pointless banter, apart from with her brother. They were always laughing and screaming all over the house all the time. But when we talked about important matters, career, or anything like that, she would light up. Sitting in the Lahore airport was a confirmation. It was the clarity of exactly how we were going to do it, and what the next step was.

In a way, my daughter and I have merged into one person. Her vision was to do sustainable development and international relations. She wanted to go into charity work. We had an agreement that we would work together in doing some sort of third-world development and environmental projects.

I am taking more time out for myself now, too. I'm getting into a routine of not always having early-morning meetings, and I'm pacing myself through the day. I go swimming and make time for fun.

I'm back into cooking. I love cooking because I've got grandchildren now and a daughter-in-law. My son and father-in-law are both proper foodies. It brings me joy to cook for the ones I love. So I'm back in my kitchen.

So that's what I'm doing. I am a businessperson making a difference. That's my main driver, which keeps me authentic and true.

You must find your true purpose. The best way is to focus on helping others and while you're doing it, you will find that place in yourself, you'll find happiness and contentment. The best healing, the cure for anything is to help others, to do meaningful work.

It's such a blessing.

There are a couple of things that I'm planning next. One of them relates to my company, Gift Wellness. We started off by giving pads to women in crisis and soon began the development of non-toxic products of our own. We then developed a soap bar line and a range of toiletries with the ethos of doing good for the planet and using less plastic.

During the COVID-19 pandemic, I had the time to take a step back and look at what I have achieved from doing Gift pads and donating products. I realize it's only really treating the symptoms, not addressing the root causes. One of the main projects I'm working on right now is the reproductive rights of women in the workplace.

We will be addressing the societal and cultural baggage that exists in relation to women's reproductive systems. Why is it still here? Why is it still holding women back? It's so embedded in every culture. The time is ripe for it because there's a real impetus from every corner of government, business, the STEM industries, and all these different sectors who are recognizing how archaic it all is.

You'll find that feeling if you focus on helping others, straight away, even if you do it in a way that you tell yourself is a survival strategy... as it was for me. You can start off doing that and before you know it, it's energizing and helping to channel negative energy, sorrow, sadness, and grief. If you channel all that negative energy and turn it into positive energy, you will find richness.

As long as the social purpose that you're looking to address is what you're passionate about, and you can visualize the effect of it, you should go for it. I had never run a proper business before. I'd always worked in the public sector and the charity sector. I didn't know how to manufacture, sell, pitch to retailers, set up an ecommerce business, what the logistics of importing and exporting were, or how to properly market our products. None of it. I had the vision. I had a video playing in my mind of what the result would look like, and it was so real to me that I knew all I had to do was learn how to make it happen.

Women do that. We're resourceful. We'll find a way to get to where we need to, especially when it relates to something that is very personal to us.

Doing this work is so personal to me. That image I saw in the magazine at the airport spoke to me. I had to do it. That's exactly the sort of thing me and Halimah were planning. I had to do it for her as if she was here, as if she was alive and she needed something so desperately. There's nothing I wouldn't do for her.

It's that level of feeling: if your daughter asked you for something, she was desperate to do something, you'd make it happen. You would go to any lengths to do it because you want to see her happy and you want to fulfill her dreams, her ambitions.

That's how passionate you must be about something if you want to make it a reality. You must live it in your head and your heart. It has to become who you are. The rest is technical stuff that you'll have to figure out along the way. No one's got any excuse nowadays. Everything is there. You can hire all the help you need on different platforms and set up a business or a project for next to nothing. Gone are the days where you have to take ads out in magazines or pay to start marketing your business. We have social media, and everything is at our fingertips. But the vision must be clear.

I know now why that whole sequence of events led me to where I am. The work that I'm doing now has totally exceeded our expectations in terms of what Halimah and I wanted to do together. It's still difficult. I still feel that pang. But the pain is fuel to me. It fuels my work and it gets me up in the morning. It makes me want to do more.

If Halimah were here now, she would say to you that you must always keep your kindness, your faith, and never be deterred by any obstacles.

She would comment on how proud she is of the work I am doing and the impact it has. She would smile and be thrilled that she has a book chapter named after her, a school in Pakistan, and a charity.

"Wow" she would say, "look at us. We did it!"

Rebellious Reflections

You can't outrun grief. It's devastating and radically life-changing. It is unforgiving and lingers with you every moment of every day.

It creates a shock wave. Body, mind, and spirit must find a way to survive it. How do you handle grief? If you were to truly absorb the unimaginable happening, perhaps, you would not survive it.

You can try to beat grief. But it's too fast, too clever. It creeps up on you in the dead of night. It sits with you every moment of every day, whispering in your ear that it was somehow your fault, that you could have done something about it. Grief haunts and never goes, because if it were to leave completely, we might forget the person we lost.

There are productive and destructive ways of moving forward through grief.

The approach Zareen took was to align with her purpose and follow a legacy she had planned to follow with her daughter, Halimah. She made a difference, and continues to make a difference to women and girls around the world. She rebelled against the idea that she would disappear, that she would die inside, that she would not be able to cope. She rebelled against grief and brought meaning into her world.

Perhaps we can use grief? Perhaps it is meant to be felt and channeled into good? Zareen has an inherent belief system, a coping mechanism that clings to her belief that this was meant to be for her. In some sense, it had to happen. Zareen created her own destiny and continues to do so. From tragedy, she emerged brighter than ever.

She became a business person with no previous business experience. She uses her business to create good in the world and is now expanding it as she steps into her social entrepreneurial status.

Zareen teaches us how we can reinvent ourselves in the face of adversity. That our work can be our solace, that giving back and charitable work can be integrated with running a business and making a profit.

What are you taking away from Zareen's story? Where is it time for you to re-emerge?

CHAPTER FOUR

Free to Be Fearless

In the Words of

Lilly Lewis, Women's Justice Advocate, UK

I stood handcuffed in front of a Crown Court prisoner van. I'd been sentenced to eight years in prison for committing a million-pound conspiracy crime.

For some reason, I felt happy. Almost giddy. After two years of being on bail and not knowing what would happen, I knew what was happening now. Even though it meant prison, it felt like solid ground.

An officer led me into my little holding cell within the van, a cramped space that separated the prisoners with barely enough room for your feet. I looked out the window. It was already night but the moon was so bright and so beautiful as it kept the loading yard all lit up.

"Well, God..." I sighed, and thought to myself, "you've given me all this time. What am I going to do with it?" And as clearly as if I were talking to someone face-to-face, I heard a reply.

You're going to support and help others.

I looked over to another holding cell where one of my co-defendants was seated. I didn't know her. I didn't know any of them. They were my boyfriend's friends from different cities. She was crying so hard, almost like she'd just heard of a death in the family.

"What's the matter?" I asked.

"I..." she sobbed out, "I'm so scared..."

"About what?" I asked, gently.

She was now crying so hard, her body heaving and trembling to the point that she couldn't speak to give an answer.

Yet in that moment, I realized I wasn't scared of anything. Not anymore. The thing I knew, the thing I could feel, was that all this was going to be something good.

Where's your mama gone?
Where's your mama gone?
Far, far away...

Yet in that moment, I realized I wasn't scared of anything. Not anymore. The thing I knew, the thing I could feel, was that all this was going to be something good.

I was seven years old. My classmates were singing, pointing at me, and laughing as I walked past. I'd only just been dropped off to school by my mum. I'd heard the song playing over the radio, but I didn't understand why they were singing it to me. I kept walking.

As the day unfolded, other children would sing as they walked past me, mocking, laughing, and telling me I was adopted, and that my mum—not the woman who had cared for me as long I could remember, who had kissed my forehead as she dropped me off at school that morning—my real mum didn't love me.

I didn't know it, but I had been abandoned in 1972 by my birth mother at 6 days old because of the color of my skin. She was white, her husband was white, and about everyone they were surrounded by was white.

In 1971, my birth mum's husband went to prison because he'd beat her. While he was away, she had an affair with my birth father, a man from

Jamaica. My mum had poor mental health and she didn't clearly understand what this pregnancy might cost her.

On the day I was born, when she saw my skin color, she realized if she took me home, I would never be accepted by my family. I was placed in an orphanage for six months, until I was fostered, then later adopted by the people I now call my mum and dad.

I had always felt different from everyone else. I never questioned it. I was the only brown face in my school. My adopted mum was white and my adopted dad was black. I was the only brown face on my street. It had never been any other way. Now there was this other element, that maybe I didn't belong to this mum and dad.

I sat with this uneasiness the whole day. Later that night, I built up the courage to ask my mum why the children were singing this song to me and saying I was adopted because I didn't know what any of it meant.

"Oh, Lilly," she said, somewhat surprised. "Oh, dear..." I realize now that she knew this talk would have to come someday. And now here it was. "Well, I suppose some of the children must have overheard me talking to one of the other mums at the school gate."

"Is it true, Mummy?" I asked. "What does adopted mean?"

"Well," she said, "one day, your dad and I went to a shop and there were all these lovely children on a shelf. But you were the prettiest. So we picked you! But you smelled terrible so we washed you up and took your old clothes and threw them away, then we gave you fresh new clothes."

"But you... aren't you my real mummy?"

"Yes, of course I am!" She said, "It's that you weren't born to daddy and me. Your mother hadn't wanted you, dear. We did. And we chose you like you were the prettiest little dolly on a shelf."

Dr. Sam Collins 79

That story never satisfied me. All I could think was who doesn't want their own baby? Why didn't my real parents want me? Why did I smell? Why were my clothes dirty? As I got older, of course, the story was more and more unbelievable and I grew more dissatisfied with the answers. Eventually, the story changed.

"We gave her an option to say goodbye," my adoptive dad once explained, "and she didn't want it. She didn't want you. She didn't love you." I didn't realize at the time that this callous answer was not to hurt me or condemn anyone, only because they simply didn't know how to discuss it with me.

But the bullying and emotional abuse wasn't only at school. My adoptive parents had two biological daughters, a few years older, who would often tell me: "That's our mum, not yours."

Another time, I had a big fight with my parents and my dad stormed into my room and started packing my things into suitcases and bags.

"What are you doing?" I said.

He glared at me, between opening drawers and yanking out clothes from my dresser drawers and stuffing them angrily into the bags.

"What are you doing?" I screamed.

"What does it look like I'm doing? I'm taking you back to the children's home. I'm not putting up with your bad behavior anymore!"

At first, I thought he was going to stop but he didn't. I started to panic. He grabbed the bags in one hand and my arm in the other and dragged me out to the car. When he threw the bag in the back and shoved me into the front seat, I slumped into the footwell, now completely hysterical, sobbing, and pleading with him to turn around for nearly the entire drive from The Wirral to Liverpool.

Eventually he turned around.

My adoptive parents looked after me as much as they could, but it was always things like this that made me feel I was, at the core, unloved. I was different. I could be traded around, or even discarded as easily as driving me down the road. I don't like saying it this way, because my parents did the best they could with what they knew, and my sisters were only children, but it deeply affected my sense of belonging.

We all know better now, of course, that if we instill information like that within a child that they will believe it, with consequences.

The first time I can remember wanting to take my own life, seriously thinking about it, I was fifteen years old. It wasn't a cry for help. I didn't tell anyone. I didn't attempt it. It was a deep somber feeling that often came up within me.

I used to like being asleep. I looked forward to sleeping. It was the closest feeling to being dead that I could come to without having to die. And whenever I woke up, I'd think, "Oh, I'm awake," and try to get on with it until I could have a nap or finally go to bed at night. Sleep was my way of escape for many years, until I discovered alcohol.

Drinking made me act differently than any of my friends. When I was drinking to excess, I got this massive high. I could drink through the pain. Ignore it totally. I could act like the woman, the person, I could never be without it.

I was always the one who blacked out and couldn't remember what happened the night before. Many times, I'd be dropped at the doorstep by friends and they'd run off. Alcohol became a friend that never left. Then I would sober up and come down ever deeper into my depression.

When I was introduced to ecstasy and cocaine and all night parties, I found myself surrounded by a new group of people. Along with them came the drug dealers and criminals—a lot of young men who appeared to be very powerful and have lots of money, lots of friends, and would pay me lots of attention. At first, it felt like someone was caring for me. A kind of attention I'd never had. But it always somehow ended up about control.

"Where do you think you're going?"

"Stay in, I want you here when I get home."

"You're not wearing that out tonight..."

Very early on in each of these relationships would first come the insecurity, and then the abuse. Though it doesn't happen all at once. Coerciveness at first, which soon transformed into name-calling, then hitting, and ultimately, sexual abuse.

From the age of 16 and for the following 30 years, I was bandied around from one abuser to the next. We met through mutual friends, parties, or blind dates, but they all ended up the same. From one criminal to another, whether they specialized in drugs or guns or fraud. Each partner was slightly worse than the one before. And they had to be, to be able to see off the previous man.

In each new relationship, I became less and less a woman who could make proper decisions for herself. I was using alcohol and drugs as a coping mechanism, convinced I couldn't survive without them. Because of my own lack of belonging, I desperately craved family and that feeling of connection by blood. So I had children with different men. I'd stay with the fathers, attempting to manufacture some idealized family life as the abuse continued.

When I was 20, I had my first daughter, Marnie. She was born in April 1992 and I married her father the following December. That newlywed New

Year's Eve was the first time he smashed my face and the first time I'd ever been seriously attacked by a partner. The blood was gushing out of my wounds, so he put me into the bathtub and used a jug to pour water over my head, over and over. I kept bleeding. Eventually, he had to call an ambulance. I stayed with him for another five years.

I met Isabelle's father next. Her dad wasn't physically violent towards me, he was emotionally abusive and a thrower. He'd smash up the house, throw plates, break the car windshield. After a while, I left him and got a restraining order to keep him away. Isabelle was born in 2000.

After that, I met Tiffany's dad on a blind date. He was a world champion kickboxer. He was big—18 stone, or about 250 pounds in weight—and incredibly strong. He was initially the most charming person I'd ever met. We drank champagne and laughed and talked and it felt... good. Tiffany was born in 2006.

At the end of the evening, he looked me in the eyes, very seriously, and said, "I want to marry you."

We arranged the date and married three weeks later. Six weeks after that, I found out I was pregnant. He was thrilled, and he was an absolute gent at the start of the pregnancy. I wasn't allowed to lift a finger. He cooked for me, cleaned the house, and treated me like a queen.

But when he lost his title and had to get work as a club doorman, everything changed.

When Tiffany was about 7, he'd taken her to Disneyland, Paris while I stayed behind as I was heavily pregnant. She was so excited to have her picture taken with Tigger from Winnie-the-Pooh, but with all the other children around, the person in the Tigger costume didn't see her and she was upset. So he walked over to the costumed person and beat him and berated him in front of the crowd.

Back home, three days before the baby was due, I was sitting on the bed doing my makeup to go to the store.

"Where are you going?" he said.

"Oh, just to get the last bits for the baby," I said.

He walked over and grabbed me by the throat, lifted me onto my feet. "So you know," he hissed, "when this baby is born you won't be fucking leaving the house." He turned me around and threw me down the stairs, which put me into slow labor. The hospital had to induce the birth two days later.

After Tiffany was born, every two weeks he would beat me, and often rape me. When I had visible bruises, he would leave me alone. As soon as my bruises healed, he would do it again. Anytime he wanted sex, he would grab me by the hair and pull me to the bedroom, calling me terrible names the whole time.

I didn't realize at the time that he wasn't a club doorman. He was involved, deeply involved, in drug dealing. The way I discovered it was when a group of men came to the house one afternoon and dragged him outside on the front lawn and beat him because he owed someone £50,000. He was told he would have his legs chopped off if he didn't come up with this money, which of course, he didn't have.

We packed quickly, got the children ready and went on the run that very night to Spain.

It didn't matter that we were on the run, the beatings continued and got worse. One evening, after we'd been in Spain for about a month, he battered me into unconsciousness.

We were in a second-floor apartment and the police couldn't get in, so the fire brigade had to come through the outside apartment window. They all thought I was dead, at first.

He was arrested, the children went with a local friend, and I went to the hospital. They do things very differently in Spain. As a wife, you don't have the option to press charges if you're assaulted, it happens automatically. They tell the abuser he must turn himself in within two weeks, which he, of course, didn't do.

So the court assigned the Guardia Civil, the Spanish police, to stay with me and my young family 24 hours a day. They slept outside the house at night. When I drove the children to school, I had an escort with a car in front and a car behind. The judge ordered them to walk within 100 meters of me wherever I went until he was found.

Through an interpreter, the judge told me she'd been a domestic abuse judge for over 20 years, and I was the saddest case she ever dealt with. She'd never seen someone who was so accepting of the beatings and found it heart breaking that I had nothing critical to say about him when they questioned me about what happened. It was because I was so often drunk and out of it that I thought it was normal. I came to expect that in a relationship there would be some abuse, it was all part of love. All part of life.

Eventually, they caught him and he went to prison for four years in Spain. While he was in prison, I had an affair with a guy I later discovered was on the run in Spain after doing a shooting in Manchester. And I was pregnant again, with my youngest son Jordan who was born in 2010. History began to repeat itself.

Because I'd got pregnant with his child, he said he wanted to come back to the UK to face the criminal charges against him, thinking maybe he'd receive sympathy or a lighter sentence as an expectant father. So I flew back to England with the children, and he was smuggled back into the country by car. When he went to hand himself in to the police, they didn't even want to speak to him. The case had been closed, so he was a free man.

He didn't need me or the baby anymore, so he left three weeks before Jordan was born.

————————— ❊❊❊ —————————

"Mum, why can't we be normal?" Issy would often say to me. "You don't need another boyfriend."

"This one is different," I'd always say—ever hopeful it would turn out.

My newest partner was 23. I was 38. He was young, drove a nice car and had lots of money. I'd met him because he was my cocaine dealer. When we got together, instead of selling me drugs, he kept me on them so I would be easier to manage. The trade-off to turning a blind eye to his criminal activities was a large, beautiful house, the kids' private school, a nanny, shopping, all at his expense. And I was kept high.

"You know," he said to me one day, "I want to get out of this life and do something legitimate. I think we should start a holiday timeshare company."

"I think that's a great idea," I said. But I should have known something was dodgy.

"The only problem is that my credit is bad," he began. "I've got so much school debt from getting my master's degree I can't even open a bank account. So look, I mean, you're older, you've got a better credit rating than me. How about we register the company and file the accounts in your name? I've already got the backing and we could make so much money... and all above board."

"I don't know anything about running a company," I said, laughing. "What do you expect me to do?"

"You don't have to do anything!" He assured me, "I need your help to open an account and start the business under your name. All you'd have to do is make deposits and transfers when the money comes in. And help me spend it, of course."

At the time, if he would have asked me to jump off a building, I might have done it. So I flew to Manchester and met his business consultant. The consultant took me to his flash office and then to the bank where he did all the talking about the timeshare business with the banker, and we opened the account. Then I flew back to Spain. No problem. I was being a good girl and did what I was told.

But early on, I knew something was off about it. At first, it didn't feel like crime as nobody was getting shot, nobody was selling drugs. But there was so much money coming in so quickly. In the first six months I'd deposited nearly £300,000. I knew something was up.

My boyfriend was very manipulative. He kept me drunk and on drugs, so it was easier to make me believe that what we were doing was fine. If I ever put up any argument, he'd say, "If you don't do what I tell you to do, I'll tell social services you're on drugs and they'll take your children."

One day, when Isabelle was about 12, she came home from a school trip very sick. At first, she wouldn't tell me what was going on, but then she said my boyfriend had given her marijuana. I was out of my mind with rage. I called the police straight away and told them first what he'd done with her, and then what I thought was happening with the business and the bank. They arrested him immediately. They didn't even bother with me at the time.

Suddenly, we were homeless. But I discovered my son's father had been arrested for an attempted murder, and he allowed us to live in his house while he moved in with his mum as he was on bail. Small mercies, I suppose.

Two years later, I was arrested. It wasn't until then that I discovered that I wasn't the only person who had set up a business and bank account. He had 10 other people working under him. I didn't know any of them. They didn't know me. Because the total amount was over one million pounds, not just the £300,000 I had handled, it meant that I was part of an organized crime conspiracy, which potentially carried a much longer prison sentence than money laundering.

I managed to get out on bail, and the children were with me. It was mostly Marnie, my teenage daughter, caring for the children, making their food, getting them and herself off to school, cleaning me up when she could.

One day, after the arrest, the police and social services came to check how we were living. I knew there was a risk they might move us to a care home. But I still drank to the point of passing out. I woke up in the police station and my children were gone.

"What happened! Where are my kids?" I said to the attending officer, startled at not waking up where I'd fallen asleep.

"You collapsed, Ms. Lewis," she said. "Nobody has been looking after your children. We've placed them into care under an emergency protection order."

I lost it. I started screaming at them to give me my children back. "This is England! This can't happen!" I didn't even hear myself; it was like having an out of body experience.

"Ms. Lewis," they said, "if you don't calm down, we will arrest you."

"I'm calm. I'm calm. Please, you can't take my babies." I started to sob. The inevitability of the situation started to dawn upon me.

"You know, the most concerning thing about this, Ms. Lewis, is how normally your children behaved. None of them were even the slightest bit worried you couldn't wake up. It's like they are accustomed to it."

The police threw me out onto the street. I had nowhere to go, so I went to a hotel for the night. I was contacted by the police the next day. A kind policewoman came to collect me. She put me in a hotel for two days and then found a women's refuge for me. When she took me in, she cried, because she could see that, after everything I'd been through, the worst possible thing for me was having my children swiped away.

I didn't get to see them again until two weeks later, supervised at a child services contact center. Issy was separated from Tiffany and Jordan, who were kept together. They looked so lost.

It may not have been perfect but it was our life. We were together and there was love. Jordan was only three, and was clinging to my leg as they tried to take him back out after the visit. I was only trying to be strong for them.

I was then told I had a six-month window to get them back. By now I was charged and under investigation and out on bail. Normally, you'd go to court to decide if the children were going under long-term foster care, or create a plan to bring them home. There was no plan the police could give me because the inevitable moment was coming. At some point, I was going to go to prison.

I don't even remember the two years the case took to come to trial. I had lost my children. I knew I was going to prison. I was in and out of the hospital. My opulent lifestyle had evaporated and now I was living in refuges and counting pennies to get a drink of wine. I tried to kill myself five times with drink and pills. One time I jumped off a seven-foot wall and shattered my heel. They put me in a secure hospital because I was so mentally unwell and such a danger to myself that I couldn't be left alone. I was completely powerless and didn't see the point of staying alive. I wanted it all to stop.

I remember waking up on the bed in the secure psychiatric hospital. I thought I'd been there for two days. Later, I found out it had been two weeks.

As I came to, I felt somebody holding my hand. This warm feeling of love washed over me. I slowly opened my eyes and looked up but nobody was there. I was told Jordan's father had recently died. He'd gone out to a party and come home, taken a sleeping tablet, and choked on his own vomit. I was convinced it was him back from the dead.

After getting out of the hospital, I went to see a psychic to try to get some clarity about him. Halfway through the session she stopped and became quiet.

"Were you in hospital?" she asked. "In a pink room?"

"Yes," I said.

"Your mum was with you." She didn't even know my birth mum had died long ago.

Then, I don't know what or why, something inside me clicked.

I'd never met my birth mum. Have my children ever met the real me? My older daughter had already told me that if I ever again tried to kill myself again, "I'm coming with you next time."

I knew then I had to change, and I had to change fast.

In the 12 weeks leading up to my court trial, I threw myself into getting better.

I started calling people and asking about help for alcohol abuse. I reached out to a lady who ran a local women's group and she put me on a fast-track program all about empowerment, mindfulness, and meditation.

I started going to a meditation group. I learned how to overcome alcohol cravings by doing little three-minute mindfulness sessions. I started to think differently, clearly. I started to enjoy the feeling of being sober and the clarity that came with it.

I knew that if I went into prison as the broken, beaten woman I'd been I wouldn't stand a chance.

As the trial got closer, I'd go to see my daughter, Marnie, who would be in tears realizing I'd soon be sent away. I'd tell her, "I'm going to prison. I'm not going to war. It's going to be a good thing. It's like a new start." Most people would be frightened, but I was accepting of it. I knew it was going to turn out for the good of everyone.

I had this other feeling that nothing else bad could happen to me. I'd lost my children, I'd tried to take my own life, I was in debt, I had no job, my son's father had died, my adoptive parents wouldn't even answer a call from me. Still, I knew something good had to come out of it.

The trial began. I was told by my lawyer to plead not guilty, and at first, I did, thinking getting the shortest possible sentence would be best.

But one by one, as victims of the scam told their stories, I started to understand the full extent of the damage caused by what I'd done.

One elderly gentleman who'd lost his life savings said he no longer trusted anybody, he was afraid to tell his children what had happened. He was now frightened even to pick up the phone because he thought it would be somebody asking for money.

It broke my heart. I felt disgraceful and disgusting.

I couldn't believe how I'd been part of something that destroyed these elderly people's lives. Even worse, they weren't my only victims. My children were also victims of my decisions. I realized what we had done was criminal and morally wrong. I was absolutely sorry. I never really have regrets in my life because I don't want to live regretting stuff, but I regret being any part of this crime.

I realized I could never pay back the money that was stolen, or compensate for what so many of my decisions had cost my family, but I could accept and serve this punishment without argument.

I told my lawyer I must plead guilty.

It was the right thing to do. While I had pages of psychological assessment from the hospitals showing all the abuse. I had letters from my hairdresser, saying how my hair had been ripped from the roots by men. I had all the police reports. I had fully cooperated. I had been recovering.

The judge saw all of it, and even acknowledged I was the only one of the defendants with any mitigating factors. My lawyer told me again and again that if I went not guilty, I'd get a more lenient verdict and serve far less time for it.

I refused.

I pled guilty to conspiracy to defraud and got sentenced to six years and seven months for changing my plea, plus 14-months for the Q amount being over a million pounds. My boyfriend was given the maximum sentence of eight years.

The first night of prison was almost like I was being hired for a new job. I felt positive after sentencing as I knew I had been given an opportunity to change. I knew God would not put anything before me I could not handle. Never from the minute I was signed in at the prison reception did my attitude change. In fact, in the remand wing, where we were all being watched for 24-hours before being moved to our permanent cells, they paired me with a younger girl because she was upset and I was totally calm.

The remand wing is a high-dependency area where they put people coming down from drugs. There were women with missing limbs, one had hardly any hair, no teeth, and scars up and down her arms. Some were vomiting.

I had never seen these kinds of people, even at the doctor's. I felt so sad for them. And it stopped me thinking about myself and my own pain. It was my turn to serve, and I had tremendous empathy for all the women around me. It was as if I worked there. I went into full supporting and caring mode.

From the start, I think people could sense it in me. There was one lady on our floor who started asking me questions right away, standing in the reception line.

"I've been arrested for the murder of my husband," she said. "How long do you think I'll get?"

I was thinking why would she ask me this? Every morning, as soon as the cell doors were open, she'd run into my cell with all her paperwork and we'd talk it over. I must have looked like I had it together.

Straight away, I got a job in the gardens, which I thought would be pleasant and meditative, planting flowers and everything. It was hard work. I remember making the officer laugh, saying, "God, we needed industrial tools to do this job!"

I threw myself into education, anything, and everything. I did customer service and a qualification at a warehouse. I did a business course. I did courses in I.T., health and safety, mental health, equality, and diversity. I even trained to be a beauty therapist.

I applied for every mental health job I could. I ended up being an on-call mentor to young girls who get shipped over to adult prison on the day they turn 18. I would be the mum that they didn't have.

In prison, I was introduced to the Samaritans, a charity group that trains people to listen. They trained me to provide confidential emotional support to others who were struggling.

I started going regularly to the gym, twice a day. When I wasn't working or working out, like during lock up, I learned meditation. I went to the library and got all the meditation CDs I could find. I listened to inspirational talks by Louise Hay. I started reading the Bible.

Not long into my sentence, I was sent the book Radio Heaven by a good friend. That book changed me. When Dr. Sam Collins told her story so authentically, I realized good things could start to happen for me. She talked about creating a vision board out of pictures of how you want to create your life in the future. So I spent hours flipping through magazines that were years old, but then finding something that resonated with what I wanted to be and where I wanted to be. I had vision boards all over my prison cell. Everyone thought it was mad. I even wrote a letter to myself from ten years on, all about my work and how I was living in this flat decorated all white and gray with a beautiful view.

Then the book got nicked. But the vision boards stayed up!

I was Ms. Motivation. I was going to make the most of this. For the first time, I was free. No drugs. No alcohol. No men telling me what to do. Of course, there were a few girls, fellow prisoners, that didn't like me. And I brought it up to my senior officer.

"I don't understand why they're so mean to me," I said. "Some of them won't even say hello anymore."

And she smiled and said, "Because you are smashing it. You walk around laughing and smiling. You never grumble. You're helping everybody. And no one understands why."

What was there to not understand? Life up until that point had never been better than when I was in prison. I was no longer being beaten, I was no longer drunk or dependent. I knew that I was becoming a better mum. I did lots of parenting courses, any parenting course I could. I was writing regular letters to the social worker who had told me I'd probably never see my kids again. I told the social worker everything that was happening and how I was changing and feeling. Eventually, I was able to see my children even while I was in prison.

I focused on positives. By this point in life, I was resilient, and my inner strength and self-belief allowed me to turn my life around. I wrote 10 things I was grateful for every day. It could be even silly things like, "I'm grateful that it's sunny" or "I'm grateful that I exercised today." I enjoyed life. I'd never wanted to be alive before! For the first time, I wanted to be alive. God, I want to live 'till I'm a hundred now! All those years I'd lost. There was so much catching up to do!

I got in touch with a family worker and they traced my birth dad. They also sent me my full adoption file from social services. All the old, typed documents. I finally learned about my mum and the real reason she'd given me up. Not because she didn't want me or didn't love me. It was because of race. It was unacceptable at that time, and in her family. She had felt that she had little choice.

So I wrote to my birth dad from prison. The prison Governor let me go out and see him, this beautiful little elderly Jamaican man. We sat in his car together talking. I told him the whole story, everything that had happened, and we held hands and he cried and told me how sorry he was.

Two days later, I rang him and said, "You know, I realize I gave you a lot of information to process about me, and everything that's happened. How do you feel?"

"I love you like a father would, Lilly," he said. "You're amazing!"

In 2017, I was transferred to an open prison to begin easing back into society. As a low-risk offender, I was given a release on temporary license privileges, which meant home visits with my children and a job to help me begin supporting them. I was fully released at the end of 2019. In 2022, I was approved to have my daughter, Tiffany, to come stay overnight. Just the two of us.

Today, my full-time job is working with disadvantaged children and teaching them about empowerment and life skills. I work for a charity which works with children who are excluded from school. I started working as a volunteer on day release from open prison. I teach them about personal hygiene, self-care, and looking after themselves, things they don't learn in school. I talk to them about where they can go for help. We discuss child exploitation, and misconceptions around sexual abuse. We do it in a child-friendly way so that these young girls know if they ever need me, in any situation, they can come to me.

Once a week, I volunteer at a women's refuge doing one-to-one and group sessions. I've been there and I know how difficult it is in a refuge. You've left everything behind and you may be in a strange new neighborhood. You may have lost your children. I tell them that all of that happened to me. But look at me now! I'm not special. I did it. We can all do it. We're not all born into privilege.

When we see women on the TV that we idolize, we don't see the backstory. We don't see what they went through. We think what we see on the screen is how it's always been for them. The truth is, being successful and finding the inner peace of being happy doesn't come easy for anybody. Anybody can do it with the right tools and enough determination.

My message to every woman I talk to, especially younger women, is to understand that you can be and do anything you want. As soon as you know what you want, focus on it. Write it down and make it your everyday goal to get one step closer.

I try to do at least one thing every single day to get my story out there as I work towards changing the women's prison system. It might be something as simple as writing to a journalist or speaking to somebody at the refuge every single day. Any change helps, even if it's just to yourself. If we all do that, every day, we're destined to see a change.

In prison, a lot of women there might see you down and want to make you feel worse. But my hand was always outstretched, picking everyone up, I realized the power of it. Being kind to other women, lifting them up, is so incredible and will accelerate your progress toward your goals. Today, I'm a woman's woman. If I see a woman at the shops or in a cafe, I'll tell her how much I love her shirt or the color of her lipstick or that her hair looks great.

If things are wrong within you, make that change. Own it and change it. You will never hear me say, "Oh, it was all of them and never me!" I take full responsibility for everything I did. Because if you don't, if you're forever blaming others, you'll never mend.

I know I made poor choices. I know when the crime was happening around me, I could have flagged it earlier. I know that if I'd had stopped drinking and walked away, my children would have never been taken from me.

It's not easy, you must own what you did wrong, otherwise you're never going to think you were wrong and how can you get better if that's how you think? So whether you are an offender or not, to understand what you've done to somebody else is a powerful way to change.

My dream for the prison system is to end it for many women. If you've got to put women in a secure place, it should be somewhere their children can visit, and where there's a true effort toward rehabilitation, to learn new ways of living.

What we're doing now is creating more criminals and wasting millions to keep the problem going. If we truly want to see a reduction of crime, we must make the system rehabilitative, not punitive.

I take any opportunity that I get to speak out. If I can change one person's perception, if I can help one person find the strength to leave an abusive partner or help one teenager who went through what I went through— whoever needs to hear about it, I'm talking about it!

When I went into prison, I was the freest I had ever been.

Freedom for me was being locked in a cell with my own thoughts and my own ideas. I'd never been allowed that before. I was never allowed to decide what I would wear or where I would go or who I would speak to or even what time I would get up and go to bed. Without the substance issues, without the controlling partners I poorly chose, I was not so afraid. I realized that there was a good person that was inside of me. I had the gift of time that I'd never had before.

One of the first jobs I got in prison was working in reception. So as the ladies would come off the prison truck, I would be the first prisoner they would see. I would try to calm them down and give them some food. I soon realized that I was seeing the same faces repeatedly.

One girl had been in and out of prison thirty-two times. Her sentences were so small that there was no room for rehabilitation. She was medicated for her drug abuse through a pharmacy, so she was never getting clean of the drugs and there was no time to do any work with her. Imagine: she's got a heavy drug addiction to heroin, she's being medicated in the prison by going to, so called, health care. The day she's released, she's no longer got health care. So what does she do? She goes back to what she knows, back to the street drug, back to doing whatever she can to get them. Again, the circle revolves, she comes back in, nobody tries to get her off the drugs. She's medicated. No rehabilitation. And out again.

I started to become the voice for these ladies and I joined every organization that I could. I became a governor's advocate in prison, which meant once a month I was able to sit with the governor and have a conversation. I was mentored by an amazing lady who worked for Appeal, which is a charity law practice. Between us we wrote a blog about my life. Then I was interviewed by the BBC.

My aim is to change the perception of women in prison. The biggest thing I would say is that if you come across an ex-offender or somebody that you could help, whether that's through employment, mentoring, or supporting them into housing, please don't dismiss them. Think about what is behind their story. Please give women like me a chance.

There's a much smaller number of women in prison than there are men. Four thousand women prisoners and eighty-one thousand men in the UK. The four thousand women tend to be the same women. So there is no rehabilitation happening for the majority. We call it the revolving door. I always say that prison worked for me. It was what I needed. It doesn't work for the majority. It doesn't work at all. I was focused and made that time work for me. For most people, it doesn't help.

There can be bias from judges when sentencing women. If I oversaw the UK justice system, I would have more community-based centers. I would keep families together, women with children. For nonviolent crimes I would rehabilitate within the community. I would have courses on self-empowerment. I would have childcare. I would help people to develop skills so that they could have a job. I would help people find places to live. I would not send anybody into prison for under a year. A lady I knew got 10 months. She's going to lose her house. She's got four children. She's had to give her pets away. She's not going to be rehabilitated, she's locked up 23 hours a day. What is the point? We're never going to see a reduction in crime. If we want to see a reduction in crime, then we need to rehabilitate.

This could happen to anybody.

I was speaking to a fellow prisoner, a lady who was a nurse. She'd been working a long shift and was tired, leaving late at night and driving home. She fell asleep at the wheel and caused a fatality. She got five years for that. She had no prior record.

It could be you. Or your mother. Perhaps your sister or your daughter.

I call it the Domino Effect, and with women, it's never one issue. Everything overlaps. It could start with domestic abuse, that might lead to substance misuse, that will lead to poor mental health, that will lead to problems with children. It's like each domino falling one after the other. It's not enough to tackle one problem. We need to look at the whole problem to make changes. So if it were me in charge, I would stop these short sentences that are doing nothing. For the people that are our lowest risk, I would get them back into the community and rehabilitate them. Get them into work.

It's common sense to me, but the people that are in power and in control of this are so scared to be soft on prisoners. They are terrified of the backlash from the general population. I'm convinced that's what holds them back. The scared public perception. When I tell my story, I try to change the perception of women in prison.

For anyone that is in a similar situation to my story, the advice I would give is pick up the phone and find yourself a woman to talk to. In every town, there will be some women's centers so definitely reach out. There will always be somebody in one of those centers that can help you. I was frightened of authority. I didn't want to speak to the police. I didn't want to speak to social services. If I'd known about a good women's center that I could have gone to for support and that was not biased, that would have made all the difference. Don't put it off for another day.

So dear reader, what is the craziest thing in the world that you would like to be or do?

Pop star or football player, whatever it is, go for it.

Because when I was younger, I wanted to be a policewoman and my father said to me, "You can't go into the police. You're Black and you're a woman." Now I wish I had because I would have been a bloody good one. Aim high. If you aim high, you'll get somewhere.

When I was in the beginning of all this, I would never have dreamed I would have gone to prison. I used to think they wouldn't put a woman like me in prison. I'm a victim. I've been abused. I was abandoned. But they do.

I'm over 50 years old now. My biggest aspiration now is to be a great mum and get all my kids home where they belong, with me. Other than that, I want to be an ambassador for women's justice. I want people to know that when I'm going to talk, I'm going to say something that everybody needs to listen to and that when I take them on, they need to be ready because I'm going to make a change.

I want to be a force to be reckoned with. I want people to know that when I say I am doing something, it's going to happen!

Rebellious Reflections

Freedom. How can we find it locked up in a prison? Freedom is a mindset, an attitude, an intention. Isn't the desire for freedom where rebellion begins? When we want to be free of something, someone?

When we want something different, something new? What is it that you want? How will you know when you are free?

Even in the most difficult of circumstances, we can become free. Even when those around her were not doing the same things as her, or when she was ridiculed for following her dreams, Lilly carried on. She spent her prison sentence meditating, creating vision boards, and helping others. Her vision had such a wide focus that she could observe not only her own room for self-improvement, but also the ways in which the prison could do better for the women in it. She saw the plight of women prisoners, the revolving door, and pledged to do something about it.

Look at her now. She's been featured on the BBC and in many other media forms. She's an advocate for women. She is now in a new, healthy, personal relationship and working so hard and beautifully on getting her children back. She is truly free.

While you may be inspired by Lilly, you still might see her in the abstract. "That's not me, that's not my situation. I don't know anyone in prison." Yet, aren't we sometimes in self-made prisons? The prison of our mind. The prison of the traditional home. The prison of an accidental life. The prison of a relationship. The prison of a job or a career that we hate where we're serving time. We tend to believe that there is no other way, that we must serve our time and suffer. Maybe there's light at the end of the tunnel in some dim, distant future. But what if there isn't? Why keep struggling through the darkness when you can create your own light?

Make the most of every moment. Don't wait until you're released.

Where is it time for you to be free?

Chapter Five

Job of a Lifetime

In the Words of
Carmen Ward,
Founder and Creator of Becoming Carmen LLC, USA

It was the perfect job, with a group of women I respected, and in less than twenty minutes I would be interviewing for it, on Zoom.

I was rested, I was ready, finding my poise, taking the morning slowly.

Suddenly, my neighbor started banging on my door.

"Carmen, I need your help!"

I ran to the door, swinging it open and there she was, soaking wet.

"You won't fucking believe it," she said. "The water is coming through the fucking roof."

"Bullshit," I said. But then I remembered how two years earlier, I had watched the new owners come in and put a Band-Aid on a house that needed surgery.

My neighbor is on Section 8, a housing voucher program, and has limited monthly income. She is a mother of five and a single mum. She needed me and she needed me now.

She needed help. She needed resources. She needed guidance in navigating the situation with her landlord. There are people all over the metropolitan area struggling with slumlords and true crisis issues with housing.

She knew that she could come next door to me and get help. She also wanted to be able to track everything that was happening. It's very important to me that we center on the needs of individuals and build relationships in the process. I knew that my job interview was happening soon, maybe the most important job interview I have ever had up to that point. But the crisis my neighbor was in at that moment, that was more important. Being there as an ear to her as she went through it was exactly what was needed in that moment.

This mother's only goal was not to have to move again. She had been forced to move every two years because of her landlord's refusal to provide adequate living conditions.

I had a decision to make. Go and do my interview or abandon it and go help my neighbor.

I wiped off my lipstick and rolled up my sleeves.

I live in Penrose Park, which is in the first ward of St. Louis, Missouri in the USA. It used to be a beautiful community back in the 1900s when it was predominantly white. It's historic. Now, it's one hundred percent Black. The average value of a home is under fifteen thousand dollars. It is riddled with crime and infested with drugs. People like me live in poverty, in crisis and in need. There are very few resources. At the same time, it's becoming gentrified, pushing black people like me out.

It's hard.

It's the system that we were taught. So trying to build a community pod in a community where black lives are supposed to matter, and in a time when we are center stage in the movement is challenging to say the least.

We have a bigger issue. Black people must learn to trust black people. And how do we do that? Where do we begin?

That's only one side of it.

The other side is that, individually, we are slowly taking steps to start to beautify our homes on the outside. We see that Penrose Park is still beautiful. We're taking baby steps to start talking to each other, and life is slowly starting to blossom.

I think the goal is to make it addictive like a drug. You've got to keep on talking to people and maintain connection so they understand that you're not a threat. That you're here to help and to add to their life so they can have a better quality of existence.

The question for me is, how do I take this community from surviving to thriving? How do we take ourselves out of crisis and into the highest level of success possible? How do we encourage people to dream?

I see a community here that has possibilities. I also see the fear and danger of having to live in this community without any support. This will be where I leave my son. This will be his home. By the time he has this and I'm gone, I hope we are a community that supports one another, especially the special needs population like my son, my baby.

I grew up without an understanding of what family was.

My mother died when I was five years old. She was addicted to heroin. I spent the years from age 5 to age 12, living with a physically, mentally, and emotionally abusive family member.

I spent those years unsocialized. I was told to sit on a step, a ledge at the end of the staircase. I was not allowed to watch TV. I was to be in bed by six o'clock. I had to stand at the table to eat, sometimes with no shirt on, in front of my siblings. I had to sleep sitting on a milk crate with my head in my lap.

I went into state-run residential care facilities. There were a few families that decided to give parenting a shot. They would take me out and try to be a parent for a minute, then when they realized they didn't want that, they'd give me back to the facility. That happened a couple of times.

Around the age of 15, I ended up in Jefferson County, Missouri at another residential care facility. I eventually left there and went with a foster family for a few years.

It was crazy.

I already had my first sexual experience in a vacant house many years before when I was 12. I thought the only thing love was connected to was spreading your legs. There were a lot of those relationships. It wasn't right, and it made me sexually promiscuous.

So young. Crazy.

I got pregnant. No clue who the father was. I had to finish high school and I knew that wouldn't be possible if I had a child. My brother came and picked me up from St. Louis and took me to Macomb, Illinois. I had an abortion. I finished high school in an alternative school in Macomb.

That's when I got my first introduction to selling drugs. It was also when I found out who white people were, for real, because I didn't mess with pink toes—that's what I called white folks. I got a real introduction to country life, white folks, drugs, the whole shebang.

We were always told you don't talk to white people, you don't trust white people. I was a pothead at that point and I didn't know anybody. I started engaging with these white folks. Turns out these people were nice, and they were doing things for me that no one else had ever done in my life.

I didn't want to stay with my brother even though I liked Macomb. People were allowing me to stay with them, like really stay with them. They looked after me. They wouldn't let me stay out after dark because it was a racist town and it wasn't safe. When I was there, I started living the college life.

Dr. Sam Collins 107

Shortly after that I met another man. He scooped me up and spent all this time with me. He wouldn't have sex with me or touch me. All he kept telling me was how amazing I was and how amazing I could be. What I did not know was the whole time he was grooming me.

He had no access to the town or to the college to sell weed. Before I knew it, I was selling weed for him. I blinked and I was selling a quarter pound a week. I blinked again and I was selling a half pound a week. I blinked again, five pounds.

He introduced me to the right people there and taught me how to buy my own weight. I started buying it myself. I didn't realize that after you start moving higher quantities of stuff, people want other things. Customers start asking for cocaine. That's when the light bulb went off. I thought he only sold weed. He didn't. He was moving a major weight of cocaine.

I started selling cocaine too, on a major scale. By the time it reached its height for me, I was moving about 18 ounces of cocaine and about 50 pounds of weed per week. That was until I turned 21 and I was arrested.

Got a lawyer. Beat the case. My boyfriend and I both put our heads down. I got pregnant again and decided I would keep the baby. I graduated college and we ended up moving to Chicago together. We stopped and walked away. I've only been back to that town once since then, and I went with my church. But I never went back after that.

My boyfriend always told me not to use drugs because of my mom dying of an overdose, but he was using drugs the whole time and I didn't know. I tried to keep my family together because that's all I had. He wouldn't get clean. He wouldn't stop. And it got hard. My son wasn't acting like a normal kid. A lot of things weren't clicking for him. I later found out through his Pre-K teacher that he was autistic.

His father said, "There ain't nothing wrong with him." He was incredibly defensive. Black people often have a hard time accepting disability.

When I finally got tired and couldn't take it anymore, I reached out to my brother. He came to where I was in Blue Island, Illinois. I brought only my clothes and a few pots and pans. Then we were off to St. Louis.

I left there broken, troubled, a mess. When I came back, my brother and his family lived in what I would call a mansion. His house was massive. He had the American dream. 2.5 kids, picket fence, family went to church, the whole nine yards.

I tried hard to be what they wanted me to be but it didn't work. Six months into that, they decided to buy a troubled woman a house and set me up in it. At that time my brother was on his way to becoming president of a big not-for-profit.

They moved me into this nice little house. It was a blessing, but I was still struggling to get by. I was begging for help with my son. Trying to figure out how to best care for him. Trying to get mental care for myself. There was nothing. No one could help me to get myself mentally together. No resources, no coaching, no support. I was on my own.

All I got was, "You got to be like this, you got to do this, you got to do that."

It didn't work.

I crashed over and over and over.

Three years into that, my brother decided to sell my house. We moved into a one bedroom shotgun, where you can see straight through the house. We had no refrigerator, no stove. Just a cooler outside for food.

It was horrible. I was still trying to be a sister, a family member, still rushing and running to go see my brother, to see our other brother who is paralyzed, going to all the family events. I was trying hard to put on the lipstick, the makeup, wear the heels, and be the presentable sister of the now president of this big local organization.

It wasn't working.

I left that house and moved to another shotgun. Left that, moved to a townhouse. I had been praying since I was a little girl that God would give me a house that was all mine. My brother bought a house and gave it to me. The problem was I wasn't together. I didn't have access to mental health care. I wasn't well. If you keep giving people what they need but you don't teach them or support them, you don't help them get healed. If you are upset that they don't measure up the way you want them to, especially if you're family or a friend, you won't help. You will destroy them. That was a problem for me.

For the next three years, I worked at a major for-profit corporation. It was like a revolving door of patterns for me. Eventually, I got terminated. Soon after, I began with a start-up non-profit providing support to their leader for about a year and a half. I helped get them off the ground, but things never quite meshed right.

I was diagnosed with major depression and it got progressively harder to balance that job. The fact that it wasn't gelling, caring for my son's special needs, and handling this new diagnosis was too much. I had to leave another job.

I had no job, no income, nothing.

Life got hard. I was making maybe $200 every two weeks and trying to make ends meet. But I never missed a bill. I made it work.

That's when my friend told me about a coaching program pilot that was starting up called Rung for Women. I was like... Hold on! Don't give up yet—something is coming! Then Rung asked me to be a part of their pilot before they launched. They wanted to make sure they had everything right for the program. I started in their pilot. Shortly after starting the pilot, I launched my own company, Becoming Carmen, with no idea of what I was going to do or what it would turn into.

Rung catapulted me. It's a holistic program giving women the opportunity to look within themselves, to become their best selves, and determine what they need for themselves. For the first six months of the program, I worked on myself. I had transformational coaching every two weeks and was seeing a therapist biweekly (sometimes weekly when I needed to.)

I was introduced to healthy eating and healthy options. Over the next two years, I lost over 60 pounds. Up to then, I had a lot of dental issues, and I was going days at a time without eating. I really got into their health program. They had a doctor on staff there that took the time to help me get physically and mentally well.

Rung for Women is a crucial access point for underserved women who want to heal physically and mentally. They help women with their career. They have all these partners that have come alongside the organization to make sure that when women finish the program, they can come out entry-level making 50 to 60 thousand dollars a year. I'm now in phase two of this program, and since I'm not going back into corporate America, they are helping me build my social capital, and expand my own business, Becoming Carmen, into all that it is meant to be.

Rung for Women is a free program. Though there is no financial cost, it is costing me my time. It is costing me emotionally (in the best of ways.) It is making me focus on what's important. I cry a lot. It's hard to heal, to get better, be better, and to see myself as complete, whole, and worthy. But it's worth it.

Everybody's rebelling now. In Black Lives Matter, the movement, we're fighting for equity, we're fighting for equality, we're fighting for options, we're fighting for people to be treated as human beings.

My rebellion for my life has been standing in my truth and what I know to be right even if it means climbing the ladder or getting success will be hard. I believe that people need to stand in the authenticity of who they are, no matter who it may upset, whether it's mother, brother, sister, cousin, pastor, police officer, or politician. Only in that rebellion can you walk into your purpose and change the world.

I think everybody needs to be more rebellious—women and men. I think we too often "follow the leader" or follow whoever we think is saying the right thing. We need to ask ourselves who we are, apart from the people that surround us, separate from the life circumstances that we find ourselves in, and be willing to stand alone. If you didn't get the job, if the pastor didn't agree with you, if your partner didn't agree with you—would you still stand on what you believe?

I want people to know and feel they are interconnected. I want people to understand the importance of connection and telling the whole story. When you only give half your story, it dilutes another person's ability to shift their life.

For black lives to matter, we must center black lives within the black community. We need leaders to shift out of politics, come into the community, and build meaningful relationships. Everyone has a different definition of Black Lives Matter. In most communities that are black, we find it hard to believe that black lives matter because the resources don't make it to us. If we matter, come, and help us.

I want people in my community to have access to all the resources, whether they be tangible or intangible. Where they can activate their dream. Where they can build relationships. Where they can support and/or educate others. Where they can begin to reimagine what community looks like by creating entrepreneurship opportunities and other things. Also where we get back to the basics. Where you can get a cup of sugar from your neighbor or go ask the kids down the street to help you cut your grass. Where we can start to provide emergency support and solidarity to each other in ways that will shift the trajectory of our lives.

How can that happen when the woman down the street is getting stomped in the face by her boyfriend, and he's got a gun so big that you ain't going to say nothing to him because you don't want to die? We need resources that can help. We need it so that when I call and ask for help, those who can pay attention so this woman doesn't keep getting stomped.

Black Lives Matter is not what is being pushed through social media and all over the news. I am the black life—this is not propaganda. Get the resources to us. Empower us. Because right now it's not empowering. It's divisive. On both sides. None of these resources are making it into our hands.

Yet somebody is getting rich.

And those are facts.

If I could talk to my younger self, that little girl sitting on her cousin's steps, I would say, "Hold on, baby. Hold on. Do not allow this world to trip you up." I would tell her how beautiful she is. And she's going to make it. I would tell her how much she matters. To never let any man disrespect her or demean her and give her a false analogy of love and relationship. I would tell her, "Baby, don't worry, you are gonna change the world. Don't worry. This ain't for nothing. It's for something."

I believe in Black Lives Matter. I believe in choice. I believe in options. For Black Lives Matter to do what it's supposed to do, we must shift and reimagine how we get these resources and support into the hands of the people who need them. Right now, it's noise. And the people we are serving are drowning. We're drowning.

And why if black lives matter?

I didn't get the dream job. I showed up late to the interview but that wasn't it.

The role was to help build community for this company; help develop their business.

When one of the interviewers spoke to me, it was almost like she was looking at me with a message from God, you are meant to be a powerful speaker. How dare you not know how qualified you are? How dare you not know how you move a room? How dare you not know that you're qualified to teach people?

"Don't short change yourself," she told me. "You are a speaker, you can help anybody, you can do this yourself, you need to be front and center, not helping someone else do that"

That changed the game for me and made me realize that I had to activate my own business immediately and not wait. Don't even wait for a yes or no answer. Activate yourself. I don't remember all the words, but I know that when I got off that interview, I knew I was a business owner, a coach, and speaker. It was time for me, for my business. I'm not working for someone else again.

The answer came very clearly.

"That job is not for you. Your words can make it all over the world. You'll accomplish your goal...

I needed you to hear what people had to say to you in that interview.

Now, do you believe in yourself?"

I cried hard at first because I thought I had messed up my dream job. I also knew it wasn't right for me. So when I got the email saying that I didn't get it, I smiled and called my friends and said, "It's not time. I knew it wasn't time."

I was going after what I thought was the job of a lifetime and that initial rejection hurt me. Shortly after, I knew that it was a setup for what I was really meant to be doing.

I did not realize the power that I had as a woman, as a black woman with a voice. It broke me in a good way. I did not get to cancel myself out by denying myself opportunities that other people knew I was capable of.

———————— ❧⸙❧ ————————

Every day is what I call, 'the pivot'—what do I need to do today to make sure that I'm whole, to make sure that my son is whole, then to make sure I'm feeding my business. I also focus on how I am feeding the collective, the community, the work, the dream that I am aspiring to achieve to help the people that God created me to serve.

Becoming Carmen has solidified and supported at least five organizations over the last year. I've also recently activated my St. Louis Community Hub of Penrose Park. I have recently submitted my first grant proposal for twenty-five thousand dollars, and I am getting ready to submit another proposal for twenty-five thousand dollars more to incubate a five-phase program to help women prepare to go into organizations like Rung for

Women. I think it is critical that women understand on the front end what they're walking into, because Rung is powerful. But if you are not prepared, it may become overwhelming. Most of us have never had access to coaching in our lives. But I can attest to its power.

So I'm offering a platform, a five-phase program to prepare women for the next phases of their life. Becoming Carmen has now contracted with St. Louis Mutual Aid to take care of all the operations of their warehouse and to bring in collective solidarity. It eliminates silos and brings people together to collect the partnership to reimagine what true community healing is and what real reconciliation looks like.

Today, I manage an entire St. Louis Mutual Aid warehouse. It's an almost million-dollar organization and I'm running it now. Me.

It's going phenomenally.

Do I have all the money that I need? No. But I went from two-hundred dollars every two weeks to a stipend of fifteen-hundred dollars. The money stretches. I am making it work. We will soon have fifteen-hundred boxes of food leaving our warehouse every week. Everything is happening. I have been working on turning it into something financially sustainable for myself and my son. I'm figuring it out, one day at a time.

All of us are shaking right now. God has called me to do something very strategic. I'm not going to be liked by everybody, but what I'm not going to do is be afraid to pull up and do what God told me to do. Blind faith is the beginning of the intersection of love and purpose.

Fear is always there. I'm terrified of everything that I'm doing. I'm terrified that I'm not going to get all the money together. I'm terrified that the work that I'm dreaming of is not going to happen. God sends people to walk with me amid that fear, through the midst of that storm.

So I say—do it afraid. Be bold enough to say, "I'm going after it. I'm going after everything that belongs to me."

In challenging myself, there is opportunity for others to do an internal check on how they need to shift to be impactful in the world. I'm offering a place of reconciliation and unification by fostering a safe place where people can be authentically themselves. That's how I am making a difference.

With this climate we're in, and everything that went on during the pandemic in the US, we must be bold enough to speak out. A lot of my friends don't look like me. They have a lot of questions because they simply don't know. They didn't grow up in the hood where I live. They didn't grow up in Penrose Park. They grew up in a different life. They want to understand so that they can learn, so they can challenge what they've been taught.

We must offer the opportunity for people to say, "I don't know." If people don't understand Black history (or whatever it may be) we don't teach them and we get angry. We try to force things into someone, instead of offering a place of reconciliation.

We must be willing to look at ourselves and do that self-check. Where am I in this, and what is my role? We can't be so angry, even if we've got a lot of reasons to be, because people are asking for information so that they can do better. With love and kindness, that's the only way we're going to reconcile and unite.

As black people, we also must go deep into where that anger comes from, why we have that anger and why we also are hands-off of teaching, supporting, and doing the things that we need to do to help others while lifting our own sails.

I want to welcome the idea that you can be yourself. It's okay that you sold dope for 15 years of your life. It doesn't matter. Cool off and tell your story, because through your story, someone will be free and then they can pull up in their purpose and help somebody else. Only when we do that can we begin again. That's the intersection.

This is a good opportunity to reimagine what we want, free of self-judgment. I am free from judging others who do not look like me.

We know that for four-hundred-plus-years this stuff has been happening, all of it. As we usher in this teaching and reconciliation, we can do it in a very loving way so that we can shift what we believe has happened over these last years. We can do that.

People only have one assignment, to love one another. We must shift and be immediate about it. We need to stop telling people what to do, and instead look inward, do a self-check, and let ourselves do the work.

I can become anything I want to become.

Never give up.

Rebellious Reflections

Carmen Ward, from a systematic standpoint, should never have made it. Coming from such a difficult childhood, into life as a drug dealer, moving around from place to place, struggling to find well paid work, being a single parent with a son with special needs. There were a lot of barriers to prevent her from becoming the business owner she wanted to be.

She works hard every day to become Carmen. She understands her journey to her authentic self. She is in constant growth. How does she do that? Some people around her could see it in her even when she couldn't. They recognized her potential when she doubted it. They told her she was amazing and powerful when she felt unsure.

What's interesting is how many people can be told this by others, "You've got potential! You're amazing!" And still, they don't listen, they don't believe it, they don't take it on. Carmen did the opposite. She heard it. She listened to the people around her, within her community and outside of it, who said, "You've got something special and you need to do something with it."

There are two powerful points in Carmen's story. First, we need to be the people who encourage, support, and empower others. We need to tell others, especially women, how amazing and powerful and full of potential they are. We are so focused on the barriers, so focused on problems of the past, we sometimes miss seeing the potential for the future.

Secondly, can you accept positive feedback? We must develop the skill, not only to deliver that level of encouragement, but like Carmen, be able to hear it, take it on, listen. Believe it enough to have it sink into every cell of our bodies, and then do something with it. Don't judge it or analyze it. Don't suspect people are not serious, or they must be lying, or whatever excuse your self-doubt can trick you into believing. Own it and understand your gifts, understand your talents, understand your skills. Work hard on improving them. Find the help you need. Find the resources that align with your purpose.

Carmen is creating unity across her community. She is here to make a difference on her street, in her city, and outside of it. She will have a wide-reaching impact across the country and the world.

If Carmen can do it, why not you? Who said you can't?

We think you can.

CHAPTER SIX

Kadama

In the Words of

Awah Francisca Mbuli,

Founder and CEO of Survivors Network, Cameroon

"If you want to go back home, Francisca," the lady of the house said, "you must pay back all the money that I paid to bring you here, and then pay for your flight home. Do you have this money?"

"No, I do not have it," I had only a few dollars left of the savings I had brought with me from Cameroon, let alone the $3,000 she was asking me for. My few remaining dollars would soon be gone on phone data cards, as I was not allowed to use the household wi-fi.

"Well, then you must work."

"I have worked two months for you now," I said calmly, "and I have not yet been paid anything."

"You are on probation for three months, Francisca. When the time comes, we will discuss your pay."

"Please, madam, my son," I pleaded with her. "I need to go to him. He has been living on the street. You have three beautiful sons. We are both mothers. Can you not understand how important this is?"

She looked down at me, took a deep breath and sighed.

I have broken through to her, she finally understands! I thought to myself, and my heart began to lighten.

"Look there," she pointed across the room. "Do you see that on the wall?"

"Yes, madame," I said, looking over at a new, very large flat-screen TV, which I had dusted and cleaned only the day before.

"That is a television. It is a commodity." She looked back at me with no feeling or expression, and said, "You are like that television."

"Madame?"

"I have bought you. If you want to go home then you must pay me back all my money. Then pay for your flight back home."

Any hope I had suddenly slid out of my body, and down into the hot Kuwaiti sand underneath the house.

It was 2015 and. I was 32 years old. The reality was I had been trafficked.

I was a slave.

Five years earlier, I was fortunate to have been accepted into a master's degree program at Buskerud University College in Drammen, Norway. As a young woman from Cameroon in Africa, I had worked very hard, had a good job before leaving, and spent a lot of money to get there. I was living in a student hostel paid for by an uncle back home while I looked for a job. I also found a local African church to attend. So I was enrolled in school and I was a happy student.

Many Africans living in other parts of the world who come from a poor background, have family back home who rely on them. When somebody leaves for a new country, even to study, their family still depends on them. They are expected to find work and take care of themselves, all their education costs, and earn money to help support their family back at home.

It had cost me so much money to get to Norway. I did not speak the language well. I found the cold, which was so different from the weather I had left behind, very difficult to come to terms with. When I did not find a job right away, I became very discouraged. Within a few months, I received word that my uncle, who was supporting me financially, had passed away, so I could no longer afford to pay my rent at the student hostel.

I hoped that friends I had made in the African church would help me. They were already part of the community and they had jobs. Perhaps their connections would lead to a job as a cleaner, or a dishwasher, or doing laundry? Something which would enable me to continue my studies and send some money to my family back home.

I had become friends with the assistant pastor of the church. One day he came to visit me in the student hostel. He knew my story. He knew that I had no job and would soon be evicted from the hostel.

"Why don't you come stay at my place?" he suggested. "I have an extra room I don't use. You can stay until you can find a job and get an apartment or return to the student hostel."

"Are you serious?" I said. "Are you sure?"

"Of course," he assured me. "It's no trouble."

I was so relieved! He was a man of God, so I had no concerns about him as a single man living alone. I could only think of how kind he was being to me. So after my last day at the hostel, I went to live with him. I had my own room. He had his room. We shared the bathroom and the kitchen.

Two weeks later I still had not found a job. I was so depressed, which was not helped by the winter cold and the dark Norwegian skies after the warmth and vibrant colors of Africa.

"I can see you are lonely, Francisca," he said. "I cannot let you go on like this. You must face the winter. Look at it."

When I did not want to look, he grabbed my face and forced me to look out of the window, to the snow and the cloudy skies. He frightened me.

"We are all humans," he said. "Everyone needs attention and affection."

That is when the abuse began.

I had nowhere to go, no one else to turn to, and I had spent so much money to get there. My family would be disappointed in me if I did not soon succeed. So I felt that I had no choice but to give him whatever he wanted.

After about ten months, I started refusing him. I couldn't do it anymore. I thought I could pretend but I was suffering so much inside. Whenever he came back from work, I would lock myself in my room. He would knock for an hour at a time and not stop. He tried to convince me to come out to him. I did not open the door anymore. I would stay in my room until he left the next day for work.

One day he left to visit his family in Ghana. When he was about to return, he sent me a text telling me to leave his house before he got home. He hoped that would make me give in to what he wanted from me, and that I would beg him to let me stay. I stood my ground. I left the house. With nowhere else to go, I spent two nights sleeping at the nearby train station.

I had made a Norwegian friend online, and without knowing who else to turn to, I called her. She was on winter break at her dad's place, and they drove almost six hours from the north of Norway to pick me up at the train station. I stayed with her for two weeks, until she returned to college. I was left with her father, who was almost thirty years older than me. He then also abused me for nearly six months.

I was utterly traumatized. I felt as if I was losing my mind. Why was this happening to me repeatedly? What was wrong with me? I begged my family for a loan and I went back home to Cameroon in the hope of regaining some sense in my life. I wanted to recover.

"Why did you not succeed?" My mother and father would criticize me when I returned home. "What is wrong with you?"

Everyone was ashamed of me, and they let me know it. In the three years following my return from Norway, I reunited with my boyfriend and gave birth to a son. My debts and living expenses amounted to more than the money I got from my job. My master's degree programme had been suspended with an incomplete grade. And my family, who had lost all the prestige of having a daughter accepted by a university in Norway, had also lost all respect for me.

"Other people go over there all the time, and they make a success of it!" They would repeat to me again and again, like a mantra. "They stay there, and they buy big houses, and they bring the rest of their family over. But you? You make us start again at square one!"

"I told you what happened to me!" I would cry.

"Oh, these things happen to a lot of people, Francisca. You could have stayed here, not gone at all in that case, and you would still have your old job!"

I was the oldest child in my family, and I had been very successful before I left. I had been taking care of my family, even my extended family, for a long time. Success was expected of me.

I had run out of options, and energy. One day a young man in the community attracted my attention. We had all grown up together, and when he would talk to my mother at her shop, she would complain to him about my situation.

"Big sister!" Adamou called out to me one day. He seemed excited. "Big sister, I have some good news for you."

I had known Adamou since he was a little boy. He lived in our community and I knew his family and he had always seemed to be a nice person. So when he came to talk to me one day, I had no suspicions. I didn't realize he had been studying my vulnerability. He was profiling me.

"You are educated, big sister," he explained to me. "I know you have seen the posters around the community about working in Kuwait. Well, I know of an even better opportunity, teaching English to the children there. And the best part is, it pays a thousand dollars a month. My girlfriend is doing it, look at her"

He took out his phone to show me pictures of his girlfriend, whom I knew was already in Kuwait. She was smiling in pictures taken at a very nice house, in a garden, standing by a shiny car.

"This is your little sister," he said with so much pride. "You know her and look at how well she has done for herself."

Everything Adamou said seemed to offer me the hope that I needed. Finally, a way out. A path to which I can fully apply myself. I was desperate, and that made me more naive.

What I did not realize was that he had trafficked his girlfriend to Kuwait and was using her as a facilitator. She was only a domestic servant and suffering there. When the people she worked for went out, she took pictures of herself around their house and in front of their car, and sent them to

Adamou. He then used them to manipulate others, like me, to believe the lie and follow her to Kuwait.

"There is only one problem," I said. "I have not finished my education."

"Big sister, it doesn't matter! You only must teach the basics." He explained that professional teachers were not needed. "You need to get your books for ABCs, your dictionary, your first reader books. Just the basics. They are only looking for people who speak good English and can teach children, and you are a mother."

Adamou came to visit me and my mother many times. Each visit he would tell us another story about how great life was in Kuwait for his girlfriend. The attractive salary, free accommodation, free travel, freedom to come home and visit anytime.

He did not want this opportunity to go to someone else.

This new job could take care of all my expenses. It would help me to regain the respect of my family I had missed for so long. It was not a big job to convince me.

This was reinforced by walking down the street, seeing the ads for jobs in the Middle East. Be a manicurist in Dubai! Hairdressers wanted in Bahrain!

Of course, I knew roughly what trafficking was but I hadn't heard or read about any specific cases and I didn't know the signs or what to look for. All I knew was that people were still in modern slavery, that some people treat other people as animals. This has always been the way where I am from.

I was confident I could go to Kuwait and start to live my life again. My family could not have been happier, because I'm the first child in a very big family. I was always the one who wanted everybody to be happy and make sure everyone is provided for.

So we agreed and began raising the several hundred dollars to pay Adamou his commission. Even though he was paid by the Kuwaiti employment agency, he told us it was also the practice for him to receive commission as an agent, for making the introduction and handling the paperwork.

Less than three weeks after Adamou's first visit, all my documentation was finalized and I was on an airplane to Kuwait. It was my son's 2nd birthday.

My visa was in Arabic. I could not read anything on it, except my name and my date of birth. I was so excited and keen to get going. I needed this change. I thought that going to Kuwait would bring back the real me. For years now I had been living in my shadow. It would give me much needed money and, more than anything else, respect. So I made no effort to double check anything. It didn't even cross my mind to find someone who could tell me what my visa said.

I found out later that my visa was one of methods used to legitimise the human trafficking scheme. The visa gives you no say in the country, you are not allowed to speak about anything. The visa gives authority solely to your employer and they have control over everything about you. When out in public (which was not allowed in any event), it strips away all your rights. The Kuwaiti citizen who holds your visa replaces you in everything, even in interrogations. You are not even allowed to speak. The visa expressly stipulated that you have surrendered all rights to your employer.

Of course, I knew none of this at the time. So I boarded the plane to Kuwait City, hopeful and excited for a new life.

The passengers were all girls, some younger than me, some older. I counted more than one hundred. It was the first time I thought anything seemed strange, but that thought quickly went. I was focused on my new self respect and how I would please my family.

As soon as we arrived in Kuwait, I knew all was not right. First, we were detained at the airport for almost seven hours before we received police clearance. We were not allowed to sit on any chairs at the airport, nor lean against any of the walls. We were told we could only sit on the floor. Whenever an attendant came near to us to give instruction or answer a question, they held their noses as if we smelled bad. Even the police did this. They looked at us like we were some form of lesser human being, not good enough to associate with them. We were purely meant for the purpose of labor and exploitation of all forms. To them, we were nothing.

What is happening? Am I not a human being like them? I suddenly felt that I might be in terrible trouble.

I heard some of the other girls talking. They were from all over Africa—Ghana, Nigeria, Senegal, the sub-Saharan African countries, and many from Cameroon. Some of them already had sisters who were already in Kuwait. They started sharing stories about their sisters.

"We are coming to do kadama," they said.

Although it is said to mean only housemaid, in Kuwait, Kadama means slave. For many Kadama, the hardship they face in their own countries makes enslavement seem like a decent livelihood. The severity of their poverty has led some women to be trafficked.

As I heard them talking, I thought to myself, "Well, my story is different. I'm different. I'm educated, I am here to teach. I am not, I cannot be like them." I was confident.

At last we were released with the police clearance. I was exhausted and struggling to get my bags together. I had more to carry than the others, because I had proper Arab dresses for teaching, some of my own food stuff, and my English aid books I had bought for the job. When I finally picked up my bag at the carousel, I heard a man calling, "Francisca!"

I waved when I saw him. "Yes, over here!"

He was carrying a little boy in his arms, about a year old. We said hello, and he asked me to come with him to the car. When we got there, he had a nice van, and when we got inside there was a young woman holding a baby, barely a month old.

He started talking right away, very seriously. "I've paid for you to come here to work," he said. "You are here to serve me. These are my two children, and that is my wife."

I was very quiet, listening to him explain it to me. I had in mind that maybe since it was a cool van, brand new, maybe he would be a cool boss. I thought, "Does a regular person come to pick up a schoolteacher? No, it would have been a representative of the school." So I stayed quiet, still telling myself everything was fine.

"You will take care of my children," he continued. "If my children cry, you'll be in trouble. Remember, I spent a lot of money to bring you here so you will follow all my rules."

Oh, my God. What is happening to me?

"Father," I said into the phone, "Father, this is me."

"Francisca! Are you okay? We thought we would hear from you sooner!"

"Father, I am calling to tell you I have arrived safely." I did not want to tell him anything else, for two reasons: I didn't want him to worry, and I didn't know what my new employers might think if I complained.

"Are you okay?"

"Yes," I hesitated. "Yes, I am okay." The man of the house stood by impatiently, motioning to me to hurry up and return the phone. I managed to say, "Give my son a hug and my love to everyone, okay? I must go now."

The man took the phone from my hand and terminated the call.

"May I please change my clothes and have a brief rest, sir?" I asked.

He said I could rest for 30 minutes. But as soon as I had changed my clothes, the baby started crying and the mother wanted to take a nap. So my rest was cut to 15 minutes.

When I came out of the bathroom the man looked at me up and down.

"You will not be allowed to wear that kind of dress here," he said. "I will buy you new dresses. You must remove your hair extensions. Also, I will make an appointment for you to have your face and body waxed this evening."

There was another Kadama in the house, a girl from Eritrea. She had been working there for some time and was to guide me on all my duties in the house and with the family. The problem was she only spoke Amharic and Arabic, so communication between us was very difficult.

I was taken to a store to shop for different clothes. The house owners wanted all servants to appear in Kadama uniform, so that if we were seen anywhere outside the house, everyone would know we were slaves. They took me to the shopping mall and bought ten sets of Kadama uniforms. They also bought new bras, underwear, headscarves, everything, to replace whatever I had brought with me. It was all far too big for me.

Then an Indian woman came to the house to wax me, as in Muslim culture body hair is dirty. She waxed every hair that would be visible except my head. I had never been waxed before and it was very painful. This happens often for Kadamas. The young girl, the madame of the house, was clear that also my hair was not to be in any way attractive to her husband and made me remove my hair extensions. So I did it. I was totally transformed. Within a few hours, the person who had arrived in Kuwait had been replaced.

There was one bed in the Kadama quarters, and I was given only a blanket and told I would sleep on the floor because the other Kadama had seniority. I slept late into the morning because I had been unable to fall asleep for a long time. My body was hot and in pain after the waxing.

Living in that house was hell on earth. They fed me bread and water and I took care of the two children for almost 24 hours every day. I did all the cleaning. When the lady of the house had her period, she would bleed into everything and then leave it for me to clean. She slept a lot too. The couple were very young and liked to go to parties with their friends, so I cared for their babies.

After about 17 days I couldn't take it anymore.

"Please," I asked the husband one day, "I need to speak with the agents in Cameroon who brought me here, can you please take me to the agency?"

The man was instantly angry. "You don't need the agents. You don't need the agency."

"Even my passport is gone," I said, "I have not seen my passport. What is happening?"

He was so furious, he walked away without answering me. I kept on asking him about it over the next two days, and the next morning he got up, dressed and said, "Follow me."

We took the little boy with us into his car and drove to the agency, which was inside a Kuwaiti shopping mall. At the agency, I held the crying baby while the husband turned into a different beast. As he spoke in Arabic, he hit his fist on the agent's desk. I could understand only the word "money" and that he wanted a refund for me.

After a long negotiation, he walked over to me, snatched the boy from my arms and left. I sat in a chair and the receptionist scowled at me. I had no idea what was happening or whether he would be back. A few hours later, he came back with my belongings shoved into my suitcase. Many of my things were missing, including my clothes, my Bible, and most of the books I'd brought. I didn't care. I was happy to be out of that house.

I stayed in the agency, seated on a bench inside a huge window along with 6 or 7 other girls. People walked by and stared at us. Then someone would come in and demand a Kadama. They would look us over and ask about our qualities and work experience. Then they would haggle over how much we cost.

A woman passed, and then returned, putting her head into the doorway, and saying, "English?"

"Yes," the agent said. He looked over to me and said harshly, "Come on, stand up!"

"I need a Kadama who can work in our home, take care of my six children, and also teach them English," she told him. And they began to bargain over me. The more desirable qualities you have, the more your price increases. Since I spoke more than pidgin English, I was worth more.

I was sold for several hundred dinars and the lady drove me to her home. On reaching the house, we sat in the sitting room downstairs and she called her children. They came in, one by one, and stood on the stairway in a line. They stared at me, then one by one, went back upstairs in a row.

"They don't like you." She said, "I should have taken a picture of you and sent it to them first." She looked away from me and yawned, "I am going to have a rest, and then I'll return you to the agency for a refund."

"I am a UNICEF brand ambassador, you know," said my next employer, looking at me in the rearview mirror as he started his car. "I have won many awards for my humanitarian efforts here and abroad."

I nodded and smiled at him. At last, I thought to myself, if he has been honored by UNICEF then he will be human to me! He must be good; he is different from the others.

An hour after I had been returned to the agency for the second time that day this man had arrived, saying he and his family had returned from vacation in Lebanon, and needed two new Kadama to care for their house. He chose me. This time, I was bought for 750 dinars - about $3,000 - with almost no bargaining.

I knew that these people would be nicer to me. I wanted them to love me and think I was a good worker. I thought, I'm already here and there's no turning back. It would be worse to go back home where I have no job. My qualifications will not be enough to get a teaching job, and I have no connections which could help me get a teaching job. So I decided it would be better to put up with things in Kuwait, and work to provide for my family and my son back at home.

The new family comprised the man, his wife, and three sons. They lived in a new, three story houses, and I was the very first Kadama for their new house.

When we arrived at the house, it was almost evening, and I was still in the Kadama dress bought by my old employer. I felt happy because it was a nice house. I looked at the awards on the wall as they showed me around. They showed me my own kitchen, my own bedroom up near the laundry. It was near the electrical grid so it was very hot up there, but still, it was mine.

The wife listed all the jobs she wanted me to do in the coming week. She asked me to clean my kitchen, then prepare myself some food and take a shower. Then after a rest I could begin work tomorrow.

"It's okay, madame, I can start tonight!" I said. I wanted to impress them, and I wanted them to love me and treat me well. So I did almost all the jobs she had assigned to me for the week before it was evening. Almost the whole house.

I didn't realize that this would make things more difficult for me. I didn't know that they had planned to hire another Kadama to share the work of the household. I had done such a fast job and had seemed so happy to do it that they decided there was no need to look for the second Kadama. And then when they discovered that I was very good at ironing they stopped sending their fancy garments and gowns to the dry cleaners. I had proved myself to be too capable.

The next morning, I awoke in pain. The mattress was very thin and laid upon an iron bed with metal springs underneath. I went to my kitchen to prepare some tea, and the milk powder provided to mix with my tea was like baby formula for newborns or for small animals. So I did not drink it or eat anything. I dressed and made my way downstairs.

"Francisca," said the lady of the house.

"Yes, madame. Good morning."

"We need to discuss a few of the rules which will apply to you in this house."

"Yes, madame."

"In this house, for you the word, 'no,' does not exist," she said. "It is not even in the dictionary. Everything is, 'yes,' when you are asked to do something. I do not ever want to hear the word 'no' come out of your mouth, understand?"

"Yes, madame."

"Secondly, whenever you see baba, my husband, you are to bow out of respect. You must not make eye-contact with him. And when he comes home in the afternoon, you are not to look at him, understand?"

"Yes, madame."

"Good. Now we must talk about my plants." We walked around the house as she explained to me the care required for each of the many types of plants, both inside and outside in the garden. So many plants.

"Yes, madame."

Every morning, I watered all the plants exactly as she had stipulated. Each week, I would wash the dust from the leaves with the hose outside or a spray bottle. One day she found a green leaf lying on the floor that had fallen off the plant.

"Francisca, what happened?" She said angrily. "How did this fresh leaf fall from the plant?"

"I'm sorry, madame, I don't know," I said.

"After my sons," she said, "these plants are like my children. So you must take care of them. Do you understand?"

"Yes, madame."

Even though I would try to get all my outside work done before the sun got too hot, working outside with the plants in the hot Kuwaiti sun was torture. The skin on my legs and feet slowly began to crack and peel, then my lips and my face became chapped and blistered. I developed painful acne everywhere.

I became increasingly unwell. I was sick a lot. I took large quantities of Panadol Extra without bothering to read the instructions, even though I knew it could harm me. I was trying to get through the day. My stomach hurt all the time because the milk I was drinking was not good. They would ask me to take mint with some hot water and drink it instead of taking me to hospital.

The entire family would have me run around the house. I would be on the ground floor and one of the boys would call from the higher floors, "Francisca, get me a glass of water." All the while a bottle of water sat across from him.

Another would call, "Francisca," where is my brown t-shirt?" And it was in the dresser drawer next to his bed.

Another would call out, "Francisca, bring me yogurt from the freezer." When he was only a room away from the freezer and I was on the third floor doing laundry.

The youngest boy, who was fourteen, never flushed the toilet.

When I cooked my own food, they would tell me it smelt bad, even when it was the same meal, I had cooked for them.

The lady of the house would give me the food from the fridge which had passed its use-by date. "Francisca, this is good for you to eat." She would tell me. "You can eat it, it's still good. I want to buy something else for the children."

The family drank only bottled water. I would bring 20 cases of water from the market. I was only allowed to drink from the tap.

It was like this all day, 18 to 20 hours, every day.

I was also not getting paid.

I knew that to have any chance of getting out, I needed help.

Sometimes CNN was on the television during the day, with nobody in the house paying any attention to it. One day, with a pen and paper I had hidden, I wrote down the contact details of the not-for-profit organizations who advertised on CNN Freedom Project. Then I went up to my room, got on my phone and emailed all of them.

I had a standard email that I would copy and paste on a regular basis to send to them. It read:

"Hello, I am a Cameroonian girl trapped in human trafficking in Kuwait. There are many other girls here who need help. I need your help to get out." I signed it: "Save a woman at a time, save a nation, save the world."

No-one responded.

One morning the lady of the house was called away to Lebanon to see her mother who had become ill.

I helped her pack her bags in silence, then went to pack bags for the two younger boys who were to go with her. They left for Lebanon that same day. The oldest boy was 18 and getting ready to leave for college in America, stayed behind. He was almost never home, always out with his friends. The husband also stayed for his work.

I kept my composure until the lady left and then I went up to my room and cried on my bed.

All I could think was that I would never get back home, I would never be able to save $3,000 to repay my agency fees, nor would my family. I started to think I would be stuck for the rest of my life.

Suddenly, the husband shouted up to me, "Francisca! Help me!"

I got up from the bed, wiped my tears from my face and took a deep breath. I hurried downstairs and found him sitting on a step with his back to me.

"Please, Francisca," he said pitifully, "I have slipped and hurt myself. Can you help me to the bedroom?"

Oh, my God. I'm not permitted even to look at this man's face. Contact is not allowed. How can I even dare to touch him?

I was standing close to him and I was scared. "I am not allowed, sir," I said.

"No, you can help me. Please help me."

He held on to me and put his hand on my shoulder to lift himself up. He limped with me to the bedroom and threw himself down on the bed. I took a blanket and covered him.

"Stay here," he said. "Stay and watch over me while I sleep." He closed his eyes and seemed to be sleeping so I slipped away for a minute but then he called me back.

"Francisca, I have hurt my buttocks very badly. It hurts so much my head is spinning! I need you to look."

"No, sir..." I said it as gently as I could as it was the forbidden word. "Please, I cannot help you. I don't know anything about it. Please, it is better for you to go see a doctor."

I returned to my room, to hide from him. I was frightened. Around 9pm I saw him easily and effortlessly get into his car and leave the house for about an hour. That's when I knew he had faked the whole thing.

He called me downstairs again, this time to the sitting room.

"I have been to the doctor," he said. "And the doctor says I need a massage."

"I can't help you with a massage," I looked around and grabbed the newspaper from the table and opened it. "But there are advertisements for many kinds of spas. Here! The Filipino massage." I handed the newspaper over to him.

"Oh, Francisca, I can't do that," he said. "Those people are dirty. You can do it. I'll teach you."

I looked at him, without saying anything, and then went upstairs to bed. I was alone in the house with this man, and I was terrified of what he could do to me.

The next day when I was working around the house, he called me up to the gym room. He had put sports mats down on the floor and laid there, fully nude, on his stomach. Next to him was a bottle of baby oil. He instructed me to take the oil and massage it into his buttocks. I couldn't believe it. Here was a man whom I was not allowed to look at in the face; now that his wife was away, he was asking me to give him a nude massage. I did it, I tried my best not to look at him. I looked at the TV in the gym room instead.

"Francisca, look at what you are doing. Pay attention to me," he said. He would keep moaning as I massaged him. "Are you not enjoying it?"

"I am not enjoying it," I said. "I am massaging you like you asked."

This happened for the next two days. Every time the oldest boy went out, the husband would go online and buy pornography for us to watch together, which in the Muslim world is not only expensive, but prohibited. I would be in the kitchen struggling to prepare dinner and he would say, "Come sit with me, let's watch." I did not want to, but what could I do? Instead I thought I could be honest about my feelings.

"Are you enjoying it now?" He'd say.

"No, I'm not enjoying it." I could see he was becoming irritated by this, so after a while, I started to pretend to smile. I wanted him to trust me. In a few days, this man, who never entered the kitchen, in the absence of his wife was making pizza for both of us to share. So I pretended everything was fine.

I was desperate to escape. I spotted a newspaper advert requesting kidney donors. In desperation, I called the number, and I ended up agreeing to let them buy my kidney for 15,000 Kuwaiti Dinars (around $50k). I need the money to pay off my employer, buy my flight back home and then to establish a business for myself in Cameroon and be who I have always wanted to be. But, thank God, I changed my mind after deciding that they would probably take my kidney, kill me, and throw me into the sea. They didn't give up until I blocked their number.

That's what desperation does to a person. I nearly sold my kidney to get out of that house.

I had to run away.

I needed to find out the address of the house I lived in. I had no idea where I was. Luckily the eldest son ordered a food delivery, and when the driver came to the house, he handed me the receipt. So then I had the address. The husband gave me his phone number, so we could text each other and send messages during the day. I felt like he was enjoying the change, and was entrusting more information to me, so I did everything I could to keep him happy, and to make him feel that I loved his attention.

In the Muslim faith, Friday is like Sunday. The eldest son and husband had gone out to pray in the morning. After prayer, it is customary for the men to meet and to eat and talk. So I found myself, for the first time, alone in the house.

I found a Cameroonian group on Facebook for Kadama in Kuwait. People who had already escaped had set it up to educate those of us who were still trapped. I had been learning about the mistreatment of other girls, and I had discovered that I was not alone. I had also started to realize from the posts on the group that the day to run away is Friday, when families are out of the house.

I went on to the group to check the posts. One of the girls had posted a message asking if there was anyone willing to run away with her. Cameroon does not have an embassy in Kuwait and she planned to seek refuge at the Togo embassy. So she asked the group: Is there anyone who is suffering and is willing to leave their house, who has money for transportation to the embassy. Can we share transportation? Yes, I replied. I was not prepared, but something pulled that yes from me. I was hurting, I was sick, I was being sexually and psychologically abused. I was also almost out of the little money I had brought from Cameroon.

She asked for my address and advised me to wear my kadama dress over regular clothes, and to put only the few essential things I would need in a trash bag: a pair of pants, a toothbrush, toothpaste. Kadama are never allowed to go outside because the traffickers know we would try to run away. So if I were to be spotted by neighbors, it would look as if I was taking out the garbage, nothing suspicious.

As I prepared my trash bag of essentials and waited for the girl from the Facebook group to arrive with the taxi, my heart was pounding. I ran through all the possible scenarios: the husband would come home early; I would be seen by a neighbor and caught; the police would be called and return me to the house, where a terrible punishment would await me.

Finally, the taxi arrived with my escape partner inside. I ran to the car and got in. It drove off fast. As I looked out the window to see if we had been caught, I took off the Kadama dress. There are checkpoints in Kuwait, and if police recognize you as a Kadama, they must take you back to your employer's house, without question.

Soon we arrived at the Togo embassy. We paid the driver and walked together to the entrance. To our horror, we discovered the Togo ambassador had decreed that no African Kadama who had run away from their Kuwait employers would be granted entry into the embassy, unless born in Togo. My companion was born in Togo so she was allowed to go inside.

I stayed outside under the harsh sun for almost three hours, I was boiling with fever. In the evening, my friend came outside and said that they would not accept us. So, we took another taxi, searching for another African embassy.

This taxi driver was new to Kuwait. He didn't know the place or how to use his GPS, and even though we gave him the address of the embassy of the Central African Republic, it took until midnight to find it.

There were no diplomats present when we arrived, but there was a group of Kadama girls inside who were trying to escape. Seventeen of them altogether, all fleeing their employers. They opened the door for us. Some had passports but no money to fly out, some had no passports. I had neither.

I had escaped but to what? I sat and waited, fighting off sleep.

The next day, I was called in by a diplomat for questioning. I told him everything that had happened to me. He asked if I had my employer's phone number, which I gave him. They must have called him because the husband came to the embassy with my passport and threatened to take it to the police with an ultimatum that I return to his house within seven days. He left, but immediately came back and left my passport at the embassy. Perhaps because he thought that it would be more trouble to explain things to his wife than to let me go.

Then, miraculously, my phone beeped with a message. It was Freedom For All from New York, offering to help. I told them that all I needed was a flight home.

That evening, I was on my way to the airport.

It was very hard for me to leave that place and the other girls. The girls who were left behind were surprised and some were angry with me. It was impossible to understand why I was leaving for home when some of the girls had been staying at the Embassy for as long as two months. Even worse, after I got home I learned that the embassy diplomat in charge of helping us return home had also been sexually abusing the girls.

After three long months of being in Kuwait, I returned to Cameroon. I was in bad shape. I was losing my mind. I was drained and malnourished. I tried to rest and recover, but my mobile number had gone viral in the community of girls still trapped in Kuwait. Day and night, I received messages begging for my help. I wanted to do my best to get them home safely.

So in 2015, I began working with Freedom for All, the not-for-profit organization in New York which had saved me. I wanted to help the Kadama girls in Kuwait and throughout the Middle East. Most of the girls had to run away, as I had done. As women, they needed toiletries and menstrual pads. The embassies could afford to feed them only rice, so they needed money for more food and essentials.

I arranged for a diplomat to send money from Freedom for All directly to the embassy in Kuwait. Then we discovered it was not being used for the girls at all. The diplomat was using the money only for himself.

So later in 2015, my organization, Survivors Network was born. I decided to take matters into my own hands to make things happen. We are working to create more awareness of the reality of human trafficking, and to highlight what can be done to prevent it. We discovered that poverty is one of the biggest factors that forces people into trafficking situations, so nearly 50% of our work is focused on economic empowerment of women and girls.

I began to visit local villages in Cameroon—leaving flyers at schools, churches, and markets to raise awareness of this issue to prevent women and children from falling prey to human trafficking schemes.

We help repatriate women and children who have been trafficked, reconnecting them to their families and support networks which can provide further help. We run a safe house, both short and long-term, where they can stay. We are looking at how we can approach governments to strengthen anti human trafficking laws, including how to expedite the prosecution process for human trafficking violators. We are also planning a vocational training school, to give women skills they can use to make money at home, so that the financial rewards promised by traffickers do not tempt them away.

I never want to leave another woman in the situation I found myself in. That pushes me on. I know what it is like. When someone tells me their story, I get angry. I need to make it change. I must do something. Even if it is the middle of the night. Victims don't always know they are victims, I didn't for a long time.

I don't know how or why I ended up in so many abusive situations. There isn't really a common factor between victims other than the fact that they've encountered an abuser. It wasn't anything I did wrong. I'm not sure what the reason was, but I believe God wanted me to experience it first hand so that I could better advocate for women in similar circumstances and force a change.

I was able to break free. I spoke out. Too often, victims understandably remain silent about what has happened to them.

I am 38 years old now and I live for what I do. I don't have another life, so I live for this one. I love it because if I don't do this, I'm not living.

My goal for the future is to see a world where human trafficking no longer exists and where women and girls are economically empowered. I want to make sure no one else goes through what I did.

There is so much joy and greatness in helping others. But also, caring for yourself is important. I want to do everything for everybody.

I'm so thankful that, with everything I have experienced, I have come out well and healthy.

You will too, whatever it is that you are enduring. Please educate yourself about trafficking. It could be happening on the street where you live. It happens in London, in Los Angeles, everywhere. Are you sure it isn't happening right where you are?

Try to help them. Try to do something.

Rebellious Reflections

We don't get to choose the country or culture we're born into. Are we who we are because we are born that way, or because of our environment? What happens when you are born into an environment that restricts women? Where there is a gender specific expectation upon you? An assumption that you will provide for your siblings. An outlook that because you are the oldest, that you must achieve more.

We can be naive about the world and believe that despite the warning signs, abuse is somehow our fault. We are conditioned as girls to become women who want to please others because they are always somehow better than ourselves. Even when Francisca was consistently abused, she still wanted to please. She rationalized her situation and tried to make the best of it.

Francisca teaches us hope, to believe in others, and to believe something better is ahead. Even when abuse, trafficking, and violence had been an integral part of her life. How does an educated woman with a university degree end up being conned and trafficked as a kadama to Kuwait?

Doesn't it make you think, "If it could happen to her, it could happen to me, or my daughter, or my friend's daughter?" Does it make you wonder if there could be trafficked women living in your own neighborhood? This doesn't happen only in Kuwait. There are trafficked women and girls all over the world, in every big city. It is big business. It is a global enterprise, with a profit and loss account. It has customer service. It has an accounts payable department. It has a brand. Modern slavery exists. And beyond the facts, beyond the knowing, we feel her story. There are many others in that very situation, right now, who have not escaped, who don't have a plan, or the means to escape.

Despite our belief systems, despite what we have been conditioned to do, despite where we end up, despite what we have had to endure, no one is the property of somebody else. Francisca found it within herself to contact someone, not-for-profits around the world who might help. Isn't it so tragic that only one of them responded?

Only one.

Yet, one is all it takes.

She rebelled, she got out. But her true healing is in the creation of her organization Survivors Network Cameroon. She is now the one who responds, who helps trafficked girls survive, come out of their situations, and thrive. She helps them to heal, and in doing so, heals herself.

We don't think much about the aftermath of rebellion. The energy it takes, the fear we must overcome, the toll it takes, the long-term healing that is required. The best healing comes from helping others. From sealing the wound, caressing the scar, feeling it burn some days, knowing it will always be part of you.

You can heal too.

CHAPTER SEVEN
Shooting Stars
In the Words of
Destiny Ayo Vaughan, Student, Ireland

It was very dark and still outside as I glanced at the clock. 4:47 am. I shivered a little as the bedroom window let in a cool breeze. My old nightie was ridden with holes.

I looked up at the night sky. Hopeful. Excited. Tonight, could be the night.

I wish to be a normal child; I would plead for hours. Please, send me a shooting star.

Every night I wished for a shooting star.

When I looked over the street across to the neighbors' house, I could see through their windows. A light flickered on as the dad once again slowly got out of bed. I knew the routine, I watched it every morning.

My neighbor was a girl the same age as me, eleven. I watched her living her life. Her mum will come into her room soon and wake her up with a little kiss. The girl didn't always look very grateful about it. She got up, brushed her teeth, put on her school uniform, and had her breakfast with nothing on her mind. Sometimes she watched TV.

I had this feeling every day of wanting to feel like her, wanting to feel normal. To be excited to be awake and get going in the morning. To walk downstairs knowing that somebody would greet me and be excited to see me. I was so envious of the whole experience that she had.

There was a school backpack hung on the chair, and her breakfast ready on the table. Her dad went off to work early and her mum made sure she was ready for school. Sometimes her mum chased her around the house to get ready. They laughed and they loved each other.

I felt empty.

What do I have to do to live the same life as you?

"Imagine if I could just be a child!" I said to myself so often I lost count.

That girl's role was literally just to be a child. My role was to make sure that I got my siblings ready for school, to make sure that when I got home the dinner was ready, and to make sure that I never, ever misbehaved.

My role was to wake up every morning and know when the punishment was coming, and tell myself, "Look, Destiny, if you don't take it, your sister will get it."

My bedroom was a very small room, not even big enough for one child. It was a bunk bed and a cupboard. That was it. No toys, nothing that would make you think a child even lived there. It was merely somewhere to sleep.

But there was enough room within it for me to dream.

I used to think that if I waited for a shooting star, I could wish for anything I wanted. I don't know where that came from. So I waited all night. I'm pretty sure half the time it was only airplanes, but I thought they were shooting stars. I used to think that shooting stars only came if you waited all night.

If I fall asleep, I'm going to miss it.

I probably got an hour of sleep most nights if I was lucky. I used to fall asleep in school and the teachers would tell my parents about it. They were not happy because they thought I was being lazy, not realizing that I was staying up every night dreaming of a better life.

Imagine if my wish comes true! What am I going to do? Will the wishes only come true for me, or will it also come true for my siblings as well? What will happen to my parents? Will they go to prison?

What if I got up in the morning and all I had to do was eat breakfast, put on my school uniform, say bye to my parents and get ready for school? What if I even had a packed lunch, a bag full of pencils and pens? What if I was excited to come back home after a long day of school? These things that seem so trivial and normal to the average child were everything to me.

That night, right after 4:47 am, before the sun began to rise, I saw one. I genuinely believed it was a shooting star. At last. My wait was over. I was stunned. It was so quick and so beautiful.

I went to the bathroom, sat there, and I realized, oh, you have to say something to make a wish...

"I wish to go to college and everything good will happen for me," I said quietly.

As I sat there on the toilet, it started dawning on me that day, the reality that the girl living across the street from me has a life that is not my life. And it's never going to be. If my circumstances stay the same, my life will stay the same—that's the best way to put it. It hit me that it's not going to change if I don't do something about it.

Maybe shooting stars aren't real. Maybe there must be action.

I have to say something.

So 11 year old me went into school that day, and during my lunch break I walked up to a good friend of mine whose mum was a teacher at the school.

"I have to tell you something," I said. "I am being beaten up by my parents."

I told her everything that was going on, but I didn't know how she took it. At that age, you don't know how people will take anything. I'm not even sure why I decided to tell her specifically, but someone needed to know. So, I told her everything.

After we talked, she didn't know what to say. We kind of went our own ways down the hall. I began thinking she might not even do anything about it.

———————— ❧❦ ————————

I was born in Nigeria in 1998. We weren't privileged. We didn't have a lot. I lived in a house with 10 other people and it was basically a few brick walls. My parents married outside of their religion which was not allowed, so my dad was hunted and shot on that account. Being in so much danger, my parents had to move out of the country. They went to Ireland and they left me in Africa to live with my auntie.

In our Nigerian culture, it was normal for girls to get married very young. When I was five years old, I was engaged to get married to a man that was nearly four times my age. I didn't know what it meant. I thought he was my friend. Every day after school, I would go visit him so we could get to know each other. I thought of him as a stranger and I didn't understand.

Then, before the marriage, my aunt said I would instead be moving to Ireland with my older sister - I didn't know I had an older sister and why I was suddenly moving to a new country!

When my dad was shot, my parents were the only ones given the visa to go abroad. They weren't allowed to bring me, likely because I was born in a different country. Where I was born is still debatable as my family doesn't seem to know either. I say Nigeria because that's the first place I remember. I don't have my actual birth certificate, only a copy. So, I assume they couldn't bring me because they didn't have a birth certificate proving my place of birth.

In 2003, I was happy to arrive in Ireland because it seemed like a good environment. Well, at least, I was told it would be. At five years old, I was happy to live with my parents and be in a new place.

Things started to go sideways quickly. After a few days of living in Ireland, my parents were very abusive. Emotionally, physically, really any type of way that they could possibly be abusive, they were.

After a few years, it became extreme. I was so afraid of this woman, my mother, that I once tried to jump out of a window to get away from her. She was coming to hit me and I was so afraid that I wanted to jump out of the window. I was trying to get as far away from her as possible.

I wasn't sure why they even decided to bring me to Ireland. I think it was part of building their illusion of having the perfect family. My parents really wanted to make sure that people thought they were great parents. They cared more about what people thought than caring for us. They wanted to bring me to Ireland so their family could appear complete.

I thought that every child went through this. I didn't know that other children didn't go through what I was going through. This is how life was. My parents used to leave us alone in the house for hours on end, sometimes days. I was always so hungry and at only six, seven, I was too young to know how to cook. When I would go to school, my parents sent me without lunch. I had one meal a day, if I was lucky—sometimes it would even be cereal. After I came back from school, I would go to work with my mum until late and then stay awake for shooting stars. Then I would get up the next day and go to school again. This was my life.

Life.

Yeah.

Everyone's life is the same, isn't it?

Once I was so hungry that I started eating the plaster on the wall because it was the only way I could feed myself. I would eat anything under the sun to feed myself. I even used to eat sand. I started eating chalk at school. My teachers even caught me doing it and would ask me, "Why are you doing this? Why aren't you eating chocolate like other kids?"

"I don't know," I would say. "I thought I would try it." I never told them what was happening.

My teacher reported me to my parents because she thought that it was a weird habit. I got into so much trouble. I remember the beating that I got that night was very severe. Teachers think they are doing the right thing when they tell your parents so it wasn't their fault.

Eventually, I started stealing other kid's lunches whenever I could.

One day, I was walking home after school, absolutely dreading going home. Along the way I was struck by a car. I was so tired, I didn't see it coming and wasn't looking the right way. It hurt and my leg was injured, but I told the driver that I was ok, worried about creating any further conflict in my life. I was so afraid of my parents that I didn't even tell them. There's a picture of my leg from the time and it was kind of bent. I told them I fell because I was so afraid of telling them I got hit by a car, thinking they would never allow me to walk outside by myself again. It would have taken away the last bit of freedom I had. I couldn't bear any more imprisonment.

I realized that eventually I would reach 18 years old.

I'm going to go to college, I'm going to get a chance to leave this house, this family. I will be free.

But then again, I also had a younger sister. What if something happens to her once I leave? I wouldn't be able to recover from it or forgive myself. I couldn't let her get hurt.

If I'm going to leave the house, she would be left entirely defenseless. She was so used to seeing me get abused, she too thought it was normal.

I had to say something.

At the time, I had learning difficulties at school, so I would have special classes during the day to get help with my English, math, and schoolwork. So, one day, when my teacher asked me to come to the special classroom, I thought it was a regular session.

Then more teachers were coming into the room.

"Is something going on at home, Destiny?"

I felt fear rise in my body. My face got warm, and I got a horrible feeling in the pit of my stomach. I didn't know what to say.

Was I in trouble? Everyone was looking at me.

Apparently, my school did have questions about my safety at home, and on two previous occasions, they had sent out a social worker to our house. But I remember before they came, we rehearsed with my parents on what to tell them.

That's one of the biggest problems. When a social worker comes into your house, they tell the parents in advance. So parents can train their children on what to say. If the social workers came and didn't tell my parents prior or took me and my sister out individually, it would have been very different. I think we would have been put in care a lot sooner. But because my parents knew they were coming, they had time to prepare and of course, they kept getting away with it.

So I was taught to lie and tell them that I had fallen or that I was always outside playing and I was a clumsy kid. If they would ask me a question where that excuse might not work, I would say, "My sister hit me, she punched me because we were fighting." That way, the social worker would think that we were the aggressive ones. It's sisters roughhousing.

If they would say, "Oh, you said something different before to somebody else," I would tell them I was lying because I didn't get something I wanted. We were trained to always put the fault on ourselves. The attitude in my house was that when something happened, no matter what it was, it was automatically our fault because we were being disobedient, too bold, or too much like children. When our parents told us it was our fault, we believed it. I was a young kid, what do you expect?

I never questioned my parents. I always thought, "Yeah, that's true, we are disobedient." I fully believed what they told me every time. A lot of kids are in the same situation, believing that whatever the adult in their life says is the truth.

If lying didn't work with the social workers, you simply don't answer.

So it took them a while to convince me it was safe to speak. But once they did, everything came out of my mouth. I couldn't contain it.

Then they were discussing what to do about what was happening in my home. I felt relieved because even though I didn't know what was going to happen, I knew I wouldn't be alone anymore. Other people finally knew what was happening.

I was also scared. Very, very scared.

In our house, if you spoke up to say something you are not supposed to, there were serious consequences. For some kids, you get grounded. For me, you're going to get beaten so bad you won't be able to walk the next day.

To be clear on the extent of the cruelty, my mum stabbed my sister one time because she forgot to wash the dishes.

Another time my parents took African pepper and put it into my eyes. They left it in for an hour, not letting me wash it out. I couldn't see anything the entire time. We endured extreme abuse. I was conditioned to behave or else I would face a new, even crueller punishment. Even though I knew these people were trying to help me, they wouldn't have to deal with the consequences if I got caught. The last time I misbehaved, I got a plate bashed into my head. I knew I wouldn't be coming to school the next day if my parents found out I finally spoke my truth.

My mum did more hitting and it was far more spontaneous. My dad was much more deliberate. With him, it was far more emotionally damaging because he planned what he was doing. My mum was wrong, of course, but the implications of what he did were worse.

I couldn't take it anymore. Something inside me decided to be brave and show my teachers the evidence.

I started showing them my scarred body. I didn't even need to speak because I was covered in scars. They spoke for themselves. It was very easy to believe me because I had so much proof to show. For some kids, their parents are much more careful about leaving signs of abuse. I guess in this one circumstance, I was lucky.

The room went dead silent and one of the teachers looked like she might cry. I was quite glad to show them so they had to believe me. I didn't remember how many scars I had until I showed them all of them.

As I showed them, I started to remember each scar, each time they had hurt me. My leg was broken and my arms were twisted. I had bruises all over my body. There was no doubt what was going on in that house.

After a while, they started bringing more teachers in because they didn't really know what to say or what to do about the situation. Suddenly, all these teachers were questioning me at once, as opposed to one trusted teacher talking to me individually. This is partly why the cycle will continue until teachers are properly trained on how to handle these situations. I don't blame the teachers. I think they didn't know how to deal with it. Nobody ever wants to be in a room and listen to a child talking about getting abused. It makes everybody uncomfortable. There isn't always proper protocol in place for teachers to know how to talk to a child who tells them they are being abused.

It was getting late and because I hadn't come home, my dad came to the school looking for me. The teachers tried to hide me. They didn't want me to go home. They were trying to get my dad to leave the school, saying I was not going to go home with him until I was checked out at the hospital. Everyone was fighting, and all I could hear was yelling. I didn't realize how serious it was. Every black child goes through this, right?

In Nigeria, many kids get beat. They get hit. It is seen as normal. I always thought it was normal because I'm not the only child I knew who was being abused. I remember when we would go to church—and this was in Ireland, not Nigeria—the number of black kids that came in with black eyes made it seem normal. There was one kid that had one eye that he couldn't even see from anymore. He lost his eyesight from how badly his eyes were bruised.

My dad refused to leave the school, so two or three teachers covered me with coats to sneak me away out the back and get me to a hospital.

After the hospital visit, I went into care and lived with a family in Waterford. My siblings were still at home at that point, and I honestly didn't know what was going on most of the time. To me, it was as simple as, "Oh ok, I don't live with my parents anymore."

It was a difficult adjustment. I think the part people find hardest to understand leaving such abuse is the way they had become accustomed to it. My whole life was abuse. It was all I knew. When I got put in care, I was getting fed every day. People asked me what I wanted to do, where I wanted to go, what I wanted to eat. It was overwhelming. Like, are these trick questions? Am I going to get hit if I give the wrong answer?

I had gone into care. I lost my siblings when that happened. We were split up. I was 11 and while I was finally going to live with normal people, they weren't my family. I no longer had the traditional family anymore. I would have to live by myself and figure things out.

I didn't know how to act because I had never been in a normal family before. It took me such a long time to settle in because I didn't know what I was doing. I was learning how to be normal.

The family that I was placed with was lovely. They helped me through a lot of things that I went through. Because of the severity of trauma that I experienced, I was battling with PTSD. I had anxiety, I had depression. Often I would try to kill myself.

This went on for my teenage years.

There were two weeks I spent in a psychiatric hospital for adults when I was 16. That's how bad I was. I remember thinking, my life is only about pain. That is all I know. I'm so young and I only know pain. I don't know happiness. I don't know love. I don't know any of these feelings. I remember saying to myself that I deserve so much better than what I'm giving myself. Because it's up to me to give myself a better life, it's up to me to find my happiness. Nobody else can find that for me now.

Yes, my parents treated me badly, but they didn't own me anymore. I think it's very important that people understand that you can't control what other people are going to do but you can control how you treat yourself. Treat yourself the way that you want somebody to treat you, whether it is in love, in warmth, or kindness. It's up to you to love yourself first before anybody else.

I think my parents had the same things done to them that they did to us. While I cast myself as a kind person, if I had stayed in that house, perhaps I would have turned out exactly like them. It would have been all I'd ever known.

My parents wanted to tolerate the life they had made. But I wanted to make a different life for myself.

I believe, to an extent, that my parents brainwashed me. Obviously, sometimes I knew that I was misbehaving, but I never believed I deserved to be whipped until I was bleeding. I think my parents truly believed that they were right.

My parents were never brought to justice for their actions.

They were able to get away with it because I was so young when it happened. I also still believed a lot of the things that happened were my fault. So when it came to bringing it to court, I didn't think they should be punished. I thought, "Oh no, these are good people, they are my mum and dad!"

The prosecutor declined my case because there wasn't enough evidence.

Even though I don't agree with things my parents did, their life in Africa was completely different. It's hard for people to understand the culture. They did not live a perfect life. My mum had suffered abuse when she was very young. My dad got shot for his beliefs when he was very young. I always try to remind myself of their pain to better understand them.

It doesn't mean that I've forgotten what they've done.

It took me such a long time to forgive them, but I have. The forgiveness wasn't even about them—it was for me. It was very hard for me to live a normal life because I was filled with so much anger.

I kept saying to myself, "Why didn't you speak up sooner? Why did you let people treat you like that?" I realized I had lived my whole life watching people who hated themselves, and who used that as an excuse to treat other people poorly. I was slipping into doing the same thing to myself!

I lived with my adoptive family for six years, and they were a close-knit family. I wasn't always the easiest person to live with. I was always testing them in some way to make sure that they were not like my parents. For a while, I didn't give them a fair chance.

Eventually, I began to feel I couldn't live my life unless I forgave my parents. I had to forgive everything. This doesn't mean I had no anger about it. It means only that I am allowed to be a better person than what I was and I had to accept what happened.

For a long time, I was in so much denial about my abuse. Meaning, I couldn't forgive if I didn't acknowledge what had happened. I had to let myself feel the anger, to have a lot of breakdowns, to push people away. To realize I would not be able to live the life I had fantasized about. I never lived a normal childhood. I couldn't have a "normal" life after what I went through. I've had to accept that.

However, I knew I could help to give another child that chance. I began working with children who had experiences like mine. It doesn't mean that I was able to take away their pain, but to be understood is so crucial to healing. We need more understanding for each other.

That is how I finally turned my life around. I realized my purpose in life.

I was in care until I was eighteen and I can proudly say that when I was 19, I started my first degree in Early Childhood Education and then I did another degree in Social Science. At 23 years old, I began my Masters in Psychological Studies while working for charities.

The organizations I work with help prevent kids who had difficult childhoods from repeating their parents' behavior. I chose to work mainly with children's issues because I was a child when most of these things happened to me. I'm a strong believer that everything happens for a reason. I always believed my role in life was to protect children. Most of what I do today is ensuring that children have their rights, know their rights, and have an adult fighting for them. Children shouldn't be fighting for themselves.

People hear me talk about my story, and afterwards tell me they are experiencing the exact same thing and do not know what to do about it. They say things like, "Before I heard you talk, I wouldn't have said anything because I would have thought that nobody was going to listen. But the fact that people are coming to hear your story, maybe they'll listen to mine!"

People think because I am not in that situation anymore, I should be the happiest person in the world because I got out. You're lucky! That's the least sensitive thing you can ever say. Think about this: you might have lived through it, but you still live with it. You still have every right to be angry. It doesn't mean you stop feeling how you feel. It doesn't mean you wake up in the morning to a new day as though nothing happened. You still must deal with that trauma. I think it's very important that people realize that we never live a so-called normal life and forget everything. It's not realistic. You live a life of deeper understanding over somebody who might not have been through the same things. You see life differently.

I went through all of this as a child. It wasn't an adult that took me out of the situation, I took myself out of that situation. I literally had to fight for myself. Children need to know that is possible. They need to know that school is a safe place to do this. They need to know about the services and helplines that are available.

We need to talk to more kids in schools so they understand what abuse is. Often, like when I was a little girl, they might tell a friend. But that child may not understand what the word abuse means. Nothing can be done unless all our children are educated on it. Schools must educate children in what is right and what is wrong. We feel we can't speak about these things to them because they are too young. Kids aren't stupid, they can understand. We need to educate children in a sensitive way that still informs them. So if they do hear the word abuse, they don't say, "I don't know what that is." Instead, they know they must tell an adult if they are being abused.

When it comes to happiness and love and developing positive emotions, it takes time. You don't wake up one morning and realize you're completely in love with yourself, you're completely happy. It is a process, a journey. When you have PTSD, and I do, there are going to be bad days. You are not going to wake up every morning and be all sunshine. And that's okay.

I always take every day as it comes. I don't rush into anything.

The odds were stacked against me. I remember when I left care, I had nothing going for me. Many people said to me, "You're never going to go to college. You're never going to succeed in life."

I feel it's very important to understand that nobody can tell you what you can and can't achieve. It's completely up to you. It's your life, nobody else's. Whatever people think of you or do not think of you, it shouldn't be an element in your life. What you think of yourself is more important, and it's very important for you to be inspired by who you already are.

You must take the time to figure out what is going to stand in your way, because that's going to stop you from achieving that goal. Then you must set out a plan.

What am I going to do? What do I have to do to push that obstacle out of my way so I can finish my goal?

Dr. Sam Collins 163

I always thought God had a purpose for me, for giving me this life. While I was wishing on that star I also thought, maybe if I prayed more, he would give me a perfect family, a family that loved me and appreciated me.

"I don't know what I did to deserve this but I know You have a purpose for me. Please, this is the one thing I'm wishing for. Please give it to me."

What I didn't realize is that he was listening to me the whole time. He had a different version. What I thought "family" was at the time was not what he had planned for me. The plan for me was to stand up for those women and children who didn't have a voice. I will never forget that being able to describe myself as a "survivor" is a privilege. There are a lot of children who don't get to use that word.

I always said to myself that if my life got better, my fight still wasn't over until I could fight for every child that needed me to fight for them. I know what it's like to feel that you don't belong. I don't want any child to feel like that. I know I can't save everyone, but I can try.

If you choose to challenge the obstacles in front of you, you must understand it will come with pain. You're going to have to address a lot of things you don't even want to change, let alone talk about.

But that's where it starts.

It starts when you talk about it.

It starts when you ask for help.

My best advice is that you don't need to be afraid to be vulnerable. You need to feel everything: the hurt, the pain, the happiness, it's all a part of being human. Vulnerability is what is going to get you to truly live your life.

For a long time, I allowed myself to be the victim and not the survivor. It used to hold me back a lot. What I learned was that my childhood was not my fault. I had no control over that. But in my adulthood, every decision I make is completely up to me.

If I could talk to my younger self, I would tell her, "You underestimate how strong you are. You can't give up yet. There's something better coming."

As a child, I thought violence was normal. One of the most important things I've learned is compassion. My foster family showed compassion beyond what they signed up for. I couldn't read, so every single night my foster mum would read to me. She would stay up to help me to do my homework. She would pay for anything I wanted. Sometimes I forgot how my mental health affected them as a family because they were always looking after me. They didn't show me how I affected them. I've learned that when I'm going through something, it's ok for me to have a breakdown. But when I come out of a breakdown, I need to turn around to those who bore witness and ask them if they are okay because I've also impacted them.

In the future, my dream is to say that I am a clinical psychologist. I also hope to be happy, in a loving relationship, with children of my own so that I can give them the life that I never had. I want to be an author by that time as well.

Everybody should live life with purpose.

Please understand that you are powerful. You don't realize how powerful you are. Anything you feel you deserve, go out there and get it. But you will have to put in the work.

Nobody else can do it for you. I wish for all your dreams to come true.

Rebellious Reflections

So did you manage to read Destiny's story without crying? I've tried several times, I even tried reading it out loud to see if that would make a difference. I couldn't contain myself. To picture her as an 11 year old girl in this desperately empty bedroom, looking up to the sky for shooting stars—looking into her neighbors' house to see another girl, same age but with a dramatically different life—beyond tragic.

How many other children like her are out there quietly suffering, not even realizing that it's not normal to be abused by your parents? I hadn't thought about that before. These kids think this treatment is normal. Destiny is very matter-of-fact when she talks about her early life. It can come across as shocking, even cold as to how she describes it. But for her, this was her every day. This was her life and she thought it was her fault.

The first time I met Destiny was on Zoom, a young woman who was adamant that if I told her story, it needed to be hopeful, optimistic—not retold in a depressing way. She didn't want it to be another drama. If you're wondering, did she go to college successfully? Yes, she did and she recently graduated! She's now working for charities to support children. She's also in the running for Miss Universe Ireland.

So many kids don't make it out the way she did. I think many days are still very hard for her, but she's so young, in her early 20's and sure to go very far in life. I can't wait to see it.

Destiny. Typically, we think of the word "destiny" with some sense of inevitability. There is powerlessness and surrender. "It's my destiny." It's written somewhere in some stars, or some book or plan, and we have no control over it.

But could it be possible that your destiny is constantly being rewritten by your actions? That there isn't some inevitable path, that no matter what you do, you end up mindlessly following. You do have control. You can influence your destiny and the destiny of others. Isn't rebellion the opposite of conforming and mindlessly following the path you're on?

To picture the hardship and abuse Destiny went through is extremely challenging. Every time she shares her story, I hear more details. I watch her progressively open and trust me, as she continues to make a difference for other kids, so that they won't have to experience what she experienced. She realizes she can change the world by sharing her story.

What was it that made her finally decide to tell someone about her abuse at only eleven years old? Eleven years old. I think it's so important to hone in on this fact: she would only tell a fellow child because she didn't trust adults. Why would she?

What do we have to learn from her? That whatever happens to you, even in the worst of circumstances, you can forgive. You can still achieve what you set out to do.

Maybe all her wishes on shooting stars were not in vain. Maybe they were heard.

Let's broaden your idea of destiny. It's not one predetermined path, but an arrival based on the array of options in front of you. As you take your steps, the path becomes clearer, the destiny evolves and changes. At any point in your life, you can wake up to a day that can completely change everything.

Destiny got up that morning and realized she was going to do something different that day.

That could be today for you. And it may not work, but perhaps it's worth giving it a try. Is there something that you haven't been telling people? It's time to open, to be vulnerable, to get help.

The secrets that we hold. The crosses that we bear. The guilt and shame that we carry. What we blame on ourselves. What we think is normal. The people that we don't want to hurt. They all weigh heavy on us. Even when her parents were abusing her, Destiny didn't want to hurt them. She didn't want to get them into trouble. But you must fight for yourself.

What is it that you have gained from Destiny?

If she were here right now, what would you tell her?

Perhaps you would give her a huge hug and tell her everything is going to be ok. Maybe it's time for someone to do the same for you. Am I right?

CHAPTER EIGHT

Ray of Sunshine

In the Words of

Pip Hare,

Professional Sailor, Pip Hare Ocean Racing, UK

I was glued to the instrument panel, watching every dial, readout, and screen, an endless stream of data as the eight-meter waves were dumping over the side of my boat.

I was constantly processing, looking for anything that wasn't right. But at that point in the storm, I couldn't see anything outside. I had to trust my intuition. Switching from the screen to my senses.

I had the second oldest boat in the fleet. And at the age of 47, I was one of the oldest competitors. I was one of very few women who had ever embarked on the Vendée Globe Race, the greatest sailing race round the world, where all competitors sail solo, non-stop and without assistance. It was also 2020 and the height of the COVID-19 pandemic.

I felt the motion of my boat. Is it picking up in the wrong way? Is that rolling a wave set coming from a different direction?

I closed my eyes to listen carefully. What was that sound? Is that creaking? Is something broken? Is that flapping? I was on hyper alert, waiting for something to go wrong. But also expecting things to work out.

I wasn't moving much. I had been frozen in the same place for two hours on a knife-edge. The angel and the devil, one on each shoulder...

Slow down, Pip.

Pip, Speed up.

Slow down, Pip!

Speed up!

I was constantly questioning them both... How far is too far? If I pushed the boat too hard and lost the rig, I was thousands of miles from help. I'd have lost the greatest opportunity of my life. I'd worked so hard to be on the start line of this race and was only halfway through.

I wasn't cruising a boat around the world solo, this was a race. There's a fine balance of competitive drive pushing me to the brink versus being cautious and quitting while I was ahead - and still alive. I wanted to prove that I could be the best I could be. Pulling the plug early would have been doing myself a disservice.

I finally decided, no, this is enough. I'm going to reduce the sail. I slowed the boat down... and then spent the next two hours beating myself up because I had put the brakes on too early. I hadn't moved for two hours. "Okay, I'm going to sit down," I told myself. I sat down and thought, "Should I be sitting down?"

That's when I got the text message from my shore team:

What are you doing? You're the fastest boat in the fleet over the last three hours!

I started laughing. This should not be happening. Not in a million years. It was funny.

I was competing with people with flying boats—they had foil wings, which lifted those boats out of the water, making them very fast. They were twenty years newer than mine, with a lot more money behind them. I wasn't being massively risky, but I knew that I was sailing harder and more aggressively than a lot of the men around me. I loved having the room, space, and ability to go at it how I wanted to. I loved it all, especially the physicality of it. I had toiled for years to get to this point. My determination and spirit would beat them all!

To be rewarded with being the fastest boat in the fleet was like a drug to me. I wanted more. It made me want to go faster. It made me believe that I could catch up to the next boat down the line, that I could stay ahead of the boats behind me. It made me believe that anything was possible.

In the Southern Ocean at that time of year, the air temperature was about six degrees. With wind chill, sub-zero. My boat was going fast, and because it was particularly old, there was very little protection on deck. As I moved, giant walls of water, 6 to 8 meters high, came over the side of the boat. If I hadn't been holding onto something, they would have knocked me straight off my feet.

I was wearing thermals, a mid-layer, a dry suit, gloves, and my hat. I had two distress beacons in my pocket in case anything happened. On my arm was the remote control for the autopilot and attached to my head was a headlamp which pierced through the pitch black night.

I normally hate being cold, but I had stopped noticing it. I had become so used to the freezing temperatures that over the whole of the race so far, I had never closed the door to my cabin. Six degrees outside. Six degrees inside. Cozy.

When weather systems came through, total cloud cover obscured any possible view I might have had. I could see those giant walls of water coming towards me, but nothing beyond. The sky and the sea were not distinguishable. It was black all around, which had stopped feeling strange.

Racing and pushing a 60ft boat on your own is a physically taxing experience. People often imagine sailing as very tranquil, easy. They don't realize how much noise surrounds you. It's incessant, and when the ocean throws the boat around, the boat throws you around. As for peace and quiet, my boat was now making some disturbing screeching and humming noises when the water came over the deck.

I was exhausted. For the last three days I had been extra vigilant. Waiting for some indication that something was going wrong. Another part of me was banking the miles. Noting when I had made an adjustment to make the boat go a little bit faster.

But for the whole leg in the Southern Ocean, I had been anxious. One of my daily jobs was to manage my own anxiety. Sometimes it was deep down within me, other times it felt like it was outside and preparing to engulf me. It was constant. I was scared, my stomach was churning, my heart was racing, my mind was buzzing. Then there was the noise and peripheral activity. It's a busy boat. It was a constant what if, what if, what if, what if? All the time I was worried. Is this too fast? Is the boat going to break? Have I gone too far south? It was seesaw between safety and performance.

Then there's the flip side. When they messaged that I was the fastest boat in the fleet, I couldn't believe it. It gave me such a rush. I'm doing this! I'm doing this better than I could ever possibly have imagined! But then ... Can I do better? Can I push myself further?

Suddenly, I was aware of an unbelievable opportunity. An opportunity that I had spent so long creating. This could be the only chance I ever get to really show what I can do. Would my desire to win beat my crippling anxiety? Could I really be the person that I dreamt about 30 years ago? Maybe even better than that? How much better could I be?

Then, of course, I needed to stay alive. I needed to maintain the boat as well as my body. I had to eat, sustain the boat, and manage the anxiety and rapidly changing emotions which flowed into my mind like the water crashing into the boat.

It was exquisite.

It was the most incredible feeling I've ever had in my life. People seldom get to walk that knife-edge. Especially so intensely and for that long. It's all adrenaline. But there's good adrenaline and bad adrenaline. For better or for worse, anxiety, excitement, competitive drive, and the need to do better - all pushed me beyond my preconceived limits.

Every sense was lit up, listening to the sounds, watching how fast I was going—feeling everything. Every cell worked tirelessly and my heart thudded in my chest.

I was at a place called Point Nemo, which is closer to the International Space Station than to any continental landmass. I was so remote, so far away from anybody and anything.

I was in love.

I couldn't see anything. I could see my sails, but I could be anywhere. It was dark like I'd never seen. I didn't quite comprehend the enormity and the scale of being where I was. I was reduced to my 60-foot surfboard whipping its way around the world. On my own.

I was truly and completely alive.

I was sailing a slightly more aggressive route than the people around me. I'd watched a couple of weather systems come through, and I watched how I sailed compared to the people I was racing against. I realized that my boat could handle more. I decided to drop a little bit further south, even though it meant sailing 150 miles in the wrong direction, to get to the finish line. I believed the stronger wind would help me make up those miles. I believed I'd chosen the best place on the race course.

I was not backing down.

My first objective was to finish the race. I had already endured weeks of brutality on that boat. It's incredibly tough to make a boat do what you want it to do. Day in, day out, pushing, pushing, pushing. Things were wearing out all the time. There was always a risk that something would break. Was it something that I could fix? If not, I was out of the race. All these variables were always circling in my head.

How you evaluate risk and what's important is crucial to race performance.

Each decision I made to push my boat harder was carefully considered. It wasn't a gung-ho approach. I talked myself into it. I logically assessed it. The boat would reach 22 or 23 knots and then a little voice in my head would say:

This is probably a little bit too fast. You should back off.

Every time I heard that voice, I'd question it.

Why?

Does the boat feel unbalanced?

Does the boat feel out of control?

Will I be strong enough?

Will I have the physical ability to take a sail down if I need to?

Why? Why? Why?

All the time I was asking myself questions. If I could logically convince myself that things could be pushed a little harder, it felt less uncomfortable, less nerve wracking, less emotionally and physically draining.

I wanted to finish the race. I needed to finish the race. It was also the opportunity that I'd looked for my whole life. If I didn't make the most of it, if I didn't end that race believing I had tried as hard as I possibly could,, then I'd have let myself down.

So I tried harder

I was scared. I don't think any one of the thirty-three of us in the race could honestly say that we weren't scared. We were all pushing our boats to the limit. On top of that, I didn't know what was in front of me. I couldn't see anything. But isn't life like that?

It was a leap of faith I had to take. I had to trust I wasn't not going to hit an iceberg or something that could sink my boat. I had to address those fears, address the fact that I couldn't do anything about them, then tuck them away somewhere. If I had thought about all the possible obstacles all the time, I would have been utterly paralyzed.

I had spent a long time preparing for the race. Most of my efforts were spent readying the boat for every eventuality—but I didn't think much about myself.

I did have a hardcore medical kit on board. I had medical training. I had to learn to self-cannulate, how to stitch myself up, inject myself, and all those sorts of things.

Sometimes I treated myself a bit too much like a machine.

So several factors created the perfect storm. I had lost too much weight. I didn't realize how much until I was out on the Southern Ocean. I was wearing layers and layers of clothes and never took them off, so I didn't notice how rapidly I was losing weight. It seemed irrelevant until I began to feel weaker.

I was trying to manage my energy and exhaustion at the same time as the demands of sailing. I couldn't do it all. My body and my immune system were starting to fail.

Dr. Sam Collins 175

I was so exhausted and decided to lay down for a minute. I failed to notice that a jellyfish - a Portuguese Man 'O War, known as 'The Floating Terror,' had washed onto the deck right where I was lying and stung my back. Instantly I had an allergic reaction to the venom.

I made the mistake of not taking my t-shirt off right away. That enabled the venom to spread rapidly across my back into my body.

My face started to swell and my field of vision closed because of the swelling around my eyes. I felt massive blisters growing all over the back of my legs.

Hives were all over my body.

My body was reacting and fighting the infection.

I had to keep going.

Days turned into nights. I kept sailing and crossed the equator.

"Avoid direct sunlight," my medical team advised. "It will make the reaction worse." So I had to stay down below all day with no ventilation in 104 degree Fahrenheit heat, with rivers of salty sweat pouring over my blisters. I was miserable.

I could only race the boat actively at night time, when it was cool outside. I looked up at the vivid and beautiful stars. They gave me hope.

It took four weeks, during the final leg of the race, to get my allergies under control. And I'd already pushed myself to what felt like my limit in the seven weeks before the jellyfish sting.

Eventually, I shared the fact that I had a jellyfish sting with the press, but I didn't tell them that I wasn't well. I didn't want to bother people. I didn't want people to focus on it. I started getting texts from friends and family members: You've got nothing to prove. Just get home. We want you to get home in one piece. All were very well meaning, of course. I hid my struggles as much as possible. There was a level of respectful space given to me when I told them, "I don't want to talk." They know I meant it. It wasn't personal. I do not want to talk. I was not in a place to give a lot of thought to how people on shore might be feeling.

I didn't really want to talk to anyone. Working with my shore team required a huge amount of trust between us. They had to trust me to tell them what was going on. I had to trust them to give me the right advice at the right time.

The shore team was allowed to advise me on how to make repairs that would put the boat back in the same condition as when I'd started. They were not allowed to give me any advice on routing, weather strategy, or how to make the boat faster.

They were only allowed to communicate with me on certain terms. There were only two or three people in communication with me. I spoke by phone to Jeff, my technical director, only four times during the whole race. The rest of the time we did everything via text message. It's a concise way of sharing information, and there's always a reference to what you've already said in the history. Particularly with my technical problems, I could show him photos and videos of things and it gave him a much better idea of what we could do.

I also had Lou, who ran the business side of things and was also a medic, so she was ready with medical advice when I was sick. Every time she advised me that I needed some sort of treatment, she would have to run that by the race doctor because we've got all sorts of stuff in the medical kit—from steroids to codeine—so the race doctor had to know what was going on as well.

But the hives kept getting worse. The blisters were so bad and I had to sleep only on my stomach to not make them worse. I wondered if I could carry on.

Will my result be jeopardized because I got sick, or made a mistake?

Would I lose all the great things I'd worked to achieve so far?

Will I lose this race?

I was annoyed with myself and I began to feel defeated. I didn't want to stop racing but I was not physically well. I'd lost nine kilos (nearly twenty pounds) in body weight. The race was taking a toll on all parts of my body. Physically, I was weak, and even though I was falling behind, I found my spirit. I believed I could catch the boats in front of me. So I pushed.

The race concluded with sailing up the Atlantic. Once I'd recovered from the sting a little, I didn't give any more of my crucial time away to the rest of the pack. We remained equidistant from each other all the way, so they weren't pulling away from me anymore, which they should have done because they were in flying boats and I wasn't. I simply wasn't going to let them get ahead anymore.

In the final week of the race, a filthy weather system descended. It was hard, tactical sailing and extremely wet and cold. There were lots of sail changes needed, and it was challenging to keep up. But those are my kind of conditions. I realized it was an opportunity and so I slowly, slowly, slowly, bought my way back up to the pack.

Each competitor can see all the boats on the GPS tracker. The boats were also in contact with each other and able to message each other. It so happened that we ended up with two different routes, north and south, to get to the finish with about three days to go. So every skipper had a choice between which route to take.

I could see the south route was quicker. But it was going to be incredibly hard work with my boat. By that time, there were four boats ahead of me on the route. I knew I couldn't catch the first two so I had to let them go. But the second two, I knew I could catch.

We're going north. We think it's safer. What are you doing? They messaged me.

Going south. I replied. I want the fastest route.

A minute later: Don't you think North is better?

Nope.

They were desperately trying to get me to go north with them. But I went south because, as difficult as it would be, I could see an opportunity. I was six hours behind one of them, and three hours behind the other. I was convinced I would catch them.

Funny, they knew it too and started to adjust strategy, sailing even harder.

And then before the finish, my spinnaker broke and destroyed all the guardrails on one side of my boat. Quite a lot of damage. And that was it, I couldn't catch them. There is nothing you can do when that kind of damage happens. You deal with it. You have no other option but to deal with it. Emotion cannot play any part. You can feel emotional about it afterwards, but in the moment, you must accept it.

The greater thing for me was that I knew I could have overtaken at least those two boats. It so happened that I didn't. It wasn't my fault. It wasn't my inability. It wasn't anything to do with the kind of sailor that I was. It's that I'd been sailing for ninety-five days around the world in quite an old boat.

And it broke.

---- ❦ ----

The Vendée Globe race is the longest and one of the toughest endurance sporting events on the planet.

It lasts for three months, you're always on. The boat is always moving. There's always something happening, whether you're awake or asleep. It's also one of the few international, top level sporting events where men and women compete on equal terms.

Ever since I first read about Vendée when I was 16 years old, I wanted to do it. I desired the challenge to persevere, but also to express my equality within the sport. A competitor is a competitor, female, or male, and that's it. That, for me, was always a massive attraction to the event. To be able to compete on equal terms.

It took 31 years of dreaming, planning, and training to get to where I was able to even enter the race, at the age of 47. The UK does have a national governing body for sailing, but it doesn't prepare anyone for races other than the Olympics. In practical terms, that means there is no performance pathway. No coaches. No grants. So I had to raise my own money, navigate my own business management, and forge my own path to get there.

Since I was a kid, I had imagined it so many times. And there was a danger that it didn't meet those expectations. I also had a complete lack of confidence in myself, my own ability, who I was, and what I was worth.

And then there were natural setbacks. I had grown up in a landlocked town. My parents had a little sailing boat, so we'd go to the coast on the weekends and do family holidays on our sailing boat. It wasn't racing, of course, it wasn't even ocean sailing, it was more a pottering around in a boat.

I was in my teens when I discovered I liked sailing. Perhaps because it gave me freedom. I started reading sailing magazines. I wanted to travel. I wanted to have adventures. I wanted to test myself and push things as far as I could, not potter around.

Through reading about sailing, I learned about the ocean racing that was happening all around the world. Every time I picked up a book or magazine and read about an ocean race, I wanted to do it. Ocean racing encompassed everything I wanted for my life. It was also clear that the only people taking part were men. The only women on the crew were cooks or in some other supporting role.

In my teens, I needed to be passionate about something. It was a time in England when everyone was doing their A-levels. Everyone was asking me what I wanted to be, and what courses I wanted to take at university. They wanted to know where I was going with my life.

I was applying for university degrees. And I could have done so many things, but I was ambivalent about it all. Sailing was my passion.

Well, I began thinking, maybe I will train as a doctor. A lot of these ocean race boats need to have doctors on board. If I was a doctor and I could sail as well, maybe they would take me. I came across a magazine article about the Vendée Globe race. I read and reread it to make sure I had understood it properly. It was about a French woman, Isabelle Autissier, who was the first woman to compete in the race. And it talked about her in the same way it talked about the men.

That was the moment I decided to do it.

I had absolutely no idea how it would materialize but I left school at 18 and got a sailing apprenticeship on the south coast of England. Since then, I've been working in the marine industry and working as a sailor.

I rapidly discovered that sailing—and especially my offshore and ocean racing sailing—is a massively male dominated sport. It's not a particularly welcoming environment for anyone, especially women. I didn't come from the same background as many of the other people who were sailing and I was cripplingly shy. Roughly five percent of those who participate in the sport today are women. Back then it was even less.

I progressed through the ranks of the professional sailing world. I became highly qualified. I started instructing and examining others, sailed, and lived all over the world, and accumulated all kinds of experience and knowledge. Still, racing eluded me. It seemed entirely shut off from me, and nobody was offering any opportunities.

When I hit thirty-five, I realized I would have to create my own opportunities, as I had with everything else.

I'm living on a boat already, I thought, why not race in my own home? I found a race that was the right entry level for me and the boat. That was one of the hardest parts, as I had to force myself to stick my neck out, force myself to say I was here and ready to challenge them.

I recognized from the outset that people were going to criticize and doubt my ability. But that didn't matter. I was sure it was what I wanted to do. I also decided that rather than racing as a member of a team across an ocean as my first step, I would sail across an ocean on my own. Until then, I had a lot of sailing experience, but I had never sailed on my own. My first solo step was to sail alone from Uruguay to the UK. It took fifty-eight days. I did it mainly to reassure myself that I was capable of it, and that it was something I wanted to do. I did it, and I loved it!

The next step was to do it again, in a race.

The next step was to do a harder race.

And after that, to get a more technical boat.

And then a bigger boat.

Every year I completed a bigger challenge. After I accomplished one, I'd figure out what to do next.

I aimed to complete every new challenge. Then I checked in with myself. Am I still doing what I thought I wanted to do ?

My route to the Vendée started when I was 18. I didn't set out on a structured performance path until I was thirty-five. From there, it took 12 years of steady growth to achieve my goal.

I pushed myself hard. I wanted to give myself the best opportunity every time to move up to the next level.

On the water, you can learn. You can learn how to read the signs, you can learn to adapt. But the greatest thing about it is that it's not personal. There are no people involved.

I think I've always worried about what other people think of me, and I've let that hold me back. I could never walk into a room like I owned it because I don't own it. I don't want to be looked at, noticed, or judged. There is no one to judge me on the water. I can be exactly who I want to be. I can do what I want to do. I can do stupid things. I can get things wrong. And it doesn't matter because I'm the only person involved. There's no one looking in from the outside. That lets me be who I want to be and not worry about what other people think I should be.

As someone who is not very confident, this feels like a confident way of approaching my goals. That's why I like sailing so much. I get to be a totally different person, and I trust myself so much more when I'm on the water. I'm the best version of me.

In the Vendée, it's unusual for French reporters to engage with English speaking competitors. They tend to ignore us. In my race they called me the Rayon—the ray of sunshine.

"Why are you so happy?" They kept asking me. "Why wouldn't I be happy?" I would reply. "I have battled my whole life to be here and I'm in the middle of the ocean doing exactly what I want to do!"

Sure, it's not easy. It's cold, wet, dangerous, and frightening. But I chose to do it and I wanted to be there, so why wouldn't I be happy about it?

Arriving at the finish line in France, I had mixed feelings. It felt very stressful. The boat was really starting to fall apart and there was a lot of traffic on the water. Plus, it was night and very windy. I'd spent the whole of the ocean avoiding the land, busy water, and not sailing into the wind. Yet at the end, I was doing all three.

I was struck by an irrational fear around six hours from the finish line that the boat was going to fall apart and I wouldn't be able to finish the race. My stomach hurt so much from the stress, I couldn't stand up straight. Weirdly, my technical director on the shore was experiencing similar fears. He was convinced the mast was going to fall. Absolutely convinced.

I approached the finish line.

I felt a rush of sadness. When I started the race, I had hoped that the Covid situation would be better and that my family and friends who couldn't wave me off at the start would be waiting for me at the finish. It was evident that wasn't going to happen.

There was no-one there.

It felt hollow. Leading up to the race, I had imagined every other part, the sailing, the hardship, the finish. I'd never imagined nobody would be there.

It was the greatest achievement of my life and I was alone for it. It was hard. People were expecting me to look happy but I couldn't do it.

Then I crossed the line.

It hit me. "I've finished the Vendee Globe Race!" I couldn't hide from that sudden emotion, pure joy. It was all there. I was so happy - and determined to do another one. I was proud. I don't often feel proud of myself. More often I say, "I can always do better." I don't think I could have done better in that race. I knew I made mistakes, but I'd learn from those mistakes and try again. Mistakes are part of becoming better at what you do. I tried as hard as I possibly could, and I took every opportunity that was available to me.

When I'm sailing, I'm a happy person. I am Rayon, the ray of sunshine. What I particularly loved in the Vendée was the competition part, pushing the boat hard and being on the edge.

I'd only been sailing that size of boat for two years. Most of my fellow competitors had spent at least four years in their boats, and some of them were even on their fourth Vendée Globe Race. I was a rookie. I didn't know how I was going to shape up against them.

I was the eighth woman out of a total of eleven ever to have finished the race. To put that into some perspective, only 12 men have walked on the moon.

For me, it exceeded my expectations. I felt so honored, so privileged, and very lucky.

I conquered the Vendée and it was an amazing feeling.

I achieved my overriding objective: finish the race.

Everything I did had to feed into that objective. It was daunting. I didn't sleep for hours. I was hungry. I was thirsty. It was relentless. I needed to keep moving on, always knowing that it would get better, it would change. I had to keep taking the forward steps.

You always need to manage your objectives in a smart way.

You need to be kind to yourself and understand that you will have setbacks. Equally, you will surprise yourself because human beings are amazing. We can do so much and we must give ourselves the opportunity to teach ourselves how to do so. That's why I love my sport so much because I know that there are so many ways for me to get better.

I'm never going to stop!

Rebellious Reflections

I don't know what a single-handed, solo, around the world ocean racer is supposed to be like. I've probably got my own bias on it because Pip Hare isn't the first personality type that comes to mind. She is completely and utterly humble and unassuming.

I first met Pip when she was speaking at an Aspire conference. She was leading a break-out group on the topic of self-confidence, which I thought would be very appropriate for her. Clearly, someone who sails solo around the world and embarks on the things that she does daily would be confident, correct?

At the event, people were allowed to choose break-out groups to join based on their own individual goals. Pip's was the largest group. It made sense, as self-confidence is a huge challenge for many people. I decided to join her group and stand at the back to hear what was happening. This woman who was giving a talk on self-confidence, who had sailed solo around the world, who had conquered every "man-made" obstacle there was to do it, was shaking as she spoke. Public speaking was clearly not her thing. What was so fantastic about that was she was giving an authentic demonstration of how someone can learn to be confident for the sake of their goals and mission in life. And that self-confidence isn't always scripted, polished, and perfect.

Pip wasn't merely sharing her tips about being confident, she was a living demonstration of it, and that it doesn't have to look how you expect. Self-confidence isn't some well dressed, perfectly smiling, machine-like quality; it is strategic and learnable.

Pip is always calculating every moment very carefully—what's working, what's not working? What are the changes she must make to keep going? At the same time, she holds the bigger picture in view. The objective? Win the race. Pip is completely focused on her larger goal and the small moment to moment decisions that add up to achieve it. The true definition of strategic.

Rebellion needs to be strategic. A big word, strategic. A masculine word with all sorts of gender subtext. Yet Pip reveals how very simple, very basic it is. Pip shows us self-confidence can be learned, that it can accrue over many days. She teaches the value of being alone and recognizing you're the only person responsible for your actions—accountability lies with you alone. She teaches us how to be positive, and grateful, and to remember all that we have worked for. She teaches us the value of competition, of winning, and of doing something difficult that very few people, and even fewer women, have ever done before.

Pip gives us insight into striving for the next thing. She told me recently that she will do the Vendée Globe race again. This time faster, better, and with a more impressive boat.

You may have limiting beliefs, too—you need to have so much money, or sponsorships, or funding, or people, or whatever it is—Pip sailed around the world in an old boat, as an older woman, when many would have considered that dream impossible.

Can't you see her on the deck of her boat, smiling in the sun with that huge sail flapping in the wind, with the ocean all around her? She found her happy place. You may not have to go into the middle of the ocean and sail around the world to find it.

What is your Vendée Globe Race? Where do you want to be first? What's your big objective?

It's time to be strategic.

CHAPTER NINE

Step by Step

In the Words of

Nasreen Sheikh, The Empowerment Collective, Nepal

No matter how hard or difficult things may seem
Even if you have no parents or anyone who cares
There is one looking after you all the time
The sun and the moon, all the stars,
The universe and all of nature is your family
The Singing Prayer by Nasreen Sheikh

It had been almost a week since the sweatshop where I worked had closed.

It was early morning and I would wake up to be in the street by 6am. I stood on that busy street leaning against a very tall wall. As I saw children going to school all I could do was think to myself.

Oh, I wish I could have books.

Oh, I wish I could have shoes.

How I wish I could be like those other children.

The children were in their school uniform, a light blue top, navy bottoms. They were my age, around 10 or 12 years old, going to school, wearing the uniform, carrying a backpack, wearing shoes, and most of all, with their friends. That's what caught my attention. I would listen to them talk, and that's also how I picked up the word "education." I heard another kid say it, and I wanted to be like that kid. Not merely to know what the word was but to know everything it meant.

I sat by the wall praying in my head all day long. There were so many passers by, so many different types of people, many of them young. In the early morning, I would see who I wanted to see most; the younger students going to college. It was very inspiring to me.

I sat and watched people for hours, doing nothing, waiting for my circumstances to change. I was a street kid in Kathmandu, the capital of Nepal. When the sweatshop closed, many of my colleagues went to find a job in another sweatshop, but I didn't. I finally had a taste of freedom. I didn't want to search out the next sweatshop and be stuck in that cycle again, so I chose to be on the street instead.

I spent most of my time on that street. Sometimes a person would give me some food and I would thank them and eat. That was my condition. I wasn't sure about my life at that time. I was waiting for something, and if it didn't happen, I thought I might go back to my village in India that borders Nepal.

In the evening I would go and sleep in the place abandoned by the sweatshop.

One early morning, I was standing in the same spot, against the wall. I felt something wet down by my feet, something coming up to me. There it was a brown and white dog on a leash sniffing me.

"No!" I cried.

In the village where I grew up, we did not keep dogs as pets. We were taught that they could bite you, hurt you, and carry disease. A dog was an untouchable animal. If you had to touch one, you would only do so to hit it hard enough to get it away from you.

"Oh, no, it's okay!" said the man holding the leash. He was an older white man with a moustache and short-cropped hair, wearing a t-shirt and a traditional Nepali lungi, which is like a long skirt for men. "He's okay. He is a good boy."

I shrank into the wall. I was so scared by that dog.

When he saw how scared I was, the man immediately pulled the dog back to himself with the leash. He said, "Please don't be scared. He's like my little son. You see?" He reached down to show me how to pet him. "Come, come, come over. Come meet him and pet him."

"No, no, no, no…" I said. "Please, I am scared!"

"You can give him a treat," he said. "And then you can pet him. See how soft he is? It will be okay." Even though I did not like this dog, or how stubborn this man was, I could hear something in him.

I looked into his eyes and saw only kindness.

Without thinking, I rushed to his side, grabbed his wrist with both hands, and said, "Uncle! Please, can you teach me?"

He was as shocked as I was. It happened so fast, but it was also like time stopped as I waited for him to say something. By now his dog was pulling him away from me.

He stood there for a long moment, looking into my eyes.

"Okay," he said. "Yes, okay. I will come back. I will come tomorrow."

And away he walked down the street with his dog.

I had not tasted an orange as a child. My parents could not afford it. I remember I would go around to the rich people's houses nearby where they would throw out an orange peel. I would take it and hold it to my face, smelling it, wanting to have one and to know what it would taste like.

Rajura, the small village I come from, is in India. There are no cars and hospitals. Women give birth on the floor. It is very poor in so many ways.

There is no clean water. There are lots of disasters and sicknesses and no way to deal with them but to try to live through them. We were disconnected from the world. In fact, people born in that village are undocumented. The people who were born in my village often don't have a birth certificate or any sort of official recognition that they exist.

Think for a moment of the challenges you would face without a birth certificate, bank account, or Social Security number. Could you go to school? Could you apply for a job or travel? Would you know your birthday?

I don't know exactly how old I am.

I would love to know my zodiac sign. When people say, "It's my birthday!" or one of my friends has a birthday, I'm always struck by a little attack on my soul. I don't know my birthday, so I can't celebrate.

My father worked as a welder for a company. He was treated very badly and was paid only $15 a month. Due to his work being so physically demanding he lost the ability to think clearly and his brain stopped functioning properly. It had a huge effect on my mother, who was uneducated, and from then on, essentially a single mother. She simply couldn't remember the dates of any of our births.

My village is poor in other ways. It is an entirely male dominated society. If a woman speaks up for herself, if she tries to bring up any of her desires, her voice will be ignored. My aunts were always being abused, even tortured at times.

My older sister was forced into marriage at the age of 12. All I ever saw were girls forced into marriage, all of them scared and shy. It felt to me like humanity was dead—like there was no goodness left in people. The only thing that mattered was what the men thought, even more than the lives of women and children.

My mother started telling me that I would be the next one to be married.

What happens in some villages in India is that girls are arranged to be married at a very young age. So the brides are all very unaware and very young. Then they have children nonstop - many have six to eight children by the time they are done. It is like you are not human. You end up becoming some form of machine, and it is very traumatizing.

I didn't want my life to be like my sister, married at age 12. I had to decide.

It was terrifying. I had to shed my old skin to grow a new skin. Developing a new skin is so tough, it's so painful and it's such a process of hardship and challenges but once you have a new skin, you feel a new you, a new freshness. Somehow, I knew my new skin was in a city far away from my village.

I was able to communicate with nature from a very early age, which made me feel I was not alone. There was a peacefulness that I reached within myself, which led me to escape my village. I was thinking that I would leave the village and have a better life.

If I were to stay, I knew the outcome. If I don't leave I will have to be like every other girl here. So there was an urgency and feeling that something was calling me. When you are connected to your own intuition and your own calling, you can feel the future. You know.

I enlisted the help of a male cousin to travel to Kathmandu, the capital of Nepal. In my village, sending children to work in a factory in the city was a normal experience. I knew if I could get to the city, I would not return.

I did not have a complete plan, but I knew the first step. My first step was to leave the boundary of my village. The next step was to go to the road, then onto the bus. Once I was on the bus, I could see the mountain down the road. When I could see the mountain, I knew there was a city beyond it.

Then I saw the city. And then when I saw the city, I thought, here I am, this is my new place.

One step at a time.

———————————— ❧❦❧ ————————————

I arrived in Kathmandu and found a job working at my first sweatshop. I felt so excited. I could work and work. I had found a way to be paid money for working. As the clothes would pile up next to me I would imagine money falling from the sewing machine.

What I had really found was a way to make less than two dollars for working 12 to 15 hours a day. I didn't even have a bed. I was sleeping on the pile of clothes I was in the middle of making.

There were so many chemicals in the fabric, I had trouble breathing. I would always find threads and clothing and chemical dust in my food.

This was my new life.

When the sweatshop's agents occasionally came, they brought hundreds of pieces for us to finish within a week. So we woke at 4am and worked until 11pm. And still the pile of clothes would not be finished, because it was not possible and they knew this. This is unfortunately the fate of many young children working in sweatshops in India and Nepal.

I desperately wanted to sleep, because when you are 9 or 10 years old, you are growing and you need to sleep. I wasn't allowed to. The other workers told me to splash cold water on my face or put on loud music so I could be awake to finish my portion of the pile of orders. Like in my village, I couldn't ask anybody about anything. There were no answers. So I started to speak to whatever shirt I was making. This was my way of clearing out my negative energy.

I cried into the clothes and said, "Whoever will wear this shirt will not feel good. I hope they can feel my tears. I hope they can feel my blood and sweat."

I worked like that for almost two years.

The agents who used to manage our sweatshop, as is typical, had to meet a certain quota from other agents that had hired them. At first, the agent came to see our work very often. Eventually he started to come less and less to the sweatshop. One day, he stopped coming. We didn't know what to think. Very slowly we came to understand that the agent didn't care about the project and had disappeared without a word.

Most of the workers in the sweatshop took their stuff and moved to another job. Even my cousin, who had brought me with him. He was finally convinced by other agents that he would have a better life and working conditions in another city, so he went there. I decided not to go with him.

I was only about 12 years old, but the street was such a free space to me. I was mesmerized seeing so many things happening, so many people moving about. The energy felt very freeing to me. I remember feeling like the whole world had opened. I had grown up in a village in the country, surrounded by a lot of space. For the last two years, I had only seen the walls of a tiny 10 by 10 room, working 15 hours a day under so much pressure. So the street was freedom.

While I spent my days in the street. I was not afraid. A little bit shy, I suppose, but because I was alone nobody usually talked to me. Also, it is not so unusual to see a child alone in the street there. But all I wanted was to be like the other kids going to school.

Oh, I wish I could have books! I wish I could have shoes... I wish I could be like those other children, and they could be my friends!

I had always prayed a lot, and since I was having a hard time I would talk to God in my head. I had my own special prayer. Sometimes I would spin around in the sun and a special prayer came to me. I called it a singing prayer, and it always made me realize I was not alone. Whenever I would sing it, it would bring me inner strength, knowing that there was some bigger force than me.

My singing prayer was how I was able to deal with fear and anxiety. That's how I created a space for myself. Knowing that the whole energy of nature was my family. Everything in this life, our little life, feels very small because the universe is so big. And I felt all of it was with me and on my side. Nature itself would pray with me and speak kindly to me.

The next day, the man and his dog didn't come back. I waited and waited and I thought maybe he would not come. Three or four days went by and I felt very sad. I would sit in the same place all day and wait.

Then one afternoon, I saw him walking quickly down the street to me. "I'm so sorry!" he said. "I had so much to do these last few days. I will take you to book study, okay?"

"Okay," I said.

"You want to start right now?"

I smiled and said, "Yes, yes, yes!"

We walked to a bookstore not too far away and went to look at all the books. I couldn't believe so many books. I wanted to know everything in them!

"Let's see. Here we are," he said, holding up a book for second or third grade students, right about my age group. "Can you read this?"

"No," I said.

He chose one from a lower grade. "How about this?"

"No," I said. "I can't read anything."

He thought at first that I might have already had some education, but he quickly realized I was totally illiterate. Finally he bought me a basic ABC alphabet book.

And the journey had begun.

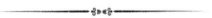

All my life people had mostly either ignored me or shouted at me. The man with the dog was the first person who ever told me, "Come over here," with any kind of compassion in his voice. Somebody wanted to communicate with me. He responded to my fear with kindness. He wanted to build a connection between me and his dog. I had never had anybody else talk to me that way.

My new teacher was an American. He had left America in his 20s and stayed in India and Nepal all his life. He spoke perfect Nepali, as well as many other languages. He had been a monk and lived a monk's life studying Tibetan Buddhism. He was a consultant for a Lama and used to translate between the Lama and the people.

I didn't know anything about the world, of course, and I was very naive and trusting. Could my teacher have been somebody who wanted to take me away, or traffic me? I didn't have any awareness that these things happened in the world.

My cousin was completely against me going anywhere with my new teacher. He stopped me going to take classes with him.

"This is how you will end up in the human trafficking!"

"He is not that kind of person!" I said.

"If you want to keep learning, then you will have to continue working at the next sweatshop. Go back to the village. You're not allowed to go with this man."

My intuition was telling me there was no danger.

"He is not a bad person," I said. "He wants to teach me."

"Well, if he cares then tell him he can come here and teach you."

So I asked my teacher if he would, and he agreed! He would come one or two days a week, and slowly we built a connection.

My teacher could have taken me to another country or sold me. That's how many thousands of women get into human trafficking. My teacher was simply a nice person. That's the beautiful thing about true humanity. I trusted him, and he trusted me also.

I had to trust him to have a big heart and to give, because it was not easy for him to come to the sweatshop and teach me every day. He made a huge commitment to me for 10 years, every single day for one hour or more. That's how I learned to keep growing and how to do things. So he also had to trust me to do something with what he taught me. It was on my shoulders to take this learning and to do something with it.

Trust is number one.

Number two is courage to ask for help. Sometimes when you are in a hard place, you must ask for help. So the courage to ask for help is so important.

Number three is not to forget an animal's true nature. Animals help us to connect and bring people together. My teacher's little dog wanted to come and sniff me. Maybe because I was dirty or smelly, I don't know, but he made the connection. He was my angel. He was one of the most intuitive dogs I have ever met, and he was so in love with my teacher.

"Why did you choose to come back?" I once asked my teacher.

"I didn't choose," he said. "I was so invested in my own education, learning language, learning religion. You were so passionate to get an education, and so was I. That's what I cared about all my life. You were a synchronicity."

Sometimes you are meant to meet certain people, to have certain experiences. The universe is always connecting the dots. He knew this, and young and naive as I was, I knew it too.

He was a monk and he did not have very much money. For him, buying a book or paper, pens or supplies was always such a gift. As we grew together and as he would teach me all these things, I would memorize them. Then it became a beautiful project for him, to be able to pass a lot of his knowledge to me. He didn't only teach me reading and writing and English, he taught me about using the computer and email and Facebook, he taught me about Shakespeare, and philosophy, and spirituality.

He taught me about living.

------------ ❧❧ ------------

Help came to me in the form of a gentle dog that led me to his kind guardian. Leslie John became my teacher for almost 10 years. Under his mentorship, I was able to learn how to read, write, and understand basic human rights.

Leslie John gave me my last name, 'Sheikh', and helped me apply for a birth certificate. His best guess of my birth date was 11/11/1991. With a reluctant bureaucracy, it took 11 years to be issued, and even then, it was riddled with spelling mistakes and date discrepancies. In Arabic, 'Sheikh,' is the name of a man at the top of the hierarchy, the chief of a tribe, or a royal family member. Perhaps Leslie intended to empower me. I didn't realize this until many years later.

All my education made me reflect on what happened to the society I grew up in, and what is still happening to 29 million girls in my country today.

Many people think slavery is finished. It is not. In fact, slavery is practiced more than ever. Clothing and electronics manufacturing are modern slave industries. And that starts with the clothes you're wearing. You might be carrying the tears of some of those slaves along with you. Even the earbuds that you wear - if you don't know where or who they come from, you can be sure that a hundred percent human suffering is included.

I feel the urgency of those people, especially the women and girls, in my part of the world. I also believe that all these problems are solvable. You can solve it. It's possible. I started to work on doing so because I wanted to show the world it is possible.

In Kathmandu, I saw women with deep trauma in their eyes, and emptiness in their malnourished bodies. I was determined to empower them. At the age of 16, I managed to secure a loan to set up the first social business in Kathmandu – Local Women's Handicrafts, an eco-conscious collective of women who create sustainable fashion and decor in Nepal. We create jobs for marginalized and disadvantaged Nepali women to gain financial independence.

At around 24, I traveled alone from Nepal to the US to share my story at an Aspire conference in Chicago. Dr. Sam Collins found me and used her personal air miles to fly me 7602 miles. I walked onto a stage in front of hundreds of women: lawyers, community leaders, and entrepreneurs. They listened in complete silence to my story, and I was overwhelmed by their response with a standing ovation.

What struck me most on my visit to Chicago was an experience at a major department store. Rows upon rows of clothes were displayed on racks. As I reached out and touched the fabric, it felt so familiar, like something I had sewn only yesterday. The store was filled with human suffering, blood, and tears.

We don't need to keep girls in that suffering, negotiating for the cheapest product possible, and making thousands of t-shirts that only end up in landfill. We don't have to do this.

In our center in Kathmandu, we use recycling. We bring women in for training, between six months to four years. Once they are trained, they make sustainable, ecologically sound products. These are the same women who would otherwise be going into a sweatshop, producing fast fashion. Fashion is one of the most polluting industries in the world. Fashion is not only harming women and children, but nature.

When I help other marginalized and disadvantaged people, it is always like going back home to my village. And I feel those people very much because I was like them. When you raise awareness, you raise curiosity. You develop an understanding that it is possible to change this. Once you raise that awareness, once you step out of fear and go to action mode, everything standing against you collapses. That is what I want to remind you of, that you do have that power.

My family doesn't necessarily understand my achievements. Eventually I was able to bring my mother, father, and youngest sister to a place of understanding, but my extended family still isn't quite there. It's my dream to return to them one day and share experiences with them, to open a third shop in my home village, and become a role model for the people living there. I wish to empower them.

Once you step into that power, whatever is against you dissolves. You become one of the most resilient people imaginable. You become a radiant person in your communities. I have experienced that with hundreds of women I have worked with.

This whole experience is like magic. It's a very pure essence and energy that I discover in myself over and over. I'm sure many leaders who are working on the ground or working at many different levels, understand that energy. Giving service to others is a good vibration. So this whole process is healing for me.

Life is a process of healing.

Right now, it's about how I can help forgotten communities. There are millions and millions of girls whose faces are not seen. People don't want to talk about them because it's painful and their stories are very striking and very hard. It takes a lot of energy and responsibility to face the facts. Not many people are ready to become responsible enough to serve others.

Our stories are not heard much of the time. Often when I talk about these problems, people are like, "Yet another problem, I can't deal with it."

I can't do it alone. I need space and support from the world to help end poverty, to help end inequality from the ground level up.

Whenever there is any pressure, never ever forget that we are the universe. The light exists in all of us. I witnessed my sister forced to marry at the age of 12, and my aunts being abused every day. Such dark, horrible experiences. The only thing that comforted me was to go inside myself with nature. Nature was there to hug me and to heal them because they didn't have a voice. So that is what I do. I go to the forest or the field to remember this connection with the universe.

These days, unfortunately, the population is increasing rapidly to the point that the villages are crowded and men have taken over the forest. The girls are even scared to go to the forest from the field. So they have very limited resources to seek help.

I ask you, dear reader, to find your secret space within you, where you feel fully you, and communicate with yourself in that space, because that is what I did at a very early age. There's always light in every darkness. I want all young girls to find that light they have inside.

I was so scared when I was coming out from that village to Kathmandu. You must be in that moment and hold that positive energy of your life. Yes, it's very hard and very challenging. We all go through so much. You can do it if you go step by step.

I don't know how to describe the suffering that I see today. Children whose physical bodies are dissolving because they don't have any nutritious food. This is the 21st century. People are talking about going to Mars, and then there's my village, where people are dying because they can't afford rice or vegetables. They deserve to have basic human rights.

So I always put it out into the universe to see what happens!

When I opened my first store in Kathmandu, it was only a tiny store. Now we have two women's empowerment centers. This is all because I was able to think bigger. If you don't think bigger, then how will big things come? To be a leader you must envision and take that power. It's one of the qualities I have learned through inspirational women.

My message is simple: you have the power to create, to give back to society, and to help others take care of themselves. I always go back to my story—as a street kid, I found a stranger to teach me, become my father figure, and help me through life. Then I was able to build up my business, Local Women's Handicrafts. Being a street kid you feel very scared. You don't have any support—forget about your parents, you are totally alone. So if I can do it, imagine all those girls with the support of their mothers and fathers, from families, from communities, how much more can they accomplish!

Now, I travel around the world to speak, and everywhere I go, women are taking over. Not only those who have been to universities or colleges, but women who come from poor societies, mentoring other women. So this whole cycle of sustainability is very magnificent and it's magical to see how you can adapt to the circumstances of the moment. Women are taking action in a very positive way.

So if the world is run by women, it will be very creative, unique, and harmonious.

We all are interconnected. Let's share and reshare, and reshare, and educate millions of people. I encourage women and young girls, everyone, not to give up. Please keep fighting for yourself, for your community, and eventually for the world. Real change comes from the ground up. And if we hear the message from the ground about what is happening, it will help us develop.

Support girls and women, please, because they are literally looking up to you.

I love men and I love women. And we all are one.

Rebellious Reflections

Mentorship. Even though we might have a distrust of people, older people, people who are a different gender to us, younger people, people of a different color, race, or belief set, sometimes we must trust that people are sent to us for a good reason. It goes both ways, for mentees and mentors alike.

When Nasreen met her mentor, something in her inherently knew that this was someone to trust, someone that could help her. She demonstrated the simplicity of being on the lookout for mentors. Some might call them angels or guides.

We do not have to do everything alone, in fact, that's both impossible and unnecessary. There are people willing to share their knowledge, wisdom, kindness, support, and often their money. They get joy from doing so. If we are so blinkered to believe everything is on our shoulders, it will take longer, be harder won, and we may never achieve the things we truly want to.

Life is about connecting with others.

Nasreen wasn't rescued. She wasn't saved. She wasn't redeemed. She wasn't discovered or found. She connected with a teacher. What are the chances?

Even when the chips seemed completely down, this 11-year-old kid on the streets of Nepal, without work, family, money—without anything—remained smiling. She met someone who was willing to help her with an education. For most street kids, this doesn't happen. For her, it did. Why?

When you meet Nasreen, she has a light shining through her that is undeniable. She is peaceful. She is grateful. She is serene. She is loving and kind. She is also utterly fierce. A social entrepreneur. A driver of change. Somehow, she can feel the plight of thousands and using that pain to do something constructive. She is remarkable.

She has dedicated her life to helping other women in Nepal through a very practical social business. She's a businesswoman, an entrepreneur, and an international speaker. She has an ability to ignite the fire within you that you didn't even know could burn so brightly.

If this young girl who didn't even know her age was able to escape from a village in India to work in a sweatshop in Nepal, to be able to run a business that could have a global impact, can the rest of us have any excuses at all?

Nasreen's story should be on the curriculum of every elementary school. She's to be studied, emulated, supported, encouraged. What is she teaching you? Do you think about what's going on now for women in Nepal? The young girls in villages in India? Do you consider the ethical changes you can make with your purchasing power? Do you imagine what you could do?

I remember Nasreen speaking at one of our virtual Aspire conferences, in the middle of Covid. She explained how she had developed the "One Million Masks Initiative." The shops that she had created in Nepal had to close, so she took the initiative online and started to sew masks for people around the world. She was so inspiring that all our attendees at the Zoom conference went to her website and started buying her masks. We managed to crash her website because we were so called to action by her. She showed us what we could do to help, and we did it!

Nasreen not only inspires us, but she gives us an important call to action. She has now become the mentor herself. Through her story, she teaches us about social entrepreneurship and how it is the future. About how to pivot to be a successful entrepreneur. She teaches us about brand integrity, values and making a difference.

Do you work for an organization? What can your organization learn from Nasreen?

What can you achieve? Can you be the mentor or is it time for you to open your eyes and your heart and find your next mentor?

It's time to take your first step.

CHAPTER TEN

Crossing the Bridge

In the Words of

Dr. Ibtissam Al-Farah,

Founder and Director, Lavender International Consultancy, UK

She looked at me like I was her next victim.

"Come with me," she said.

I didn't know what to do. I froze. I felt alone and scared. I did not understand how I had got caught up in this web. Somehow I managed to say, "I am still waiting for my interpreter."

"The interpreter can't make it," she snapped, looking impatient.

"What will I do?" I asked.

"It's not my business," she said. "No one can help you today."

I was a refugee in England and I was being investigated for fraud, for working illegally.

This is a mistake! I had been working as a volunteer, teaching the children of people from the Muslim community where I lived for no pay. I was at the very start of my refugee journey and I had financial support given to me each week by the UK government so I could survive with food and necessities.

I had received a letter summoning me to an investigation meeting and I didn't know who had reported me. I wondered why anybody would do such a thing. How could this happen?

I was at my local job center in Sheffield, waiting to be called. I was terrified.

The investigator assigned to my case was a white British woman with short dark hair and a very angry expression on her face. Her hands, arms, and even her chest were covered in tattoos. Her ears were pierced with very large and heavy looking plugs that stretched her earlobes. Where I come from, people with tattoos are not to be trusted.

I was so frightened by the investigator and I didn't know what to say. I felt like I was in a bad dream and unable to move.

"So... let's go. Follow me."

I stood and she led me into a small and blank interview room with a table, a few chairs, and a video camera. It was like a crime TV show and I wondered if there was a two way mirror.

We sat down across from each other at the table and she said, "We're going to record this."

She read me my rights, which I did not understand very well.

"I'm sorry," I said, "I don't speak good English. But I will try my best to understand."

"Okay, okay," she said impatiently, and pressed the button on the video recorder.

Click...

This English woman didn't know me. My story. My background. What I had been through to get to this place.

I call myself a self-made girl. I was born in Ethiopia. My mum was born there as well. So three generations were there, and then we moved to Yemen. My mum was the head of the family, and her mum was the head of the family before her. They were strong women, but life was very difficult for them. My mum passed away when I was eight, so I don't remember much about her.

As a girl I was angry and quiet. I was never allowed to express my anger, cry, or show my sadness. I wanted to survive. I wanted to do something different. I loved to read. So I used to read anything available to keep myself busy and avoid the reality of my life.

I've read all of Charles Dickens, Agatha Christie, Victor Hugo, and Greek philosophy. I used to live in my books. It was safer than the world around me. I used to imagine how I wanted to live in the future. Inside my books, I would dream my dreams.

Yemen is a society which oppresses women and girls. We've got no voice. I'm not even going to say limited freedom, we have no freedom. No access to anything. So, blindly, you must be a follower. Within my books, it was different. There, I did not have to follow others.

I needed to be quiet because if I argued, I was beaten. I refused to leave school, even though educating a girl was not valued. I refused to wear a hijab. No one from my family had ever gone to university and no one was going to pay for me to go.

So I saved money. No woman from my family went out and worked. I got a full time job and saved enough to enroll in University full time. I worked two shifts from early morning to night time, then studied late into the evening and on weekends. I also bought a car, which was another bombshell to my family.

Are you crazy? Are you mad? You're going to drive?

I started traveling around and explored the outside world on my own. My family couldn't believe it.

I couldn't drive to my village to see my sister. I would have loved to, but as a woman, I was not allowed to do so.

I used to drive my car with my nephew sitting beside me in the passenger seat until we reached a point about 45 minutes from our village. Then I would stop so we could swap seats and he would drive me in my car to the village, to my father's house. I would have to cover my face as well. These were the rules.

One day I decided to drive myself.

So I drove there alone in my bright red four by four Jeep. When I arrived, my sister came out to greet me.

"Ibtissam. Well done. I'm proud of you."

Her husband, who is the leader of the tribe, came out with his gun toting guards

"Who drove you here?"

I said it was me. He wanted the guards to drive me back. I said, "No, it's not dangerous." My car is a four by four. He looked at me, then at my sister. She also said, "No, she doesn't need help." My sister is a capable woman and knew what she was doing. Then I drove back. I broke all the rules.

Eventually, I developed a successful career working with International NGOs. I held very well-paid and respected jobs in Yemen. In one of my jobs, I managed the finances, and I was the only woman in such a position in the whole country. I was dealing with millions of dollars. This scared some people. The system was corrupt, and they did not like me, a woman doing such a job.

I was threatened repeatedly, but life had to go on. I didn't let it put me off.

One evening, a friend, the chairperson from the women's project where I used to volunteer, called and asked if we could meet up. So before heading home, I stopped in the city to see her. I parked my car and went inside to chat in her office.

As we were talking, one of the women ran into the office and yelled, "Ibtissam!"

"Yes?" I said, confused but calm.

"Your car! It exploded!"

We went outside. My car was engulfed in flames. Someone had put a bomb in it.

People were putting the fire out with an extinguisher, rushing to keep it from spreading. I walked back into the office while everyone was panicking. I was calm. I had been saved by an unknown grace.

On another occasion, I was invited to a conference. When I arrived at the hotel, there was no sign of any conference.

I went to the reception desk and asked them about it.

"No," they said, "there's no conference today."

As I stood there confused, two guys came up to the reception desk beside me. I heard one of their voices casually say, "We changed the location of the conference. You can come with us."

I ran.

I had many near accidents. I was often threatened, interrogated, and manipulated to be kept under control.

Other times I received ominous phone calls.

"Hi, how are you doing?"

"Fine, who is this?"

"We wanted to say we know where you are and what you are doing."

Then the line would go dead.

Slowly, I started to realize they knew things about me that only I knew. They knew I was alone in my office and home. They were somehow watching everything I did 24/7.

I am a calm and quiet person but eventually, even for me, it was too much. No-one can live this way.

I had to get out. It was too dangerous.

All of this led me to decide to leave Yemen. Though it wasn't really my decision. It had to be that way. I had no choice

No one in my family knew where I was going. I didn't take much, a small suitcase that I used for work trips. The only person who knew was one friend. She said, "You have to be safe and you should leave."

That is how I ended up as a refugee.

Claiming asylum is not something you want to do. It's not an easy, quick fix to change your life. It's the last resort.

You leave everything. Not just your stability, not just your job. You leave your life, memories, family, and friends. You leave the warm smell of your homeland. You leave your own home empty-handed.

———————— ❧❧ ————————

When I first arrived in Sheffield, England, I was completely lost. I moved straight away to my own community. I was told it's better to go to your own people to be safe. Being within the community and able to speak Arabic freely would make things easier.

I started my new life there. I felt safe. I volunteered in the Islamic Center and started teaching Arabic and Quran. At first I taught children, then I moved on to teaching adults. I didn't have to bother learning English. Most of the shops were owned by Arab and Muslim community members, and I had access to their legal services as well. Amid the total culture shock, I had at least one small place where I felt I belonged.

Everything is good. Everything is organized for me.

I began socializing with the other women there, trying to make friends and new connections. People tend to know that my country, Yemen, is considered one of the poorest countries in the world. There's extensive oppression, particularly patriarchal oppression, which limits the freedom of girls and women living there. So when I settled in England, I assumed that women in my community there would be more open minded.

That turned out not to be the case.

I was more educated than most of the women there. Not only in terms of having a university degree but also in terms of life and work experience. I had worked in the public, private and government sectors, and traveled the world for work. On top of that, the way I thought, spoke, had discussions, and composed myself made me feel completely different. But despite the isolation, I never lost my sense of pride in who I was.

I wanted to integrate into my own community, not the British or white community or the local Sheffield community. I started attending a Yemeni women's meeting every Saturday. It was more of a social gathering, really. But even there I felt isolated. The way they thought and the topics they discussed were so different to me. Of course, they all spoke Arabic, but due to their lower level of education the subjects discussed were more like gossiping. Talking about other women, talking about their husbands, fashions, talking about...nothing much, really.

That's not me. Even in Yemen, I was never in that kind of social circle. I do not gossip about people.

This was not my safe place. This was not where I belonged. I had felt safer in Yemen. I still wanted human connection and friendship, but I couldn't find it anywhere in what was supposedly "my" community. That meant I had a lot of work to do to progress the English language to broaden my social circle, I was only in the beginning.

I didn't know any English and because I was already an adult, it was difficult to pick it up. The whole environment was discouraging. I did my best at speaking English and hoped others would help me learn along the way. But my relationships in Sheffield weren't on that level.

I did very well in my volunteering and teaching the Quran in the Mosque. I taught many children. Some families started taking their children from other mosques and sending them to me because they had heard about my teaching. I didn't merely teach their kids how to memorize it. I told them stories so that they could understand it and think about it for themselves.

Eventually, I was asked to help run the school program at the mosque. My career in Yemen as a financial manager had taught me how to run any kind of business, so it wasn't difficult. They would ask me to help review paperwork and authorized me to sign certain transactions.

I used to think, "Oh! This is a good thing to do, for myself and for others. I am helping the children, their mothers, and the community. Allah will reward me for this!"

But soon, it started to go wrong. As I became more popular among the women and children in the community and was given more responsibility for the school, the men seemed to feel threatened by me. I didn't realize this until later.

One day, I received a letter from the fraud investigation department. I didn't even know what the word 'fraud' meant at the time. I went online and looked it up and I was shocked. I couldn't understand how or why I was being investigated. It transpired that someone had accused me of not paying taxes.

All I could think was that there was no way this could be! I'm a volunteer, working there in all weathers. I am an unpaid babysitter for many of the children. Why is this happening? Can't they see I am only trying to help my community and live my life?

They used my inexperience and my poor English against me to start trouble.

———————— ❧ ————————

The investigator at the Job Center turned the video recorder on and sighed as she flipped through my file.

"Before you start, I brought my certificates and some of my personal documents." I handed her my work experience certificate from Yemen that I obtained through the UN to show her who I am, where I had been in my career, and that I had impressive references from a well-respected Canadian Consultancy group I had worked with.

"I don't know why I'm here," I said, "and I don't know why anyone would say this about me. I'm only doing voluntary work at the school and I have never been paid. You can see from what I have brought that this is who I am."

She started asking me questions, some of which I didn't know how to answer at all. I was incredibly nervous. This stern, tough-looking, tattooed woman was intimidating and I had no idea what she might do. But as we talked, I saw her facial muscles start to relax a little.

At one point, she reached over to switch the tape for the camera but turned it off instead. She paused, looked at me and said, "You know, off the record..."

"What?" I said.

"I believe you. I can see you don't know anything about this."

"No, I don't."

"I think you are being set up," she said.

"Set up?" I said, "Why? I'm doing good for people! I'm teaching the Quran. Allah should save me!"

"Well, you have no idea where you are or how it works here," she said. "It's nothing about Allah saving you or not."

"What do you mean?"

She said, "When I read your name and knew I was going to investigate you, I thought to myself 'I am not going to let you go without a charge. I don't like people who are claiming benefits and doing wrong.'" I couldn't believe she was telling me all of this openly.

"I have had bad experiences with these people, as well," she said. "When I walk in the streets of that area, I don't feel safe."

I couldn't believe this tough looking woman felt scared in my part of the city, but I realized she was right. It wasn't safe there. I began to trust her.

"Why do you want to help me now?" I said.

"Because" she said, "I think you are in the wrong place. In some communities—particularly your community—they are afraid of strong women."

"In Yemen, of course," I said, a little confused. "Not here in England."

"Oh, no, no, no," she laughed, "here, too!"

She then showed me some documents from the school. "Is this your signature?"

"Yes," I said.

"Okay, let me show you another document. I want to help you. Do you know who this signature belongs to?"

"Yes," I said, "that's the head of the Islamic Center."

"You sure?"

"Yes," I said, "he's nice."

"He's the one who reported you."

"What?" I was shocked.

"He's the one who reported you."

I paused, stunned.

"Why?"

"As I said before, these people don't like strong women. And if you want my advice, if you want to succeed in this country, if you want to make your own name, if you want to be who you are—think again. Be careful where you are."

"I see."

"I'm going to tell you how to get yourself out of this because I've got nothing against you after hearing your story."

And so this angry, tattooed British woman told me what to do to get out of trouble, and I did what she said exactly. Not long after, I received another official letter saying my case was closed, there was nothing against me.

That was such a big moment for me. Sometimes we meet people who can point us in the right direction. We're not expecting them, what they look like, or how they sound. We had both made judgments about each other based on how we looked and our backgrounds - and we were both wrong about each other.

I'm always amazed when things come from nowhere to save me, escorting me to new ground. I paid a price, but I realize there is always that light at the end of the tunnel. I only need to be who I am. I don't need to pretend to be someone else.

It is difficult to believe there are people who want to limit your freedom, like the people who reported me. To discover that someone hates you so much that they try to limit your freedom is a strange experience. Especially when it's someone you know and trust.

I have always believed that you should never judge a book by its cover. Yet that's what I had done when I looked at the investigator, and she had done it to me when she saw my name. Then, by listening, she trusted me. I realized, by truly listening, I could trust her.

This is magic—honestly.

And that was that. It was a big moment for me. I decided to leave the Islamic Center. Even though it was like, well, what am I going to do now?

A few days later when I was walking in the City Center, I found myself in the tram lane. Next to it was the University of Sheffield Department of Lifelong Learning building. I went inside to look. They had leaflets explaining the classes they offered. Not only did they offer English classes, but there was also a Women's Studies course! I wonder what level of English they would accept?

I walked up to the receptionist desk and said, "I'm sorry, I'm new here so I don't know what to do."

"It's quite alright" she said. "How can I help?"

"Well, I love education," I said, "but I don't know how to access education here."

She said, "Oh, well, here is a leaflet for you for some English classes."

"Brilliant!"

Leaflets in hand, I felt a new found confidence and sense of direction as I made my way back home. I started focusing on my English and took on a new volunteering position. I joined an English conversation group to practice English with university students and retired people. It took place over coffee. It was the kind of social gathering I needed. The conversations were far more my speed.

We met at a Christian church in town, which welcomed everyone: refugees, asylum seekers, even people who were lonely and wanted to talk to someone. All could come and sit together.

To get there, I had to take a bus from my community to the other side of the city. I looked out of the bus window as we passed the Arabic speaking parts of town and the Islamic Center.

We were about to go over a very old bridge, which empties into a big, long street, when I noticed a woman sitting on the bus with her kids. I recognized them. I had taught the kids at the Islamic Center. They were related to the person who reported me.

"How are you doing?" She said, "We haven't seen you in a long time."

"I'm fine," I said, adjusting my hijab, pretending I didn't know her relative was the one who reported me.

"What have you been doing?"

"I'm doing voluntary work," I said.

"Oh—where?"

"At the Christian church," I said.

"What?" She said, a little too loudly. The bus was full of people! A few heads momentarily turned.

"What do you mean, what?" I said.

"You left the Islamic Center, and you are now doing volunteer work at a Christian church?"

"It's a place I feel comfortable," I said. "Where I feel safe. It's not about it being a place of worship. It's the place I go to learn and grow, where it is located has nothing to do with me."

As we crossed that old bridge, I realized I had done something huge! I crossed the bridge from my comfort zone, the so-called "safe" community, and went into the unknown.

I had gone to a place where I could discover myself. When I talked to others and told them, in my broken English, about my life and achievements and goals, it dawned on me that I had achieved a lot.

I was so proud of the person I was, and who I was becoming.

———————— ❧❦❧ ————————

Years later, I was by myself, browsing in a shopping center in Sheffield.

"Sister! Sister!" I heard a man call out.

When I turned around, I was stunned. It was the man from the Islamic Center who had reported me.

"Sister!" he said, catching up to me. He smiled as he walked, his arms open, motioning to me to come and speak to him. His wife had continued to walk down the street with his children. "Do you remember me?"

"Yes," I said, "Of course, I remember you."

"Yes, good," he said. "And how are you? What have you been doing?"

"Well, I have my Ph.D. now," I said.

"Oh, brilliant!"

"Thank you."

He paused and looked at me very seriously and said, "Sister, for the last six years I have tried my best to find you. I wanted to ask—it would mean a lot to me if, well—if you could please forgive me?"

I looked at him and realized I felt no anger towards him. "You know what you've done. And it is not me who forgives," I said.

"Forgive me, it means a lot to me. Samaheni," he said.

"I forgive you, but I can't forget," I said.

"Thank you, sister. This means a lot to me."

And it meant a lot to me, too, because I had never confronted him over what he had done. I thought it was very brave of him to talk to me. It gave me some much-needed closure.

I progressed quickly after I had crossed that bridge and started my studies. I was interviewed for and accepted into the Women's Studies course. Then I applied to and was accepted by the University of Sheffield where I received my MA degree. My educational journey continued until I was awarded my Ph.D. I am now Dr. Ibtissam.

I was so pleased when I finished my presentation to my Ph.D. examination board. The examiners told me they were very impressed with my work. They even recommended that it be published. They said, "We really enjoyed reading your thesis. It has the potential to contribute to academic literature as well as having real use at the policy and practitioner level." That was thrilling for me!

Now, I work in my community as Co-founder and Director of DEWA (Development and Empowerment for Women's Advancement) in Sheffield. We have been working with asylum seeking and refugee women. I also run my own higher education consultancy and provide one-to-one academic support for international students. I teach others about their rights and sometimes, how to fight for them. I'm doing what I believe I was made to do: to use my professional skills to support other people. I'm an experienced person and I believe in my right to study, my right to education, and my right to be respected as a woman. I'm well respected by others. I've earned that respect.

I'm a member of many committees with the city council and other social enterprise groups. I love it when people value my life journey.

My advice is to challenge yourself. Be careful when you choose to take a risky step, even if life has forced you into that risky position.

I'm trying to create a better me for tomorrow. I deserve it. I deserve to live happily. I deserve to be respected. And so do you.

We must believe in ourselves. Life is not fair for many people. Don't wait for things to happen, it doesn't work.

Find your way, trust yourself, and go for it.

Rebellious Reflections

Quiet leaders like Ibtissam smash the stereotype that to be rebellious, we must be loud, we must raise our voice and shout and campaign and march. That is a part of rebellion for sure, but Ibtissam's rebellion has been different. She quietly got on with the business of achieving her goals.

Girls didn't stay in school in her family or go to university. Women didn't buy cars or drive on their own. Women were not in powerful jobs. Did that automatically apply to her? No. She quietly got on with her own interests. She paid for her own university education. She worked when other women didn't work. She was always asking, "why not?" She didn't accept the status quo.

This story could easily have ended happily with this young girl from Yemen working her way into a very successful career in finance. It would have been great, but the story didn't end there. She resigned from a job that did not meet her values. In fear for her life, she left everything to live in a completely different country. Without shouting, screaming, or any fanfare. She acted.

Can you imagine working so hard to achieve your dreams, going to university, getting a good job, then leaving it all? Can you imagine becoming a refugee in a new land, unable to speak the language or get a paid position, and then accepting something more basic than what you had been doing throughout your whole career? Maybe you think you're being smart by going to your community and speaking your own language, and then someone from your community tries to harm you as you try your best to fit in.

What do you do? Blame others, fall victim, become like everyone else? Accept it? Ibtissam crossed the bridge into a new culture, new work, and a new education. She learned how not to judge a book by its cover. She shows us that allies and angels come in all shapes and forms. Maybe not in the ways we expected, but they do arrive.

Ibtissam has continued to thrive and was recently awarded her Ph.D. in England. I have a Ph.D. myself and I know that is no small feat. To do it in a second language ,in a new country, is astounding. It gives the achievement 10 times the value, maybe more.

Not long ago, Ibtissam was speaking at an Aspire conference. When she was on stage, I asked her how it was when she first arrived in the U.K. She paused, looked at the audience of hundreds, and continued her talk in Arabic.

I didn't understand what she was saying, and I began to feel a little panic. Very few people in the audience could understand her and it started to feel uncomfortable. What was happening?

When she finished, she looked around and asked, "How do you feel?" She explained that the confusion that we felt, the near distrust we felt, was what she experienced every day as a refugee in the U.K.

I was astounded by the genius of this demonstration. I hope that Ibtissam has taught you about many things and that you will be more accepting and understanding of refugees who travel so far and go through so much.

If you're a quiet leader who's assumed you need to be loud, take note of this power. Don't try to change, it will never work. Instead, truly step into your own form of power.

What is your bridge to cross?

CHAPTER ELEVEN

Spandex Gate

In the Words of

Jen Coken, CEO, Embrace the Ridiculousness of Life!, USA

In August of 2019, I started the application process with the US Customs to get my Global Entry card for a trip to London. The earliest interview appointment I could find was 200 miles away and scheduled for February of 2020. That's when the pandemic hit.

Finally, in July, I was able to make an appointment closer to home in Baltimore, Maryland. But due to limited staff, it was scheduled for March of 2021. When the day arrived, I had no idea where I would travel. The pandemic was still a thing but I wanted to be all set once the travel restrictions were lifted.

The interviewer called me to her desk and said, "Ma'am, do you have any arrests on your record?"

"Well, yes, I do," I said.

"Thank you very much for telling me the truth," she said. "Can you explain the circumstances, please?"

"Sure," I said. "When I was 19, I tried to steal a pair of spandex pants from the local department store, so I could go to Heavy Metal Night at Filthy McNasty's. You know, it's all about the pants."

The guy at a desk behind us laughed out loud.

"Ma'am, we need a letter explaining the outcome of the situation."

A guy leaning against the credenza behind her snorted out a laugh and said in a soft voice, "But Janet, it's nearly a 30-year-old charge."

"But she's listed in the FBI database," she said, looking back at him. He shrugged his shoulders. She looked back at me.

"Look," I said, "I don't even remember where it happened anymore."

"I'm sorry," she says. "We need a letter and some documentation."

Okay.

I was not going to be deterred. So I spent days calling all the county offices that I could remember. Nobody had a record. A lawyer friend tracked down where it might have happened, so I gave the city office a call. I was told that their records were lost in a flood in the basement ten years ago. Another dead end.

Another friend, ex-FBI, confirmed that I do indeed have an FBI record. Not because of all the protesting, or because I worked for Greenpeace, or my political activities in college. Nope. My arrest record is for stealing spandex.

I call it Spandex Gate.

I was getting nowhere, so I called the customs woman back, "Nobody has a record of it. There was a flood ten years ago and... that's it."

"Ma'am," she says, "I need something for your file. You are going to get your Global Entry, but I don't want them to question you over it."

"Well, what should it say?"

"I don't know Ma'am. I can't tell you what to say. I'm going to send you to customer service, hang on."

So, it's press one—boop, press six—beep, press five—bloop. After a 25-minute wait, the customer service woman on the other end of the line answered. I tell her the whole story, and she says, "Well, we can't tell you what to put in the letter. You must talk to the officer that you were initially speaking with."

Fine.

I called back my friend at the Global Entry Office at BWI Airport. "My understanding from customer service is you have the jurisdiction to tell me what needs to be in the letter, ma'am. What do you want it to say?"

"Oh, okay! Here's what I need..."

I got it sorted of course. Eventually.

Story of my life. Always hustling. Always busy. Doing my thing. Not much time on my hands.

That was all about to change.

—————— ❧ ——————

There we were, in the middle of a pandemic, and I was leading webinars about handling anxiety. I was a speaker at an Aspire conference. I was doing all the things that I needed to do to find my people.

Every morning, I gave people a dose of inspiration that I called "Java with Jen." From the moment the lockdown started in March 2020, I was doing at least two webinars on managing anxiety and imposter syndrome every week. I also produced a six-part vlog about racial injustice called "Frankly Fridays," in which I interviewed people on racism in the arts, in the prison system, marijuana laws, and bias in writing and publishing. I started a book club called "Being a Great Ally." It was so important to me to get voices heard and to educate.

In July, I hit a wall.

One morning, I had a call with my business manager. I was sitting out on my balcony, "Kyle, there's a whole bunch of stuff we're going to stop doing because I'm exhausted. I can't keep up this pace. I can't."

Okay, like what?" he asked.

"We're not doing this, this, this, this..." It was a laundry list of stuff.

He said, "I'm glad you said that because the team has been freaking out and didn't know how to talk to you. And they elected me to do it."

"Perfect," I said. "Look, I'm taking off for a week's vacation. I was supposed to go to a friend's house but with Covid, it's now a staycation for a week of self-care. So I'm going to sleep Sunday night and go be a tourist in my own town. I don't know what's open, but I'm going to sleep in on Monday. I'm going to wake up and go whichever way the wind is blowing."

I got into bed thinking about my options... Did I want to go to the Kenilworth Aquatic Gardens to see the beautiful blossoms that look like a Matisse impressionist painting? Did I want to go for a walk? Did I want to go find new hiking trails?

As I turned over in bed, I felt a massive pull up my side. Almost like that stitch feeling you get when you're running.

What was that?

I took my fingers and I started following it, and following it, and following it. I got to my nipple and there was a hard knob. I hadn't noticed it before. I went to a mirror and looked, noticing my nipple was pointing downward and a little bit on one side.

Why have I never noticed that before?

I remember having felt something the previous month but it was movable. I Googled it and it said don't worry about it unless it's immoveable. Well, this was immoveable now. I knew right then in my gut what it was: breast cancer.

I could not sleep at all that night. I was waiting for 8am to call my gynaecologist as the starting point. I was going over and over everything in my head. At some point I fell asleep.

The next morning, after I made my appointment, I sat on my balcony sobbing. I honestly didn't know who to call. I had a lot of friends and a tight family, but I didn't know what to say. I didn't know what I needed. I didn't want to worry anyone.

I sat there thinking about the future. What does this all mean for me? How is it going to impact my business? Was it really cancer? Was I going to have a "chemo brain" where I can't concentrate? How would I make ends meet? Could I move in with someone? Should I break my lease?

After three hours, I found the nerve to pick up the phone and call my stepmother.

"What's going on?" She asked.

"Are you near Dad?"

"Yes."

"Please step away from him." My dad has bad anxiety. He wouldn't call it anxiety, but he's my dad, and he's 83, and he worries about me.

"What are you going to do?" she said after I explained my situation. "Can you get someone to go with you to the appointment?"

I called a girlfriend, Monika, who lived near the doctor's office. Due to Covid she couldn't come into the office, but she waved to me from behind the glass in the lobby.

The examining nurse said, "I think it's a clogged milk duct, but I will send you for a mammogram and an ultrasound."

Whew. I dodged a bullet. Time to celebrate! Monika and I went out to lunch and had a drink. Yay! We met another one of our friends nearby and went out to dinner.

Two days later, I drove myself to the radiologist's office thinking it was no big deal. Get the mammogram. I was feeling relaxed when the radiologist came in with the results.

"Miss Coken," she said, with her mask on, "I'm not exactly sure what this is, but I'm going to send you for a biopsy. And even if it comes back benign, I'm going to send you for an MRI."

I jokingly said, "What? Look, my mum died from ovarian cancer. I'm well versed in the whole situation. Give it to me straight, doc. What is it, like, 80 percent?"

She looked over her mask and said gravely, "Much higher."

It was all I could do to keep the tears back. I checked out of the doctor's office with tears running down my face, but I had my mask on so nobody could see my lip trembling. I got to my car and started bawling. The first person I called was my business manager.

"I don't know what's going on," I said. "We may have to reschedule everything."

Then I called my parents again and told them both, then my aunt and uncle. By then I was exhausted. It was such an ordeal to retell the story and have no answers to their questions. I kept the group tight because I didn't want anything to get out into the public domain for fear that my existing clients would disappear. I needed to continue to run my company.

One of the few people I did tell shared my news with others without my permission. I started getting random Facebook messages and emails, including one from her ex-husband.

I reached out to her and asked, "Did you tell people about what is going on?"

"Yeah, you know, only people who care about you."

"Honey," I said, "it's not your news to tell. Why did you tell your ex-husband?"

She said, "I guess I should talk to my therapist."

"Yeah, you should."

I started to realize that people were so used to me being there for them, they still expected me to hold the space while I told them my news. I talked to another friend, and she got upset, really upset. I was trying to talk about some business stuff, and she cut off the conversation.

"I need time. Give me some space to manage my upset."

And I thought, you know, go get someone else to give you space to manage your upset. I am not going to do that. I'm not. I can't. I'm the one with the life-threatening diagnosis. Besides, you are not allowed to be more upset than me.

One friend I told didn't know how to support me, so she reached out to another person whose best friend had died from breast cancer. And thank God for her. She told me I needed a CaringBridge website, which allows you to update people on your health status, so you don't have to say it a million times to a million people.

People wanted to know how I was, how they could help, what they could cook for me. Smartly, we had everyone donate GrubHub gift cards. When

I felt like cooking, I could, because I have such a specific diet and a lot of food allergies. When I wanted something brought in, there was enough food.

I did a video for people coming to the CaringBridge site saying, "Hey, it's Jen, and I'm sorry you're finding out this way, but I have breast cancer. And if I could do anything, I would call each one of you individually. And if I could be with you, I'd want to sit down so we could cry together. But it's too much for me. I don't want to keep talking about the negatives."

So it became a mantra: "If you want updates, go to the CaringBridge site."

I was very closed about it. I didn't talk to a lot of people. I did not tell my clients. Not because I didn't want them to be concerned. No, because the best thing for me right then was to be there for them and not have any attention focused on where I was at. I eventually had to tell my step mum and my cousin to quit calling me and asking me for updates.

"Oh, well... I don't feel like logging in."

Most people know me as someone who's very public about things. I thought my whole life as a grassroots organizer had prepared me for my mum's cancer. I then realized it was my mum's cancer that had prepared me for my own journey.

One of the most important parts of my journey was not talking with others about my cancer or my treatment. I insisted people went to the Caring Bridge site. It was traumatic for me to talk about what wasn't working. I only wanted to give voice to what was possible for the future. As I have always told my clients: "You are what you speak!"

I get messages from spirits through songs. After my initial diagnosis, with no idea what my prognosis was, a song started playing in my head that I had never heard before. At least I couldn't ever remember hearing it before.

I was in the shower. As I was sitting under the water, crying and hopeless, I heard, "And thank God I'm breathing... don't take me too soon because I'm here for a reason."

When I heard the actual song, "One Day" by Matisyahu, for the first time, I dropped to my knees and wept. But not in sorrow, in gratitude. Because I then knew, without any doubt, that I was not going to die. My time wasn't up yet. I knew that I had more to do.

I played that song every morning as I took my shower and let myself sob as much as I needed to.

By the end of August I still didn't know what the situation was, even though I was seeing so many doctors. I had never been sick a day in my life. I've only had elective surgeries on knees and a foot. I'd never had to deal with taking medication. It was new for me to have to take care of myself.

I rearranged my schedule. I only did calls from one to five, because some mornings I woke up and cried the whole morning. I got myself together enough by noon to take a shower, put ice on my face and be there for my clients. That was all the time I could manage. I started to realize how exhausted I had been feeling for a long time. I still didn't know how it was going to impact my company.

My dad called me very upset one day, "If it wasn't for the pandemic, we would be there. And Gina would be cooking for everybody and your freezer would be full." I didn't even have the wherewithal to cook for myself.

September rolled around, and I had two surgeries. My small group of girlfriends would not let me go to any appointment without one of them.

Somebody was always waiting in the car for me. My best friend came in for both surgeries (they didn't entirely clear the margin with the first surgery).

In mid-October, the doctors did something called an Oncotype DX score, which shows how likely it is that the cancer will recur. My score had to be 17 or lower for me not to have chemo. I didn't want chemo. I know what it does. I watched my mum go through it.

By this point I could barely keep it together, but I had to keep the company doors open. I had people on my payroll and knew I could not cut them off, but I still hadn't told the outside world.

Finally, I got a call from my breast cancer doctor, the head of the breast cancer group at Holy Cross Hospital. There, everybody talks to one another, they meet as a team, so I knew all the doctors were in sync with my current state.

"You're a 16, you don't need chemo."

"I'm going to need radiation, right?" I asked.

"We don't know how much."

Okay, now I've got it. Finally, I was the author of my own journey. I'm five foot ten. I have breast cancer. It's stage 2A. I don't need chemo. I'm going to need radiation. That's what's so. My life has always been about contributing whatever has gone on with me to others to make a difference. So it was time for me to go public.

My team and I created the hashtag #checkyourchest as a campaign because mammograms were down 40 percent that pandemic year. We wanted to encourage women to have mammograms (and if this applies to you, be sure to get regular checks)!

In November, I met with my oncologist. She was awful. She talked to me like I was six and this was show and tell.

"Sooooo, what does the Oncotype DX tell us?"

I looked over at my friend Leigh, who made all the notes from my appointments to help me update people on CaringBridge about how I was doing mentally.

I rolled my eyes and fired the oncologist.

In December, I hired a new oncologist, and was getting radiation Monday through Friday. I had five friends; one took me each day of the week. It helped break up the monotony of regular treatments. One friend brought his dogs, and we'd go for walks. With another friend, we'd go grab a coffee.

Because it was the end of the year, work had slowed down. I'll tell you something, by the end of that year, during the time I had breast cancer, I doubled my business. I went into 2020, having lost 80 percent of my business following the withdrawal of a big corporate client due to the pandemic. I finished the year with twice the business. How do I think this happened?

I made, "Make Imposter Syndrome Your Superpower," my niche. I worked with a team member to create a quiz, started doing podcasts and webinars, warm called people and started getting clients. One client who took my quiz became a VIP 1:1 client and then hired me to do organizational development work within her company, which I am still doing!

It took everything I had in me—the 20-plus years of coaching, my faith, my friends, my knowing that this diagnosis was here for a purpose, and that I had chosen it, because that's my belief system. I realized the reason I chose it was first, to know how much I love, and second, to know how much I'm surrounded by love. That's what it's about—love.

Now I take Fridays off for me, to listen to my body.

My act of rebellion was not allowing myself to be victimized by my health, but rather to allow myself to move through the spaces of my health. There were moments where I felt like a goddamn victim. You know, "So my mom and now me—really? It's not supposed to happen to me." I had all the genetic testing that said I should've been fine, but guess what? 85 percent of breast cancer is not genetic.

My left boob is a little smaller than my right now, and it has a slash through it because the tumor was attached to the nipple and areola complex, so they took it out. I get to choose whether I want reconstruction once everything is clear.

I am not sure if I want reconstruction. I've been toying with the idea. The breast surgeon did say once they do the left side, they must suck some fat from my belly to make it match the other side, and then they're gonna must do a lift on the right. So I was like, "You know, can we do a little lipo too? Maybe get a little tummy makeover at the age of almost fifty-seven?"

I kind of like that idea.

I'm about to do a big photo shoot. All because one of my girlfriends made a comment while we were talking about the surgery and I was like, "Do you want to see it?"

She says, "No, I want to think of you as healthy and whole."

I thought to myself, if I don't have a nipple and an areola, does it mean I'm not healthy and whole?

There is such a focus on women's breasts. You must have all your pieces together to be healthy and beautiful. Of course, there was no malice behind what she said, and she didn't mean it in an offensive way. But it made me think. Later, I talked to my PR person and I said, "I have a vision of me doing a topless photo in the shoot." We're going to be in Charleston where there's a 2,000-year-old tree that we'll use as the background for a campaign. The only thing I know how to do is to contribute my darkest moments so that other people can see the gift in it, like I have.

You always have a choice about how you will respond to any circumstance, no matter how shitty. You truly do have a choice. But it's hard to realize that while you're amid it.

I think the most powerful choice you can make sometimes is to take a nap. Seriously! You can choose to take a nap. You can choose to sit quietly. You can choose to watch crap on TV. It's not necessarily always about showing up for others. Sometimes it's showing up for yourself and sometimes that means to enjoy doing nothing.

When you're amid it, the best thing you can do is take time for yourself—to sleep, to cry, to be angry. Every day is different. Expect to be in an unpredictable mood and be okay with it.

I wouldn't change anything I have faced in my life. I think if I had to give my younger self some overall advice, it would be this: "You need to care much less about what other people think and take better care of yourself."

think about you is none of your business. What you think about you, make that your business. You're the one you must look at in the mirror.

I think there's always room for women to be more rebellious from the viewpoint of standing up for something we see as possible. Even when others tell us it isn't possible, don't believe them.   If in your heart of hearts you want to be that thing, to do that thing, to go after the thing: do it.

Be your own person and the right people will love you for it.

The wrong people will leave.

And that's a blessing.

Take care of you.

New story of my life. Always hustling. Busy. Doing my thing.

In case you are wondering if I ever got to Heavy Metal Night at Filthy McNasty's, I did. My friends gathered $50 to bail me out of jail so that I didn't have to spend the night there, but I borrowed someone else's spandex pants!

Rebellious Reflections

Do you like to be busy and on the go? Jen Coken—woman, activist, writer, entrepreneur, speaker, coach, comedian par excellence—multiple roles, multiple hearts. She moves through life fast, effectively, humorously, and impactfully. In control or out of control, she is always asking, "What can I do now that will make a difference?"

Breast cancer made her stop. Boom! The room filled with smoke; the machine wrenched to a halt. That's the impact of a health crisis. Shocking. Absolutely, totally shocking. Because suddenly and without warning, control is gone. Everything stops. The world slows down, almost blurs around you, and there's nothing you can do except wait and perform the "best practices" you are told to do by someone else.

Does the rebellious woman have a pause button? Breast cancer pressed that button for Jen. How does rebellion deal with imminent death? Jen refused to entertain it. She refused to comply with all social standards around body image. She refused to deal with everyone else's grief and pain about her. The ability to cocoon, to slow down, to be healthy, to take a minute and be with friends, to rest, recover, and re-emerge became stronger than ever. She did that.

So, is it time to hit your pause button? Is it time for you to cocoon? Or is it time for you to support someone else's cocoon?

Twelve Miles

In the Words of

Sarah Kitakule, The Kitakule Foundation, Uganda

I looked down at my father's face. He was dead.

I left university in Slovenia immediately and rushed home to be in Uganda.

They had not closed the coffin. They had waited for me to get to the funeral to look at him before they lowered him into the grave. I said my goodbye quietly.

You've gone before I could pay you back for all the sacrifices you made for me to have a better life.

I pledged never to bring shame to his name. I swore that, in the future, people would look at me and say, "Yes, that man trained his child to care about her role in life." I resolved to continue his legacy.

My father recognized early on that I had leadership skills. He told me, "You have the potential to be a minister Sarah, I want you to have a good education. Education is the ticket through life. Even if you don't get married, it will enable you to take care of yourself without having to depend on anybody else."

I'm not rich. I come from a humble background. When I die I want to know I have made a difference. I am one of those girls who wants to impact other people's lives.

I come from a small village in Uganda, yet I have built a school and become an international speaker. It's unbelievable what you can do when you put your mind to it.

I'm a first-generation graduate. My dad was the only person who went to school in his family. He had eight children and he somehow put all of us through school. We all achieved first degrees, second degrees. We all have careers.

My father did not have those opportunities. He started school at 12 years old and had to walk 12 miles every day to get there. Despite that, he was determined. He became a great trade unionist, and whenever he traveled in the world, he came back with stories.

"You have to get an education," he told us, "because it's only education that can liberate you from this small village and take you places."

The villagers used to laugh at him because he had daughters and he wanted us to be educated.

"Why waste your time?" They mocked. "These girls will only get pregnant. They're going to get married. Why are you sending them to school?"

My dad would say, "Shut your ears, daughters. Don't listen to them. Go to school, education will liberate you."

And it did.

My father, who had to walk so far each day to get to school, saved enough money to send me to boarding school. He took me there, carrying my suitcase, when I was six years old. He told me as I cried that I wanted to stay with him, "Never mind! You can suffer now, but you will thank me later."

I can't thank him enough for it because it changed my life forever. It changed the lives of my children and grandchildren forever.

Education transformed me. I am passionate about it. That's why I am on a mission to empower people to empower themselves, starting with education. I'm very cynical about what goes on in the world, about the UN bodies and all their declarations. But I know that as an individual, I can make a difference.

We can each as individuals make a difference.

After boarding school and college, I worked for various international organizations including the Commonwealth Secretariat in England. I saw the way people struggled.

I kept thinking, what can I do to give back to my community?

As my time at the Secretariat job was coming to end, I found myself wondering, what could I do that would fulfill me? For a long time, I had known that I was good at helping other people. Friends often commented on how I had helped them, or advised them, or made connections for them, or introduced the right people to each other, or generally made the most of any opportunity.

I realized that I was happiest when I was helping other people. So how could I do that best?

I began to learn everything I could in my home country of Uganda. Given what education had done for me, I decided that was what I needed to work on, closely intertwined with gender and women's economic empowerment. I started to think about creating my own school in my village in Uganda.

But building an actual school? It felt like an impossible dream.

I started by putting together a small library. The library slowly evolved into a school. The excitement of the children who came, desperate to learn to read, spurred me on. Some of them had never even seen a book before. So I knew that I was on the right track. The decision to invest in an expanded library was an easy one for me to make.

My dream was to transform the place where I grew up. I would expand my little library building. It would have a radio station, which would broadcast to the local community about what they could do to improve their lives. It would have a music room, for a children's orchestra. I dreamed about all the rooms it would need, and the different types of vocational training it would offer.

I could see it all in my mind. It would be a nice place. Well painted and not like a typical African school building. It would have a garden with plants and birds singing.

People in the village gave their own time to work on the building which housed my little library, to see if it could be expanded to accommodate my ambitious plans. They reported back that it was too poorly built to convert and extend. The whole house might come down in the process! So that wasn't an option. Then I thought, what if we put up a big building with a multipurpose hall?

I hired an architect with my own money. Once the designs had been done, I had to find a way of financing the build, to prove to people that I was serious about bringing my vision to life, and in the hope it would encourage others to join me.

People want to follow those who are doing something, but not when there is nothing on the ground. They want to see something tangible. So I sold my apartment in London and invested the proceeds in building the structure. I had no regrets. This was my dream. This was my vision. And I was happy when it helped persuade other people to come on board.

The hardest thing was the length of time it took! When you want something done, you want it done quickly. Once I'd started, I realized it wasn't that easy to fundraise. It wasn't easy to get people to contribute. That meant that the project took longer than it should have, because the resources were not coming in as fast as I had hoped they would.

It's very hard to look at a building that is not finished when you have already built it in your mind. I envisioned it with beautiful painted walls outside and a garden with benches for the children. That was my dream, benches around the building and play space. I also dreamed of installing showers, as some of the kids don't have proper bathrooms at home, that way they could bathe before bedtime.

I struggled to see my vision through to completion. It was one of the toughest things I've ever done. It was lonely. It was scary sometimes. I worried: even if it got finished, how would it be sustainable? I didn't want it to stop.

I wanted it to be able to continue for generations. I wanted people to see what we'd done and say, "Here is something that those siblings created a long time ago, and it has withstood the test of time." That was only attainable if it was sustainable and managed properly. It needed good governance structures, the right staff, and the right trustees who would continue the vision that started with a few of us.

Finally, the building was constructed. I couldn't believe we'd done it. It is a huge building that can house seven grades of school kids. It is well decorated and colorful and soon we'll have the official launch. I'm sure so many of my friends from England will be amazed when they come to Uganda and see what we have achieved. Whenever I look at it, I find myself thinking, "It's unbelievable what God can enable people to do when they put their hearts into it. When they commit."

———————— 8ᵉ⋲8 ————————

My dream came true and the school now stands.

Recently, a big thing happened. It was late afternoon in Uganda. I had borrowed a TV from my brother and we put it up on the wall. It was a small screen, maybe thirty-two inches, but it was good enough.

We had invited the children to come to the school to watch the Footsteps event that Dr. Sam Collins and Aspire held for young girls. That would have been unimaginable a few years ago. For these children from a small village to be able to sit there and see young women from all over the globe sharing their stories and ideas... It was fantastic! They didn't know about the technology. They didn't know what Zoom was, or what webinars are.

This was a huge deal for our village. I watched the excitement of the kids as they arrived, one by one. Some of them came with adults who also loved it. I watched their faces as we connected to the conference. Then, they were able to see Dr. Sam Collins and the other speakers talking at the conference. There was such a look of amazement on their faces that they were able to watch it while it was taking place live.

I looked at them sitting there, as evening turned into night. The solar powered lights for the library enabled them to experience the full conference in a clean and safe environment. That was the best feeling!

As the evening went on, some left because it was getting dark. Not everyone could stay to the end, but I was impressed by the number of people who did. They stayed because they were learning something new.

I realized something, too: this all happened because of me.

You may be thinking that this doesn't affect you as you are not Ugandan. Maybe education is not your thing. But listen: We must all do something.

Many women around the world are legally restricted from having the same choice of jobs as men.

There is still a gender pay gap.

Many women living in sub-Saharan Africa die in pregnancy or childbirth. Women are dying as you read this.

How about automation displacing women from formal employment? Many women have lost their jobs. Many don't even have access to phones or basic technology. How are they going to manage?

And this is only some of what is happening.

Doesn't it make you want to do something?

We can't all work on education, but how about water? How about the women who are being trafficked? How about the women who want to learn to do business but have no skills or tools? There are so many things in the world that you can work on.

That is why, when we experience life, whether it's through jobs, the training that we get, the schools we attend, or the people we learn about through the media, we gain knowledge. We work on solutions when we become passionate to do so.

I'm sure many who saw what happened to George Floyd in the US were moved to risk their lives during Covid-19 to protest. Who cannot be moved by what happened to that man? When we see such things happening in the world, we are moved. And then we react.

My father took me out of my village so that I could have a better education. So as an adult, I thought I should figure out how to improve education for my village.

You start with what you have. You don't have to wait to get something bigger. You don't have to depend on somebody else giving you a lot of money. You just must start.

I asked myself, "What do I have?"

I had an apartment.

So I sold it.

It is emotional, because when I look at some kids, I see myself in them. My God, I could have been them if I hadn't gone to school. I can see that they are desperate for knowledge, they are desperate to know. They are desperate to find out about other people, other cultures, to access the knowledge that is out there. If it had not been for this new school, they wouldn't have any of those opportunities. This is what drives me.

The Aspire Footsteps event showed me that there's a lot that can be done. People today can teach children how to read from somewhere else—they don't have to be based in Uganda. They can sit anywhere in the world and teach these children. There could be nursery schools or elementary schools in Kampala and beyond that would connect with us. Kids could have teachers from other schools.

Most of the kids in my village are way behind their peers, globally. This technology could be used to enable them to catch up at school. The kids could come here and participate in teaching from the best schools and the best teachers in the world. My next step is to see which schools are willing to partner with us, and to find retired teachers who can offer their time.

I met a lady at another Aspire event. Through her, we're considering recruiting some people from the US who could teach reading to our kids in

Uganda. It opened a whole world in my imagination of what could happen at this place.

There is a lot that you can do very easily that will improve people's lives.

This kind of thing has never been available in that village—never. Now this building can seat 500 people or more!

Who are we to have that size of space? I can do this, what else can I do? How can I utilize the space which has been given to me? The contributions have come from many people. How can I ensure that it will continue to create a positive impact? How can I look back one day and feel confident that it has changed people's lives for the better.

I have learned that I must stay committed to my vision and not give up even if few people share it or think it is worth supporting. You will still find those resources. I can't thank my brother enough. He is a doctor in the US and he has given a lot, which enabled us to pay the workers. You can only volunteer to a certain level, and the commitment from these workers has been immense and deserves a fair wage.

I have learned to live my life as me, and not to be envious of other people's lives, to appreciate that their life is like that and mine is like this. I have learned that having a vision I want to fulfill is what makes me happy. I might not be as rich as someone who has invested in stocks and shares, rather than a library and a school to support lots of women and children. I'm quite comfortable with that. I know that if something happens to me and people say, "Sarah was instrumental in changing our lives," I'll rest in peace because that is what I want.

This was the most important thing I realized: the lessons I learned through difficult stages and experiences always moved me towards my goals—not away from them. I had to work to change the way I see difficulties.

My prayer every morning is, "God, give me more time because I have lots to do. But please, make it effective time. Make me strong and able to do a lot so that I can change my community."

When you get that urge to make a change, ask what do you want to change? As an individual, what do you want to be different? It could be a very personal thing. Are you in a miserable job? You want to do something else? You need that urge to change, whether it relates to the people around you, your environment, or the social norms and systems around you.

What, then, do you do?

I have learned through all the Aspire conferences I have attended that I must stop procrastinating, and just do it. I have to start where I am. Start with what I have and what I know.

Good intentions are not enough. Make the call, make the move. Don't sit around. Stay focused on what is important and ignore what is unimportant. There is too much information around us nowadays. Focus and choose your niche. If you can't find your own niche, find a cause you can support. Avoid the comparison trap. Forget what other people are doing. Determine to do something on your own, to act for no other reason than the fact that you believe in the goal you have in mind.

Then, find an accountability partner. Find a choir to sing with you. People who will keep checking on you. People who ask how you are doing. Currently I'm working with a friend online, developing our visions together. She is helping me work out how to brand my foundation. This is someone I met at an Aspire event.

Some people will laugh when you say, "I want to do this." When I told people I wanted to expand the library, some said, "Why? In a rural area? How are you going to build it?" They expected me to build a shack.

The sky's the limit! Don't forget, you must have a plan to give structure to your ideas. Sit down and plan even the simplest challenges. Write down your plan and your steps.

Then you must keep running, persevering and stick with it. It's not going to be easy. It will be tough. Sometimes you will feel alone. Sometimes you feel like giving up. Sometimes you will think, how am I going to do this?

You will find a way, or you will find an excuse. Make sure it isn't the latter.

Persevere and never, never give up. That was my motto when I was at school, and it still lives with me every day. I will never give up until I see the lives of those children changed so that when I finally go into the ground and up to the heavens, I will know that I have transformed lives. Just like mine was transformed by that man who walked 12 miles a day to get an education.

Rebellious Reflections

You should see Sarah speaking at an Aspire event. She holds court. She has a regal stature, somehow sitting higher than everyone else. A big presence in the room. Everyone around her is heads down over their notepads, writing everything she says. She's quite remarkable. No one questions her. Nobody argues with her. It is as if a queen is speaking to you. And she's very frank, blunt even. She's extremely entertaining too, but she doesn't realize that.

"Don't babysit your ideas," is one of Sarah's phrases. "Don't make excuses. Let's get on with it." She does it very cheerily too. She doesn't seem to struggle through it like others, even though she has her adversities. She enjoys her life, taking action and knowing why she's here and she gets immense satisfaction from it.

She has an inability to talk about the past. It is difficult to get her to talk about what she's done and how she did it. She's always focused on what's next. What am I doing next? What's my dream? What's the next ambition? What am I going to do? That's remarkable. She's not one to talk about her achievements and her successes. She's very much about the practicality of achieving things now or in the future. No fanfare. No self-promotion.

If you think about it, forgetting what is behind you keeps you in action. When you're living in the present, you're paving the way for the future. Sarah teaches us about the satisfaction within action. The feeling of doing something, of moving forward, the momentum that creates. She shows us that an accumulation of small actions will lead to big results.

Sarah is living a big life. Her school should be emulated across Africa and beyond. Her motivational sayings should be catalogued in a book because she has so many. My favorite one is: "If you go to your neighbor's house and eat their cooking, you may never eat your mother's cooking again."

She means that it's always good to try new things, because you might think that what you've got is good, you might think your mother's cooking is amazing because you've never tried anybody else's. When you try something else, do something else, you start to realize there's a big world out there and maybe your mother's cooking is not so great. It makes you think, "Maybe I could do better—be better."

You must stretch yourself. Discover new perspectives, keep pushing, focus on the future. Love life. Remember that material things are not important. We can derive much more satisfaction from what we have created and achieved for others.

Dr. Sam Collins 253

Her rebellion is also respectful in that her father gave her a legacy. He walked 12 miles to school in Uganda every day and ensured she didn't have to. He was a pioneer of his time to recognize his daughter should have an education when others didn't. She carries that legacy for others.

I can hear her voice now, saying something like, "You may be impressed, but it doesn't matter. What matters is what are you doing? Are you thinking about it? Are you babysitting it or are you doing something? Do something."

What is it time for you to do?

CHAPTER THIRTEEN

Bad Mother

In the Words of
Karen Sherman, President, Akilah Institute, USA

I had built up the climb up Kilimanjaro in my head. It was so much more than a mountain. And particularly after I lost the CEO job, I had something to prove.

I can still climb that mountain.

It became a huge metaphor for me. Taking my family up Kilimanjaro. I hadn't climbed a big mountain like that before or done anything like it. I hadn't even done much camping before. But I had it in my mind that this was something I was going to do.

I was in good shape. I worked out. I was training. But there's a big difference between going for a nice run and climbing an almost twenty-thousand-foot mountain to the highest peak in Africa with your husband and three sons. Just a small difference.

We geared up and got ready to go. An outfitter helped set us up and we picked the long way to the top. We thought it would be better for acclimation purposes and make it easier for the boys to get used to the climb so they could make it to the top.

For some parents, taking three kids to the mall is a big deal. In retrospect, taking an 11-year-old boy on an eight-day trek to the top of a mountain might sound outrageous. The twins, my 14-year-old boys, were great. They were typical brothers, chumming it up and the next minute arguing. They were big fighters growing up. So much so that a lot of other kids didn't want to be around them. They're such extremely different people. Along this trek up

Kilimanjaro, they were hiking buddies. They were doing it together. For once, they were both getting along. They had a common goal.

And then I got altitude sickness. I started feeling bad the higher up we went. I couldn't eat. I wasn't drinking enough water. I was light-headed and sort of swirly. I thought I might have malaria.

Must (step) climb (step) mountain. Must (step) summit (step) mountain.

That's the kind of person I am.

It was freezing. Base camp was at around 15,000 feet. It was excruciatingly cold at night. It had also been unusually damp. All of us were wearing layers of the same damp clothes for six days.

We slept in our clothes. We slept in our hats. We didn't brush our teeth. I had brought all these face creams and lotions, thinking more like a ski bunny than a mountaineer. And because we didn't bring our own cold weather gear, we had to borrow these big, puffy coats, so I looked like the Michelin Man all bundled up.

The way it works is that you trek for several days to reach the base camp and then climb to the peak. Summit day finally arrived, and we were at the base camp. On summit day, you wake up at midnight to start hiking. We were making it work. Slowly, slowly. "Polay, polay," as they say in Swahili. As we got higher and higher, we started to pass other climbers on the side of the path throwing up.

It started out pitch dark, our headlamps on at the outset of the hike. We trudged along, walking single file following people up this skinny trail. We had guides who had climbed Kilimanjaro multiple times. In fact, for the summit, we brought an extra guide in case somebody needed to turn around as it happens often.

At seventeen thousand feet, my youngest son Kai was not doing well.

We took a short breather, he sat against this rock as pale as a ghost. He'd thrown up on the side of the trail and sat staring blankly at the ground. He didn't say "stay with me," or ask me to come over. He didn't do anything.

Things did not look good.

"He needs to go back," said one of the guides. "He can't go any farther."

We stopped and talked about it. I thought, Okay, I should go down with him. That would be what a good mother would do, right? Bad mother for bringing an 11-year-old to Rwanda. Bad mother for bringing him up a mountain. Selfish mother for wanting to continue and feeling slightly irritated and maybe even resentful that I might have to stop.

Certainly not one of those good mothers back at home in the US who stay with their kids to do their homework and do all those good things that good mothers do. Of course, I'm the selfish mother, the bitch mother, the mother who's not there.

But I'm never coming back to this mountain again.

It's not like, "Oh, next year I'll come back and try again!" That's not happening.

Must. Summit. Mountain.

"Okay," I said, "Kai's going back down with the guide. We are going on without him."

—————————— ❦ ——————————

I think of myself as an ambitious person, or at least I used to. Early on, it may not have necessarily been for the right reasons.

I think we as women sit around waiting for people to acknowledge us, to reward us, to give us our rights, to give us a balanced life, to say "I notice that you're feeling x, y, or z."

We don't claim it, and own it, and change it.

I wanted to go to Rwanda. I wanted to climb that mountain as a family. But I wanted to live there with the kids and not with Bill.

For me, going to Rwanda to work was like, I've got to do something different. I've got to change something for myself.

I want to do this.

I put a lot on the line with it, obviously. It wasn't only the move; it was about the work. It was about my marriage to my husband, Bill. It was about a lot of things that I felt weren't working for me any longer. I was being honest with myself. I was unsure that I could take care of the kids by myself. Asking myself that question, "Could I be that person, the single parent?"

I'd never been that person.

Here's my superpower, but also my weakness: I didn't think through what it might be like to be on my own with three kids in Rwanda. Having traveled to South Sudan and Congo and all those other places with my work already, it wasn't out of my realm of comfort.

My rashness carried me forward. I have a good flight instinct. I know when I've got to get out of there because this or that isn't working for me. My marriage wasn't working for me. This life wasn't working for me.

I needed to see if there was a different way to do this, to do something differently.

When people start telling you all the time, "Oh, you should run this... you should be the CEO." You start staying to yourself, "Hey, maybe I should be the CEO."

At the time, I worked for the not-for-profit, Women for Women International, an organization that helps women survivors of war rebuild their lives. I was based in Washington DC. The organization was going through massive changes. We had a series of consultants come in to tell us how we should fix ourselves and do things "better." This was yet another fix which created a kind of awkward dynamic. The founder was transitioning to a new role. The founder was stepping back. I had been COO for four years before that role was eliminated. I then became head of global programs. The board was going to bring in a senior, more experienced person to support the CEO, who later stepped out altogether. They ended up bringing somebody else to be the President and COO.

It felt like a slap in the face.

Of course, I was going to throw my hat in the ring for CEO, as did this other person that they had brought in as President and COO. So I was competing against this person internally, which was awkward, as well as external candidates.

At the same time I was also going through the initial stages of menopause without realizing it. I wasn't sleeping, and generally was not in a great place. My marriage was also coming apart. We had not been doing well for quite some time, and I felt a little bit of that "now or never" in terms of having to make some key decisions about our relationship.

I honestly felt that to get to a different place, mentally speaking, in my life and in my marriage, I needed to go to a different place. I needed to leap - to put it all on the line. We had worked on our marriage through therapy over the years, but I hadn't yet done the hard work of figuring out myself and who I wanted to be.

I did know this: I did not want to be a part-time mum and share custody. I had worked hard through infertility and other things to get my kids. Giving up being a full-time mum was the biggest thing that kept me from wanting to move forward on changes to my relationship. Even though I was traveling extensively, I still couldn't envision seeing my kids every other weekend. I couldn't fathom that.

All this came to a head when I was sitting in the WFWI office and two board members came in to tell me they'd selected an external candidate for CEO.

I was devastated.

"We want you to stay," they insisted.

This new CEO will want a clean house, right? I said to myself. She will want to build her own team—and rightly so. All I was thinking was how do you stay with an incoming CEO for a job that you had put in for, then lost?

I had invested so much of myself in the organization over the years and didn't know where to go from there. Rwanda was my path forward.

When it came to moving to Rwanda, I stated what I wanted, what I needed, and I worked to make it happen. Systematically, I went to the board chair and then I went to the President and COO, and I figured it out. Lastly, I went to my family.

There weren't a lot of places I could go safely with Women for Women International, and bring the kids with me, but that's what I wanted to do. Afghanistan, Iraq, South Sudan, Congo? Sorry, no. I didn't want to live there with the boys. It was either Bosnia or Rwanda.

"We're building a women's opportunity center in Rwanda," I said. "It's kind of lagging. We could use more leadership there."

I didn't even mention it to anybody. It was all my brainchild. I didn't talk to my husband about it, didn't talk to my kids about it. I wanted to go.

On the car ride to the airport to visit my brother in Boston, I blurted out, "I think we should move to Rwanda."

My husband was livid, of course. He didn't have any time to adjust or think about it or think about what it meant for our relationship or our family, which is a fair point. Absolutely a fair point.

The boys at the time—my 14-year-old twins and my youngest son, 11—were sitting in the back making enthusiastic comments. "Yeah! We're moving to Rwanda!"

The boys were intrigued by the idea. I think I caught them at the right time. My twins had finished their last year of junior high. So they didn't have any connections to high school yet. If they were more entrenched in high school, it might have been a different conversation. My youngest was in fifth grade. He was flexible. It was a good point in time.

Then I needed to go through a process of convincing my husband that whether he wanted to go was not the issue. The issue was I needed to go, and I wanted to take the boys with me. I don't know if he internalized it the same way I did because we weren't too explicit about it. I saw it as a trial separation.

Can I manage the boys? Can I raise them on my own in Rwanda? What would that be like? Where do I want to go from here with my marriage? Where do I want to go from here with my career?

For a long time, my husband and I had been more good friends and social entrepreneurs, or collaborators, versus husband and wife. There were intimacy issues. Our parental templates were different. I'm much more confrontational and engaging. I was on the kids regarding academics, where he was more of a people-pleaser. I was the disciplinarian. He got up and made them pancakes. A lot of power-dynamic issues that played out in multiple ways.

"The issue isn't me being less powerful," I would often say to him. "The issue is for you to find your own power."

I always felt like he was easily the more likable, or lovable parent. I'm the prickly one. At least, earlier on. I don't think it's as true now because they understand who I am. I felt maybe they were always a little scared of me because I'm clear, direct, and I was always honest with them.

I thought they would miss their dad and probably have a hard time being with me the whole time. I also felt like that year would be an incredible year for our relationship that would shape us going forward. We would get to know each other in very different ways, being in Rwanda.

And my boys would finally get to see my work up close.

When we talked it over, we decided that, yes, it would not be such a horrible thing for me to go. And then later, for me to take the boys with me and him not to go. The idea of moving to Rwanda itself was not such a crazy idea after all.

We were on a plane two months later.

My husband came over with us for the first three weeks to help us settle in and figure out certain logistics. Then he went home, and I was there alone with the boys.

After my husband had gone back to the States, I had some support. We had a woman who helped me by staying with the boys overnight if I was on a work trip, and she would pick them up from school and care for them after school when I was at work.

Every house in Rwanda comes with a guard and ours would play soccer with the boys on the lawn. He was also something of a gardener and kept everything watered. Life for the boys wasn't too dissimilar from home. The boys went to the International School of Kigali. It was a very small school. There were kids from all over the world, many from other African nations.

It was an interesting school with fascinating classes. They took Tai Chi as part of their curriculum. They met all sorts of interesting kids, some of whom they're still friends with today. I wanted them to see my world and experience different cultures.

On weekends, we spent a lot of time exploring Kigali. We also started training for the trek up Kilimanjaro that coming winter, so we'd go running. I'd take turns running with the boys or boot walking one of the many hills in Rwanda. It became our one-on-one bonding time. I would go running with them and we would have that time together. That tradition has continued to this day. I often take individual runs or workouts with my boys to spend time with them. Something about working out together unleashes real conversation, and gets us away from the usual, "Yeah, Mom... Sure, Mom... Whatever, Mom..." type of conversation we all enjoy so much as mothers!

They didn't realize it was a trial separation from their father. In fact, I had moved out at one point earlier in our marriage when the kids were younger and had rented an apartment not too far away. We explained it in a weird way, saying both of us were in an intensive work period and we've got to work late, so we're going to take turns in the house. They were young enough they didn't question it then. This was a real separation.

I felt empowered, but it was also scary at the same time. I was a little lonely, too. As time went on, the kids made their own friends and wanted to go out and do kid things, which they should have! I made some friends there, too, and started building my own network. It's not like you want to see work colleagues every weekend. I had to work hard to build a social life. It was interesting to realize my husband was the person always responsible for our social life as I had always been traveling for work. He'd set up the social engagements on the weekends and playdates for the kids, and we'd all arrive at the appointed hour.

I now had to do those things, which I had done very little of over the years. It forced my hand in good ways because, frankly speaking, I was dependent on Bill and his caretaking. The epiphany was, "I need to get my act together. I can preach all I want about self-sufficiency for women and here's me not being self-sufficient." Self-sufficiency was at the heart of the Women for Women International development model. The irony was quite clear to me.

Bill also initially found it lonely, but he liked it in some ways, too. He was working out whenever he wanted. He didn't have daily familial responsibilities. He took the opportunity to take some trips and other things with friends. In the end, he coped quite well. Not a bad gig, right? He did miss us, so he came to visit a few times.

That had its own challenges, those re-entry challenges. Every time I would come back from a trip, I'd have these re-entries into home-life type of challenges. I'd have to enter back into the family. Like, there's Bill and the boys—and then there's me.

When Bill came to Rwanda, he would experience his own re-entry challenges. You feel like you're dealing with an established unit and must break through those relationship auto-piloting habits that get built up over time. In some ways the boys and I were the Four Musketeers because we were living our lives together. Then here's Bill coming in trying to insert himself. I'm sure he would feel that way when I would come back from one of my trips. For me it was like, "Hey, see how it feels?"

Over the course of my career, I've gotten the whole you're crazy for leaving your kids thing all the time. Particularly from other women. "You're leaving your kids? What kind of mother are you?" It's mostly contained in the awkward glance, or snide comment here and there.

Bad mother.

I was at the bus stop one time meeting the kids when they were coming home from school. Because of my work, I was rarely there to meet the bus. A woman who was also there picking up her own kids started making chit chat.

We weren't friends, more like acquaintances.

"The boys were having some trouble with an assignment," I mentioned. "So I was helping them with their homework last night."

"Well," she said, "my kids don't let me help them with their homework anymore. You're never around though, so it must be more of a novelty for them."

Jesus Christ! I don't even know that she realized what a stinger that was. She didn't realize, of course, I was checking my kid's essays and helping them with their homework while sitting in South Sudan for my work with women survivors of war. Working in conflict zones, addressing the challenges of genocide and battles with corrupt politicians was my daily "To Do" list. Go fuck yourself, lady.

There were people in my family who used to say to me, "Oh, you're never going to have kids because you're always gone." Kind of looking at me from the surface and saying, "I can't recognize a good mother in the choices that she's made." People often see things from their experience, not from someone else's. We're always overlaying our own lens on the issue, saying,

"My life doesn't look like that. There must be something wrong with that person for making a different choice."

My own sister once said to me, "Well, Bill does everything..."

"Well, he actually doesn't do everything," I said. "He does some of the things that you do around the house." Bill did her version of everything. I did the other things she had no insight into. It's very easy to judge. I see women judging other women all the time.

Bill was and is a good guy. He was and is a good caretaker. And for a long time, I thought, if he's the good one then I must be the bad one. I beat myself up so well over that.

The truth of it is, it takes two people to make a marriage. If it's not working, it's rarely about one person unless there's something egregious and obvious going on. If it's not working, it's usually not working because you're not working together as a couple. The chemistry doesn't work anymore. The power dynamics don't work anymore. Not everything is fixable. I mean, it is so random in so many ways how we end up in relationships with people.

Bill and I tried for a long time to have kids and it was hard.

Part of it was we had waited for ten years. I was traveling a lot and we were both building our careers. So we waited to even try for kids. Once we started trying we found out I had endometriosis and couldn't get pregnant right away. So it took years.

The twins. It was a long road and a fertility struggle to get them, and I really wanted them. Sam and Eli were born. Three years later, at a check-up my doctor looks at me and says, "Someone's pregnant."

And I was like, "Who?"

Well, it was me. So boy number three showed up a little bit unexpectedly, which was great. We had moved into a new house and were creating a library or office space which ended up becoming a nursery for this little guy.

While they were growing up, I had a good relationship with my boys, even being more of the in and out mom. I saw taking them to Rwanda as a great opportunity to bring them into my world for the first time. I had kept those worlds very compartmentalized when they were little. So the chance to expose them as individuals was front of mind. It was also an opportunity for them, I thought.

I don't think I fully appreciated what it meant to be a mother until Rwanda. It was a big turning point for me and for my relationship with the boys. It meant everything. I started to realize that if I had been one of those women who was out working and doing what I was doing without really being able to give them an insight into what we were doing in Rwanda, there would be something missing. And I realized why I had struggled so hard to have them in the first place. I wanted that family. I wanted that grounding. And I can tell you, as time has gone on, I value and appreciate them more and more.

The climb would fall on my 50th birthday. And we had always done family adventures together. I wanted us to go up as a family and include Bill.

There was something very magical about being on the mountain together. Sam and Eli became hiking buddies and they really kind of put aside that squabbling and ended up as partners in crime. That was really the first time I'd seen them actively work together towards a singular goal. It was inspiring to see. I do think it fundamentally changed their relationship as brothers.

A lot of people wouldn't have done it, or maybe even brought their youngest but I knew they could handle it. We'd trained for it, we'd practiced for it. Of course, we could do it.

Dr. Sam Collins 267

I don't believe in low-balling your kids' abilities. I see a lot of parents doing it. They're too overprotective. Don't do this, don't do that. I really believe in setting a high bar for your kids, whatever it is. I've tried to do that very intentionally.

I can remember hearing somebody from the Gates Foundation say one of our challenges with education and children broadly is that we set low bars. And then when they fail to accomplish even that, we're surprised.

I'm a high bar kind of gal. But you probably got that about me already.

"Kai," I said. "Are you okay to go with the guide back to camp?"

"Yeah," he said, queasy and breathing heavily.

"Okay, I love you."

"Love you, Mom."

"I'll see you at base camp," I said. And I gave him a bundled up hug. I watched Kai walk down the mountain a little bit. Then I turned around, took another step, and faced my demons, faced that death march up the mountain.

It only got harder.

But at last we made it.

The twins were ahead of us and summited first. Then me and Bill.

So you take some obligatory pictures of yourself at the top, touching the sign at the summit. Then you slog your way on down.

It was a lot of work, but also thrilling and amazing and I'm so glad I persevered. Did it solve all my problems? Did it fix my marriage and fulfill me and set me up for the rest of my life? Of course not. But it made me realize something: one of my best qualities is that I am tenacious to a fault. I'm a dog with a bone. That is something that I will always carry with me.

I was going to summit that fucking mountain even if I had to crawl my way up.

Because I felt like—even at my worst—I can do anything. I can't say that I was wracked with guilt as I continued climbing. I did wonder, "Jeez, I sent my son down without me. Was that the right thing to do?"

In that moment, I chose self-preservation above all, which meant continuing to climb that mountain. I wasn't worried about my son's safety, these were experienced guides after all, but I did question my own judgment. There are a lot of mothers who put their children's needs above their own. That's not inherently a bad thing. That said, I do think as women, putting our needs at least on par with our children's, giving ourselves permission to even have needs, including unmet needs in our families and relationships, is a step in the right direction.

I could see that woman in my mind, the one from the bus stop, "You left your son behind on the mountain at 17,000 feet? Bad mother!" At each step, I could feel her condemnation.

I don't share with the other moms what it is I do. Because, of course, I want to fit in with the other mother's, the good mothers, because I want to be liked. I am also wrestling with my own guilt for leaving my kids for work, my own feelings of insufficiency.

There are a lot of mothers who probably would have made a different decision. The first reaction from many people who have heard this story is,

"You're not likable. I don't like that about you. I would have made a different choice."

That is the crux of the issue: somehow I'm inherently unlikable because I put myself first? Because I made a different choice than you might have made? Or do you feel like you would love to make a choice like that, but you are too afraid to make it?

I don't fault them for that. In fact, I questioned myself. I knew a lot of "good mothers" who were well liked would never do what I did. But I would also like to ask for a little grace, too. I had my own things to work through. Does this make me a good mother? A bad mother? Or maybe the mother that I am? A-different-than-you-mother. I suspect a lot of people would not have even brought their kids to Rwanda. That is the kind of mother I want to be.

Back at basecamp, Kai said, "I would never have wanted you to come back with me. I would have felt terrible if you had to do that for me."

It was a good experience for all of us, even for Kai. He has ever brought up not summiting or ever dwelled on it. It hasn't scarred him. Getting to the top was more important for me than for anybody else. It was something that I needed to accomplish.

Kai is an aware young man, and I think all the boys understood how important this was to me to continue.

Whether it's climbing a mountain or what I do professionally, my boys respect the choices I make. I don't know if they always did in the moment, but they see their mother as being strong, competent, out in the world, and doing good things. I think it inspires them. and I think whether you're a mom or dad, choosing yourself is good role-modeling for your kids.

I had always felt like the "bad mother," the bad parent. I was the "No," parent. I was the one who set the boundaries. I'm the one who, frankly speaking, after seeing so many kids all over the world who were suffering, who didn't have the level of privilege or hope or opportunity that my kids had in America, felt like they're easily spoiled. They're entitled. The contrast was stark. I've seen kids in Afghanistan barefoot, selling toilet paper between cars on the street.

I'd get home and my kids didn't blink to say, "Take me here. Do this for me. I want those shoes, and this and that and this, too."

I spent a lot of time trying to unpack the difference between "needs" and "wants" with my children. Bill was all about the wants. Do you want this? Sure! You want that? Okay!

That was a big source of tension for me and the sort of reconciling of my work, the difference between us and how so many other people lived around the world. That world and our world, in the land of plenty.

You don't want your kids to feel deprived. It's about framing. Understanding the context and giving your kids a total perspective so they understand how fortunate they are. To teach them that choices you get to make are a gift, because there are so many people around the world that don't have that gift of choice.

Rwanda was our experiment. If I had to do it all over again, I would do the same thing and make the same choices.

You don't have to continue to be stuck in a state of mind. You can change if you want it bad enough. You can unstick yourself from a sticky situation. It does take courageous acts. There will be tradeoffs. There will be difficult decisions.

I have friends who are in difficult situations, professionally, in marriages, in various realms of life. There is a vortex we create by saying, "Well, I can't do this. I shouldn't do that. I can't move here or leave there." Those are all mental constructs.

Yes, there are real obstacles. They may be financial. They may be familial. They may be moral or other things. The courage to leap is something that is so important for women. If there are things that hold you back, they are by and large more internal than external.

Women can be our own worst critics. We can be both self-judging and judgmental of other women. It's a fundamental flaw. If we were to really give room for women to make different choices, allow them because we trust them and we respect them and we understand that they're good human beings, then the world would be a better place.

I'm personally not so worried about male judgments. It's the women who are hard to hear. I used to get that all the time from women. You're never at the bus stop. You're never around. What kind of mother are you? You're going to Rwanda? You left Kai up there?

I wasn't the one organizing the playdates or necessarily cooking dinner every night or doing those things that mothers are "supposed to" do. But I'm also the one in South Sudan checking my son's essays, taking them on hikes, running alongside, doing all sorts of things mothers aren't supposed to do. It doesn't have to look the same.

I love this quote: "We don't see things as they are. We see things as we are." We look at life through a certain lens because that's the way it works in our life. But your lens is not necessarily the way it's supposed to work in other women's lives.

There is another quote from Madeleine Albright, who said, "There's a special place in hell for women who don't support other women." When you denigrate women's choices, whatever they are—whether you're staying at home, working, traveling, climbing mountains—you're doing a disservice to women more broadly and, quite frankly, to yourself even more so.

In that sense, in one way or another, we're all survivors. You may be asking yourself how you can overcome your own obstacles and challenges to influence the causes that are important to you. How it's possible to work to change other people's lives or even your own. I've asked myself that question on so many occasions, and I've come to realize that repairing the world starts with us. It starts with us as individuals and as women with healing the wounds of our own past, with addressing our own limiting beliefs.

When I was experiencing my own crisis—my work, my marriage, my family— all the issues felt like they were crashing down at the same time. It felt that everything I had worked so hard for was coming apart. I knew instinctively that I needed to do something different, maybe even something life changing, and try to have a fresh start. Although I didn't understand it at the time, what I needed was a reinvention.

Because I was able to take this leap, because I was allowed the space to figure out what I wanted, my husband and I are in a better place in our marriage now. We separated and then reunited after my year in Rwanda. My sons and I are closer than ever because of this experience. They have all grown into exceptional human beings and young men. I could not be prouder of each of them.

During the year I spent living in Rwanda, I oversaw the construction of a first-of-its-kind women's opportunity center and began writing my book, Brick by Brick, which is now published. I'm currently based in the USA and am President of the Akilah, a women's college, and center for female leadership in Rwanda

I believe that women, wherever they are, whatever their circumstances, are inherently powerful and courageous. The belief continues to be the driving force behind my commitment to women's advancement.

Beyond continents and cultures, beyond war and peace, what separates us truly is choice– the ability to choose from the simplest expressions of our daily preferences to the more profound and life changing choices that shape us as women, as mothers and human beings.

Many of us women have had to build or rebuild our lives, one step, one small change, one brick at a time. Though outside forces may have shaped us and even oppressed us, we've held onto our dreams, forged our own paths, taken risks, and led change in our families, communities, and countries. Many of us have fully embraced our choices.

All of us can do the same. We can repair ourselves, we can reinvent ourselves, we can channel our energy and our passions into the causes that are most important to us. We can make a difference in our own lives and in the lives of others, and we can support our sisters around the world. My work has deepened my sense of perspective and appreciation for what it takes to be a woman in this world today, even when that womanhood is threatened or diminished by one's family ,culture, or society. It also reminds me daily that while making tough choices can be daunting, the very act of choosing, especially for women, is the great privilege of our lives.

Rebellious Reflections

I love Karen's story, because I too often must make the same kind of decisions about work versus kids.

For some people, it manifests while working a job in a corporation, navigating the challenges of a healthy work-life balance, time management, and being able to attend your kid's extracurricular school stuff, which is, you know, often scheduled during work hours. For Karen, it was working a job helping women survivors of war, and arguably, in some of the most dangerous places for women in the world. This was a regular, everyday thing for her. She kept it secret from other mothers because she experienced "mothers' guilt" with the best of us.

So I love the moment when she's climbing Kilimanjaro, deciding whether her younger son should go back down because he's struggling, and she doesn't want to go down with him. Continuing her climb goes against all social norms of what mothers should do. Shouldn't she stop and go back down with him? A tremendous question. What type of role models do we want to be for our children? Shouldn't we be showing them how to persevere, to be resilient, to keep going?

Though he may not have understood it at the moment, in the long term, her son realized how terrific what she did was. Even though she could hear the mothers at the school gates judging her, she would not have done it any differently. Those turning points are critical to notice.

Resilience. She carried on. She set herself the challenge of climbing Mount Kilimanjaro and did it. She's a role model and a fierce advocate for climbing mountains, whatever the mountain might be. Karen teaches us to do serious work, but to not take ourselves too seriously.

She's willing to put herself on the line, to share her messy stories, to be judged. In fact, she shared that many people told her they didn't like her when they heard that she carried on climbing and her son went down the mountain. I liked her more.

What's your Mount Kilimanjaro? What is your personal challenge that, if you were to achieve it, you would prove to yourself that you can do anything? It could be a physical challenge like this, it could be emotional, mental, spiritual, or all the above.

If I was ever given an opportunity to pick a global team of people to work with on women's equality, Karen would be at the top of my list. She's someone who you could call out of the blue and say, "I need to meet you in X city, and I need X amount of money." She wouldn't question it. She'd be there, and if she had the money, she would give it to you.

Karen teaches us that we are allowed to be imperfect people and mothers. Thank goodness! Because so many trailblazers come across as superhuman, far out of this world and far from being anyone that we could be. We realize through her vulnerability, through her self-growth, through her mountain climbing, through her resilience, through the challenges in her marriage, mothering, and as a professional, she truly is a rebellious trailblazer. And a wonderful friend.

What is your mountain to climb?

CHAPTER FOURTEEN
Motherboards
In the Words of
Eileen Brewer,
Accelerator Director, Takween Accelerator, Iraq

"That sounds very dangerous."

"Have you thought it through?"

"You shouldn't go! Aren't there other places you can work?"

Undoubtedly, I would have asked the same questions, as little as two years ago, of anyone who had told me that they were planning to work in Kurdistan, Iraq. At the age of 60 and by themselves, no less.

But the people who asked me the questions didn't really "know" me.

The typical response from those who know me well: "Of course you are going to work in Iraq!" If I have an opportunity to make a difference or dive in to try something new, I'll dive in. It doesn't matter where the work is located.

I have two sides to my personality. One side wants to help advance the status of those who most need the help and have the least resources, particularly women and girls.

My "other" personality is completely adventurous. I love to travel. There is no greater joy for me than jumping into the middle of other cultures and challenging myself and my beliefs. I am constantly open to change. I want to listen deeply, knowing I may change some of my long-held beliefs. How beautiful it is to listen to the perspectives of others and respect their experiences, while also sharing my knowledge to help them build businesses.

I used to do consultancy work for US Embassies and international NGOs, traveling to multiple countries to provide training on entrepreneurship. I journeyed to each country for one or two weeks, then briefly came back home to California, then went back out again. This afforded me the opportunity to travel to many places doing what I love to do.

When Covid hit, all my trips were canceled. I knew I didn't want to go back to work in Silicon Valley. I had worked hard to transition my career from there and into something about which I felt very passionate. Since trips were being canceled and borders everywhere were closing, I began searching for work where I could help entrepreneurs in another country and continue doing the entrepreneurship training I so loved.

Two job opportunities arose: one in Kurdistan, Iraq, and another in New Zealand. I interviewed for both, talking at length to people in both countries. But the phone call that came through in May of 2020 was: "Would you be willing to take the job in Kurdistan, Iraq?"

Outwardly, I was very cool. "No problem," I said, "sounds great!" Inwardly I was terrified. This was a much bigger leap than I had planned to take. I hung up the phone... and panicked! What have you done, Eileen? Why would you say yes to that? Are you completely insane?

New Zealand during Covid was one of the safest places you could be!

But I know myself very well. I will always choose the more difficult job because I know it will challenge me to grow professionally and emotionally.

Instinctively, going to New Zealand was easier. I would be helping people who spoke the same language as me and who have more resources. This didn't feel like a true alignment with my purpose. As much as New Zealand sounded awesome and beautiful, loving water and island climates as I do, it felt like an easy way out.

Kurdistan, on the other hand, is landlocked with few opportunities to enjoy fresh water during the blazing summers. I volunteered to move to a place where it was 45 degrees Celsius (113 degrees Fahrenheit), for at least five months out of the year.

Yes, a big part of me was scared. "You're leaping further than you need to."

When I feel fear I try to investigate what the fear is. In my experience, it's usually caused by some lack of knowledge. So I do research, whether it's for a new job, a new skill, or a new country. In Iraq there is a region called the Kurdistan region, in the northern part of Iraq. I learned the Kurdistan region was much safer as compared to living in the southern region.

I talked with women who lived in Kurdistan. Everybody told me it's safe. It's amazing. You're going to love it. Don't miss the opportunity! Not one single person, including Americans who had lived there for a decade, not one hesitated. No one told me it was scary or that they didn't feel safe, or that they had one too many close encounters. No one! So by doing the research, I decided to go ahead and take the job in Kurdistan.

When I was in high school in the 1970s, I was the only girl on an all-male water polo team because a female team did not exist. I wanted to play water polo, so I challenged my male colleagues and they put me on their team. Today, a lot has changed and there are female water polo teams. In the 1970s, it was not merely progressive to have women on the team, it was unheard of.

In California, where I grew up, you had to be sixteen before you could drive a car alone. I learned, however, that you could ride a motorcycle alone at 15. I wanted to be able to get out and about solo, and not depend on other people. So when I was 15 years old, my older sister taught me how to ride a motorcycle and I bought one. It did not take long for me to have my first accident, where I suffered a broken leg. I spent my 16th birthday in a cast from my toes to my hip. I was in that cast for six months and unable to leave my bed the first month.

One week after they gave me a cast that allowed me to bend my knee, I was off on my motorcycle again. Why not ride if I could? Who cares if there was a cast on my leg? At least that leg was well protected!

Around that same time, my parents divorced. My mom moved out and left us with my dad. My three oldest siblings were already out of the house; only the three younger siblings, including me, remained. My dad was a blue-collar worker and worked two, if not three jobs, at a time, trying to make enough income. We were teenagers so we were pretty much left on our own to raise ourselves.

At that time, I was very much doing whatever I wanted, running around and partying and missing school. One of my high school girlfriends invited me to come and stay with her family since I was spending so much time at their house. After two weeks, her parents told me, "We're already licensed foster parents. If your father agrees, we can put you in the foster system so that we can get some money each month to help pay for your food and general upkeep." My father said, "Sure," and he signed the papers.

I stayed with this family for about a year and when I turned eighteen, I left school and hitchhiked with my 17-year-old best friend. We left Los Angeles and traveled all over California, Oregon, Washington, and Banff, Canada, for four months. Then we came back into the US down through Wyoming, venturing into the Dakotas and Nebraska. We were just a couple of girls with backpacks hitching rides with strangers.

While that trip was fun, we also experienced a lot of fear and a lot of scary situations. We found ourselves in some extremely dangerous scenarios, close to being raped and attacked on multiple occasions. Talking our way out of situations, running, and hiding saved us more than once.

One time there was a truck driver who picked us up. He started coming on to us on the ride and suggested we stop at a hotel, so we said, "Yes, but let's get some alcohol first." When he got out of the truck to run into the liquor store to buy booze, we jumped out of the other side of the truck and ran as far and as fast as we could, then hid in some bushes. Another time a guy pulled a knife on us and when he slowed down to turn onto an empty dirt road, we jumped out of the van and ran. Luckily, he decided not to chase us.

Scenarios like those happened four or five times. We never stopped, we never gave up, we never said, "Okay, we're done, we're too scared." We laughed it off and put our thumbs back out there the next day. Coming out on the other side of these experiences taught me courage. I learned I could face new or scary challenges and survive. I learned how to be self-sufficient. My stories all ended with me being safe which I know is not true for many women. I know I was one of the lucky ones and I am not cavalier about it. At the time I did not think about it, however, as I have gotten older, I recognize how very lucky I have truly been.

My early career started with jobs in machine shops and manufacturing plants where I was usually the only female on the shop floor. I worked with large sheet metal rollers, punch presses, and heavy equipment. I liked the physical work, the challenge of learning new skills, and showing the guys I could do anything they could do.

As I moved into office roles, I met women who were willing to mentor me. They taught me how to behave in a professional work environment and how to do complete job functions properly. These women educated me about giving back and helping others succeed instead of watching them fail.

Even my older sister mentored me and helped me find work. In 1998, she worked at a tech company where nobody got hired without a college degree. She was also pretty rebellious and hired me on her team even though I did not have a degree. She told them I would be good. "Very good," actually. She did that for me. She went against the norm and took a lot of flack over it. She was right. I loved program management and I am exceptionally good at it.

Because I did not have a degree at the time, I had nepotism written across my forehead, and my colleagues did not want to talk to me. I eventually found allies and those who were willing to teach me. I went back to college, and through night classes, I got my bachelor's degree in information technology. I really enjoyed the work and stayed on that career path for 20 years in Silicon Valley. I especially liked the hardware part of technology and have always held roles involving managing hardware manufacturing.

Every job I have ever had has always been bigger than me at the moment I started. Not having the skills, not having the background, not having the education, I was always jumping in and saying, "Yes," eventually learning the job and getting good at it. I always got excellent performance reviews. Then I would outgrow the job and need to do something else more challenging.

I gained confidence by observing others on the job. I used to sit in meetings listening to other people, men, because there were never women in the higher-level roles. I listened to the men speak and looked at the reports they were delivering, always thinking, "I can do that. I am not seeing anything they're doing that I can't do."

I will often take jobs that I don't know everything about, even though it can be intimidating. I also know I would be bored very quickly if I already knew everything. I love the challenge and the opportunity to learn.

Teach me new skills. Show me new things. Challenge me, even though my gut reaction is fear, my body freezes on the inside, I can feel my chest get tight, and I can feel my fear rise. I will stay in that seat, listen intently, and learn how to do what I am being taught really, really well. Then, show me something else. Then show me something else, again.

I need to do it this way. I need to learn how to do this to survive. It is only after I achieve something, or understand it fully, that I get this joy inside. Whether I make a complicated spreadsheet or a great presentation, there is that joy of learning a new skill and it feels good to look back at that work and say, "I did that!"

Immediately, then, I want to turn around and figure out, okay, to whom can I give this? Who can I teach? I will show the next person because others showed me. I will read a complicated book, build a presentation deck on what I learned from the book, and share it with others in a more easily digestible format. Especially if it helps women advance in their careers where they might be getting overlooked by male leadership. I have mentored dozens of women on how to overcome the challenges they face in their careers.

I don't want anyone to feel stuck, or like they can't achieve because they don't know how to do something. I don't want them to get left behind. I want them to see that they can do this. They can grow and advance. So go ahead and admit to me that you don't know how to do it and I'll show you how.

In 2012, I was a Director of Program Management at a tech company when I started volunteering for the US State Department's TechWomen Exchange Program, doing one-on-one mentoring for women coming from other countries to Silicon Valley. I had worked in Silicon Valley for 20 years and I knew there were entrepreneurs and start-ups all around me, but I had always worked for bigger companies. I wasn't involved in the start-up ecosystem.

The TechWomen participants were telling me about their funding experiences. They were trying to start businesses, they were trying to get funding, and they were hitting a wall. Men wouldn't invest in them. Men wouldn't take them seriously. Because I had never put myself in the start-up investment space, I didn't realize what was happening right down the street from me.

I was intrigued.

"Screw that!" I thought. "I'm going to help fix this problem!" I ventured into this start-up ecosystem where I had no experience because women were telling me they were not being treated fairly.

I began investigating the start-up gatherings in my community. Meetup groups were extremely popular at the time, so I used the platform and got myself into any meeting for which I could register for free. I sat in the room and listened.

Then I read books to find out what the rules were. What are the boundaries? Tell me the rules. I want to make a difference, and I want to support female founders. I want to be a female investor investing in female founders. What do I have to do? It's a process, I learned. You must understand and read as much as you can, listen and ask questions and find a way in.

One of the requirements is that you must be a Securities Exchange Commission (SEC) accredited investor before you're allowed to be an angel investor, which is an individual who provides capital for a business start-up when most investors are not prepared to back them. I learned I was shy of the financial requirements to be SEC accredited so I went to my boss and said, "I need a raise."

"Why?" he queried.

"Because I want to invest in female founders, and I need to be SEC accredited. I want to help women," I confidently responded.

He said, "Okay," and gave me the raise!

The State Department's TechWomen program leads annual delegation trips to the program countries of these emerging female leaders. Each year, one hundred women from twenty-one different countries come to Silicon Valley to work in our companies as we mentor them for one month. They then return to their home countries with their newfound knowledge and skills. On these overseas delegation trips, 20 or 30 mentors fly into one of the countries for one week to provide additional training.

I went back to my boss again and said, "I want to travel to these countries to provide training and get more girls interested in science, technology, engineering, and mathematics (STEM). I want to go on these State Department delegation trips."

It had nothing to do with my day job at all. I was a Director in Program Management at a security hardware and software company.

"I want to go to Rwanda for a week and teach girls about hardware," I told him.

Again he said, "Okay!"

My boss considered my proposal seriously because a lot of the tech companies have a corporate responsibility department with a focus on community outreach. The company wants to prove they're encouraging community engagement, volunteer opportunities, paying it forward, and helping others. They encourage their employees and motivate them, even to the extent of offering an extra five-day paid vacation per year, if you're using that time for volunteer work.

When I first started mentoring for TechWomen, I paid all my expenses out of my own pocket. However, since my boss could see I was becoming very serious about the TechWomen program, the company first paid about 20 percent of costs, then 50 percent, and soon they were paying 80 percent of my travel expenses to go on these delegation trips.

I worked for a man who had the emotional intelligence to say, "What do you want in life? What do you need to be successful? What do you need to pursue your career dreams? And how can I help you get there?" He role modeled the servant leadership style which I fully embrace and practice with my teams now.

———————— ✦ ————————

TechWomen took me to Rwanda on my first delegation trip. I was trying to figure out how to instruct these girls on technology because I didn't want them to be afraid of hardware. I wanted them to understand that they could open anything and learn about the parts inside that make it work. On that first trip I took a hair dryer and a clock radio. We flew into Kigali, Rwanda, and got on a bus ride for a couple of hours down dirt roads to Gashora Girls School. There were some three hundred girls living in the compound. There were only cold-water baths, dorm-style sleeping with bunk beds in long, wide open rooms, and cinder block classrooms. But they were well-equipped compared to most of the schools I've been to since then.

I entered a room of thirty girls planning to teach them about simple electronics, thinking that a hair blow dryer and a clock radio would be a great entry point. I had them on the table.

One of them held up the hair dryer and asked, "What is this?"

"You know, it's—to blow dry your hair," I responded.

She says, "What do you mean blow dry your hair?"

I tried to mimic how a blow dryer works and they all giggled. I realized they had never seen a blow dryer and had no idea what it was. Many of them came from homes with no electricity, let alone the need for a blow dryer.

By that point, I was feeling silly but we took the blow dryer apart anyway so they were able to see the heater coil and understand the concepts. We did the same thing with the clock radio. We had a lot of fun talking about a variety of small household electronics, with me trying to mime a toaster or mixer.

On my next trip, I decided to try different electronics to teach them about technology. I was comfortable with hardware because that was my background and I had access to old servers and desktop computers. I started breaking open the servers and computers and filling my suitcase with old motherboards to bring with me on these delegation trips. The motherboard is the large green board to which all the other components are attached. There are additional "daughter cards" that can be attached to the motherboard. I explained it to the girls like this: "when your mother can't do all the chores and she asks you for help, you're the daughter helping the mother do the chores. This is the daughter card, helping the motherboard get all the work done." They immediately understood!

When I first took the motherboard out and held it up, the girls were terrified. They looked at me like, "You want me to learn about this? I don't know anything about it. Don't ask me any questions." Panic was written all over their faces. I recognized that look of fear!

We put four or five girls at each table with one motherboard and handed out simple instructions so that they could read and understand them. I have female peers who have never touched hardware, and they get assigned to each table to coach the girls. During a 30–40-minute session you can see the girls (and peers) light up, because they're touching the hardware and they're putting processors and memory sticks on and off the board. They are learning the meaning and function of each component. I recognize that feeling of success!

At the close of the session, I can stand in front of the room, hold up the motherboard and say, "Who would be willing to show me what the processor is?" Twenty hands shoot up simultaneously, eager to come up and talk about the processor. They want to engage and share what they have learned. Because I traveled with those motherboards in my suitcase to countless girls' schools in so many countries, thousands of girls have been introduced to basic technology concepts. I can't tell you how exciting and satisfying that feels!

Everybody thinks that I'm super successful and lucky. That it's easy for me to get work. In fact it is not and it's less luck than sheer drive. It has always been incredibly hard for me to get work. I have to apply to hundreds of jobs each time I am hired, even now.

When Covid hit in 2020, I once again found myself with no job and no income, so it was a case of figuring it out, overcoming my fear, and going to Iraq. I had no one else to depend on for income. I had to decide.

I was hired to build the first start-up accelerator in Kurdistan. An accelerator speeds up the growth potential of a start-up so that it can progress much faster. Think of it as a boot camp in market readiness and investment development. This was a huge opportunity for me. It felt challenging because I had never built an accelerator before, let alone, in an environment where I didn't speak the language and there were limited resources. In Iraq, the power goes off five or six times per day, and you must sit in the dark, waiting until the power comes back on again.

In all of my jobs, I need to know the boundaries and rules. For weeks, every meeting has cantered on me asking my colleagues to define the rules, so I can push the boundaries and make the biggest impact possible with the funds and programs we offer. If the grant says we must deliver one 12-week program, can I change that to three 4-week programs? That sort of exploration-versus-acceptance gives us the ability to better meet the needs of the community.

There are always those gatekeepers who will say, "I completely understand you and support you from a personal perspective, but when I put my grantor work hat on, you can't do that." Others will tell me, "Keep pushing, keep going, push against what you're being told." They coach me in this way because they see the benefits of making the changes; however, they don't want to stand out as being rebellious; they leave that to me. I'm trying to do what is best for the people we are serving and if that comes across as too rebellious, so be it.

I have learned that sometimes it is easier to ask for forgiveness instead of permission and I take that into my decision-making process all the time. Every job has gatekeepers and clients and we sit in the middle of those two, often opposing groups. When I see a way to help more clients I might forget to ask before I make a change.

Being born in California as a white female was completely random and arbitrary. I have loads of privilege. Privilege I didn't even know I had until I was exposed to people from different countries and cultures. As soon as I became aware of these privileges, I started figuring out ways to share them, to try to give away things to which I had free access. There was no way I could become aware of the disparities in access and treatment and not do anything about it.

Others are born in countries where they have no control over their poverty or lack of resources. They had nothing to do with the situation in which they find themselves. So, if I can get to them and I can give them what I have been given so freely, why wouldn't I? That's the ethos I have lived by since being exposed to the vast differences across our countries and cultures.

Then there's the self-sufficiency part. Knowledge increases self-sufficiency. If women can support themselves, if they can have good paying jobs, they won't have to stay in abusive relationships or be forced into marriage or into degrading jobs. Women have a way up and out when they are exposed to new opportunities.

The girls who worked on the motherboards didn't know that they could be engineers, or that they could design products. Now, thousands of girls around the world know that they can be engineers and that they can be contributors in their communities.

In all of my jobs, I have leveraged my rebellious streak. I rebel against being told I can't do a certain job just because I haven't done it before. My work history illustrates my ability to learn, grow and adapt to new roles.

For women who may not be naturally inclined to be rebellious, I would suggest starting with small steps that are a little out of their comfort zone. If a woman is being talked over in a meeting, she should speak up and ask her to continue her thoughts. If you feel alone, find allies and like-minded people through volunteering or online groups. If somebody is doing something you wish you had the courage to do, ask if you can join them. Some people are scared to go to a public protest but feel a passion for it. I have made signs, walked miles, and led many chants during the recent marches for the #metoo and Black Lives Matter movements. I did not ask anyone's permission, I showed up and started marching and chanting. You can bring a friend with you and do the same thing.

If that's what it takes, then let's do it.

Don't stop being rebellious if you get push back from family or friends. I am in several Facebook groups about single women traveling. There are thousands of women in these groups. At least once a week, there is a young woman who asks about how to deal with her family who doesn't want her to travel alone. The family projects its fears onto a woman who is willing to see the world without waiting for permission or a partner. The post states, "I want to travel, and my family is telling me it's selfish, or it's dangerous, or it's irresponsible. You should have a regular job. You shouldn't be a nomad." How do they deal with this family negativity and guilt tripping?

Every week I reply to these posts the same way:

You get one chance to live the life you want.

Make it your life, not somebody else's.

Don't bend. Don't cave. Don't ever give up!

Do not make choices based on fear, especially someone else's fear.

Make choices based on knowledge. Do your research and share the knowledge.

When I took the role in Kurdistan, their Covid cases were very high, so I didn't immediately move into the country. However, I needed to get closer than California due to the time zone differences. I lived in nearby countries for months before moving into Kurdistan. I didn't plan it that way, however, I became a digital nomad, working full time and living in Croatia and Turkey for 5 months before moving to Kurdistan. I had never been to either country and took that leap of faith I have grown so accustomed to and lived as a nomad. Every week I would take a bus ride to a new city and find a new home. I lived alone, ate alone, and exercised alone. I overcame fear on nearly a daily basis. At times I struggled to communicate. I struggled with reading labels in the markets. I struggled with finding the next place and how to get there. It would have been much easier to stay in one place for months versus moving every week, however, I figured if I was there, I should see as much as possible. When I was exhausted, I allowed myself to rest. When I was lonely, I had calls with friends back home. I pushed myself through the process and am truly grateful for having the courage to experience it all; the hard and the easy days.

I am now finishing my time in Kurdistan and looking for my next opportunity. I have made many friends and will miss them dearly when I move on. But the time has come for me to find new challenges and make new friends.

I have applied for new roles from Alberta to Zanzibar. When I do my job searches, I set the location filter to "worldwide" and find the roles most suited to my skills and sense of adventure. I apply to those for which I may not have all the skills, and those beyond my reach, so that I will continue to learn and grow.

I don't feel like I'm invincible, but I do feel like I'm never going to let fear stop me from doing anything. I'm going to educate myself. I'm going to pay attention to my surroundings. I'm going to make good choices, but not let fear be the only reason I don't do something.

My history has proven to me that if I'm willing to walk through the fear, I'm always happy on the other side of that decision.

I'm in my sixties and still wake up every day wondering how I can help others and give back what was so freely given to me!

Rebellious Reflections

When I grow up, I want to be Eileen Brewer!

Brewer the Rock Star. The Silicon Valley executive. The making a difference woman, entrepreneurial activist in Iraq. She's had rebellion in her blood from an incredibly early age. She is always learning, putting herself into new situations, asking to be taught, and willing to listen so she can understand the current limits to stretch them, extend them, and often break through them.

How can you stretch and break the rules if you don't first understand what or where the problem is? How can you even understand if there's a problem without understanding why the rules don't work?

At 60 years old and on her own, she took a job in Kurdistan, Iraq. She is focusing on her skills, her strength, her passion, her talent for technology and entrepreneurship. She's helping people, inarguably, in one of the most difficult countries on the planet. She could have chosen a much more comfortable option. Instead, she chose the bold path. The more challenging, and, as she would say, more fulfilling option.

Eileen wakes up alive, conscious, and ready every day because her environment demands it, because her job demands it. She's taught herself to speak up. Before she knew how, she practiced in front of the mirror. She's the definition of moving outside of your comfort zone.

Her comfort zone is huge. It is global. Many of us would find her comfort zone terrifying. We'd have so many reasons not to. So many excuses. Plausible excuses with which other people would heartily agree.

Eileen knows what she is doing and where she's going. She's always looking for the next thing—expanding her skills, her life view, her world view. This expansiveness is a form of rebellion, too. People who don't know "how" will judge her decisions. She will move forward regardless, rebelling against other people's judgments. Not just "because," not to be difficult, but because she has a reason.

Next time you have a difficult decision to make, and you might avoid a path that is difficult or frightening, think of Eileen. Remember it may also be fulfilling, unique, and powerful beyond measure. Remember that legacies are long lasting and that you will inspire others to follow you. Every day you will wake up, pleased about your decision. You will live life in a beautiful mixture of excitement and fear, and that's okay, because that's what makes you alive.

Are you truly alive? Do you wake up each day with gratitude and excitement for what's to come?

It's time to start living.

Chapter Fifteen

Choose Life
In the Words of
Aletta Raju, Labor Law Specialist, South Africa

"You got engaged last night," mum said to me, only semi-lucid.

"What are you talking about, Mum?"

"Oh, my goodness, you got engaged last night," she repeated.

"Mum," I said, laughing. "I didn't get engaged."

Mum always thought I would be alone because I had spent a lot of my life single. But at 39, I wasn't even dating anyone at the time.

"I know you did," she insisted. "To that really nice guy..."

"Mum," I made a joke of it, "I wish I had gotten engaged last night!"

I fed her a little bit of pureed vegetables, a butternut squash soup I had made before coming to the hospital with my sister-in-law, Vanessa. Mum didn't want to eat much, and she couldn't chew, so she had two or three spoonfuls.

Mum had rectal cancer and had gone into remission as it was only Stage 1. But now she was suffering from an infection contracted during her treatment. Her condition was making her thinking become increasingly muddled.

She had been put in the ICU two days beforehand. We were able to get in for a brief visit with her until the staff asked Vanessa and me to leave so they could do some more tests. I lived a few hours away, so I saw no sense in going home and coming back. Vanessa had some shopping to do, so we decided to split up and I headed to the gym. I needed to do something to pass the time and to try and keep myself together. I would only be away for a little bit.

When I got there, I rode on the bicycle for a bit, but I couldn't concentrate. I went and sat in the sauna to try to relax and recoup my energy for going back to the hospital. It didn't work. I had an inexplicable pain in my stomach, and I didn't know how to get rid of it. I felt an impending sense of dread, as if I knew something was going to go wrong with my mum.

The pain worsened so I started with some deep breathing. As I sat there alone in the hot sauna, I somehow started talking to my mum. I don't know why, but I wanted to have a conversation with her.

"I don't know what's happening," I said. "I'm feeling so helpless. There's so much more for you to experience." I could see her face in my mind's eye. But she wasn't replying, only listening.

"I want to throw you a purple party for your birthday next month," I said. "Remember the purple party? We're going to celebrate your life and make purple cupcakes, and everything is going to be purple like you love!"

I started to cry as I spoke. "We've got a month to go," I said. "Only a few weeks until your birthday. We must do this for you! So please, Mum, I know you're in pain and I know this is hard for you, but please, can you choose life, for you? Don't choose for me. Choose for yourself."

I finished my conversation with her and wiped my eyes. I had to get back to the hospital. I had to be quick. I showered and went to my locker, standing with my towel around me as I took a glance at my phone. There were 20 missed calls and messages from both the hospital and Vanessa.

My heart sank. I felt as if the blood was draining from my body, and I suddenly felt dizzy. I berated myself for not always keeping my phone with me and for leaving the hospital.

I dialed back frantically.

"Where are you?" Vanessa said.

"I'm at the gym. What is it?"

"You need to get back to the hospital right now, quickly. I'm not sure..."

I went numb. Oh, dear God, please let everything be ok.

I can't explain how I got dressed, packed my stuff up, and got into my car. I don't remember doing any of it. I remember finding myself in my car, driving like a maniac and praying. Please, can there be no traffic? Can I go through all the green traffic lights? I need to get to the hospital. It was as if somebody else was moving my body in this car through the streets towards the hospital.

I quickly parked my car and ran towards the hospital entrance. A friendly security guard waved and smiled as I bounded towards the elevator. I flew down the corridor and arrived breathless at her room.

Vanessa had been talking to her before I arrived. My mum always loved her like her own daughter, and mum was the mother Vanessa had missed out on growing up.

Vanessa asked Mum if she wanted to go to heaven to be with Daddy and Aldrin, my brother.

"No. I do not," she answered.

"Well then, Mum," Vanessa said, "you must fight. Your blood pressure is dropping, and you must fight. Aletta is here now, so keep fighting."

Mum couldn't speak. Her eyes were wide open and dilating. I held tightly to the side of her bed crying, looking at her, begging God, the universe, anyone who would listen for her to stay alive, as the doctors worked around her.

Dr. Sam Collins 297

Then she looked at me with a vacant gaze and I knew she was slipping away from me. I went hysterical.

"Mum!" I said. "Choose life, Mum! Please, choose life! For you! You have so much left in you, so much left to experience."

Choose life, Mum.

Choose life!

"Please," I turned to the doctors, "Is there anything you can do? Can you put her on life support? Can you do anything?" I begged them.

"I'm sorry," one said. "Her blood pressure is too low. If you put her on life support, she's going to be non-responsive." I knew my mum never wanted that.

She had always said, "If anything happens to me where I can't live properly, don't keep me alive."

It's beyond traumatic watching a parent die in front of you. I felt so helpless. There was nothing I could do. There was nothing I could say. She closed her eyes and the machine stopped right there while we were all in the room.

Another regular day for the hospital, but the most traumatic moment of my life.

I blanked out and sat there. Numb and in shock. Her body was lifeless in front of me. Disbelief flooded over me. Perhaps it was a mistake and at any moment, she would come back. I waited and waited.

After a while, the mortuary came to take her away. They didn't want me to stay to watch that process, but I refused to go. I stood there until they wheeled her out. I had to see it to prove to myself that it was real. She wasn't coming back.

She was gone.

That was it. She didn't choose life.

I've lived a lifetime of loss.

When I was 31 years old, I lost my dad who died of a heart attack while playing golf, which was one of the things he loved doing most. Soon after that, my brother Aldrin was diagnosed with cancer. He was in remission after a transplant when a driver skipped a traffic light and struck the car he was in, giving him fatal brain damage. Five years after we lost Aldrin, my mum was diagnosed with cancer. After she died, I was the only one left.

I lost everyone I loved, and I was alone in the world.

From the age of 13, I took on the rescuer role in my family, the people pleaser. I grew up in South Africa in a family environment where there was a lot of anger from my dad. He was a politician and an activist who had grown up in extreme poverty. My grandfather came from India to South Africa as a laborer, and my dad saw the extreme disparity in equality. He lived in survival mode.

We grew up in a situation where if my dad was happy, the rest of us were happy. If he was angry, the rest of us walked on eggshells. He was constantly fighting and battling the systems of injustice, and when he came home, he took out all his anger on us. He didn't realize it, but he put us in our own version of survival mode.

I loved my dad, and I'm grateful for him. But he didn't know how to express himself. He was so passionate about correcting the injustice in South Africa, and he went out and did what he needed to do to make a change. But when he came home, we were his emotional punching bags.

My mum, on the other hand, was the silent nurturing power in our house. She loved us unconditionally. Growing up, my brother, being the only other boy in the house, became my dad's target. No matter how seemingly miniscule of a mistake or misbehavior, Aldrin would get a beating from my dad.

My pattern in my life became survival, making peace, making sure everything and everyone was okay at home, and making sure that my mum and my brother were okay.

After my dad died, mum went to therapy. She started painting. She created beautiful landscapes and portraits. She was a natural artist who found herself at 61 years old. More than the fear of losing her, I wanted her to choose life because she deserved it.

She had so much more to experience.

The whole time we were fighting my mum's cancer, I never gave it a thought that she was going to die. Even though she was diabetic from the age of 19, and they had to be extra cautious with her treatment, she was only Stage 1. It's still too early for cancer to cause any life-threatening issues, right?

What she didn't tell us was that the chemo and radiation treatment had internally burned her. She never spoke about it and never gave any indication she was hurting. It wasn't until one day when it got so bad that she mentioned it to me, and I had to take her to the hospital. She was only there for a week, but the infection got so much worse. Within two days they had put her in the ICU. A few days later, she was gone. She was only 64 years old.

I later challenged the hospital because I believed that they might be negligent. I wrote a letter stating that I thought the heart specialists should have checked the level of the blood that she was receiving more carefully. Perhaps they didn't take special care with her or give her body a chance to heal between treatments. I was livid and I needed answers.

I received a letter back with all the reasons that they could find. I challenged that letter, and we went back and spoke to the doctors. But they had answers to everything. Eventually, I had to let it go. None of it was going to bring my mum back.

I had so much guilt. Maybe I should have done something differently at the time? I trusted that the doctors knew what they were doing. So, who was I to keep asking whether they're doing the right thing?

In hindsight, I wish I could have spoken out or done something differently. But I also am working to heal that part of me, because I know I did the best I could.

I had to make peace with my mum's death.

I had lost so much. But without knowing it at the time, I had also gained a lot. It took me a long time, but I started to feel more grateful for all the things I did have.

My whole young life was always based on someone else. I was always trying to be happy for their sake. Everything was supposed to be happy and peaceful at home. I tried to stay happy after my dad passed away. I tried to stay happy when Aldrin had this cancer and recovery and passing. I tried to stay happy so that my mum was okay. If she was okay, I was okay. It was always based on someone else. I did it all so unconsciously.

At my dad's funeral, I remember people whispering into my ear, "You have to be strong for your mum and your brother..."

At my brother's funeral, they whispered, "You have to be strong for your mum and Vanessa..."

When my mum died, I thought, "Who do I need to be strong for now?"

That was a huge revelation for me because I realized I needed to be strong for myself. It was rebellious for me to start choosing my life. I had to reinvent myself. I didn't know anything about myself, not even the little things like what I enjoyed spending my time doing, or hobbies, or foods. I had an idea of it, but I didn't know myself well. I had conformed myself to what was happening to others in my world.

I was somehow convinced love meant setting myself aside and making everyone else happy.

My mum was such a good person. When we cooked together on a Friday night, she would say,

"Why are you sitting at home? Go out!" She knew I was quite a sociable person and I had lots of friends. I used to love to go out. But when she moved into the house with me, and as we started our home together, I would always rather be with my mum on a Friday night. After a crazy week at work, I loved going home, being in her company and enjoying all the yummy food she used to cook for us.

"Don't worry about me. I'm fine!" She would say.

But I did worry about her. I focused all my attention on my mum. I made life decisions based on my mum. It was the same behavior that I learned in my childhood.

But when everyone was gone, I was able to make decisions in my life based solely on what I wanted. Had my mum still been around, my patterns would probably have remained the same. Now I had no one else to worry about, and no one else to factor into my life.

Now it was finally my time.

Okay, I'm alone now. My nuclear family is gone. What's next?

There must be more to life than this. I deserve happiness. I deserve love. I deserve to enjoy my life. I'm choosing life. And that was my new beginning.

But what does that mean? I had never chosen my life before that. I was always going from one crisis to the next.

From when my dad died, to my brother's cancer diagnosis, which forced us to stop grieving my dad (it would have been too much to bear, trying to cope with it all at once.) Then we were focusing on my brother's cancer journey, the fear of losing him, and then his death. Then it was my mum and her illness. One to the next. It took up all the time and energy I had.

Now it was like... What the hell do I do now? What is there left for me to do? My little nuclear family had evaporated, and I didn't belong anywhere anymore. I was completely lost and disconnected from the world.

So, I started making choices for myself.

I chose life.

Choose life became my mantra.

What do I want?

What shall I do today?

I wanted to travel. I wanted to find love.

I decided to take a trip by myself to Machu Picchu, Peru.

"Are you sure you want to do this by yourself?" Some well-intended family would ask.

"Yes," I'd say. "I want to go on a trip by myself. I've never traveled so far alone or made a trip of my own, and I want to experience it."

In Lima, I did the entire Machu Picchu climb by myself. The trip was serene for me - I sobbed for a whole day in the hotel room. That was the first time that I really cried after mum was gone. All my barriers were broken down. It had been so dark for me, and suddenly something shifted, and I realized, "Look at where you are, Aletta. Look at you! You're on the other end of the world by yourself experiencing something completely new. And amidst this pain and this darkness, there is life all around you."

It was a journey, a pilgrimage I needed to take for myself.

Everything changed. I had a paintbrush, and I could paint anything I wanted without any roadblocks. I had a clean canvas.

What's next for me?

What kinds of people do I want in my life?

What do I want to do for work?

I left my job and started my own business. I had to choose life.

I started a relationship with someone I had known for 20 years. It took me on an adventure of love and showed me how I deserved to be cared for and respected.

I was free to make any decision I wanted about my life. Where I wanted to go, where I wanted to live, what career I wanted to have, what experience I wanted to have learning new and different things.

I had to learn about self-love. I had to learn about the roles my parents played in my life. I had to heal from the relationships I had with my parents. I had to deal with sibling guilt because I was "the good kid."

I am still on my journey to honor my life amidst loss and constant change, but each day, I am becoming a better and stronger version of myself.

My life taught me that circumstances can change in a split second - and that change can either paralyze you or allow you to grow and evolve. I choose every day to let my light shine.

I choose life, will you?

Rebellious Reflections

Can we unconsciously grow up pleasing everybody else? We think that that's the way to operate. We also believe that pleasing other people gives us joy. Pleasing other people gives us identity and gives us purpose. But at the same time, we can easily forget ourselves, spending so much time and focusing on others, we lose who we are, or in some cases, never develop our own purpose and identity.

For Aletta, and others who will identify with her story, it took a series of truly shocking and terrible losses for her to realize the importance of putting herself first to begin to live her own goals, dreams, and ambitions. With her whole family gone, she was left with no other option than to really think about what she wanted for the first time in her life. This was her rebellion. At that point in her life, she started to ask herself the questions: What do I want? Who do I want to spend my time with? What do I want to do in the future? And these questions can seem simple to ask. In fact, they are very difficult to answer, especially in a time of grief.

Aletta traveled alone for the first time in her life. She went to Machu Picchu, doing something that she thought she would never do, climbing the mountain. She found love. She left her job and started her own business. Somehow through a terrible time, she fulfilled her dreams doing all the things she wanted when she was truly focused on herself.

Her rebellion was to go against the norms and patterns of her own life, which had formerly been to please other people. Her rebellion was to not let the great loss of losing her entire family beat her. Her rebellion was ultimately to choose the life she so desperately wanted for her mother. Her rebellion was to make peace with the death of her father, brother, and mother. And to live a life of fulfillment and purpose.

As I reflect upon grief, I realize the difficulty of doing what Aletta did. She must have felt so alone, and so confused as to why this had happened to her. To lose your entire family is unimaginable. We must celebrate Aletta's great strength, tenacity, and gentleness as she embarked on her new life and new story. She now lives a life of purpose doing the work that she loves, helping other people through their own journeys of grief and survival.

CHAPTER SIXTEEN
Amazing Grace
In the Words of
Dr. Sam Collins, Founder Aspire, USA

This part is scary.

As I write, I'm not sure that I will publish this final chapter. I feel compelled to write it for a few reasons. One is purely selfish: I think it's going to be cathartic, and I'm interested to see if I am even capable of recounting what happened.

I feel brave enough to tell a final story that isn't pretty. It's messy, I became very unwell, and it stressed people I dearly love. It's a story of a rebellion that didn't go so well. And yet, it stretched me to truly understand what being rebellious truly means to me in my life, work, and world.

Pulling Rebellious together and bringing it into the world has been my own journey of rebellion; an adventure around the world; an extraordinary experience meeting woman of all backgrounds, ages, and nationalities.

They shared their stories with me. They bared their souls. We laughed and cried together as they talked about girls' education, modern slavery, sailing solo around the world, breast cancer and spandex pants. About child marriage and finding your dream job. About going to prison and finding more freedom there than before. About facing religious bias, and death threats every day.

They talked about what makes a good mum or bad mum. The importance of staying true to their core beliefs and values, and the steep cost of doing so. They paid in so many ways. With their money, their reputations, their confidence, their mental health, and their physical and sexual safety. By contracting breast cancer. By the shocking murder of a daughter and being trafficked to another country. They were frightened refugees who fled in fear of their lives to places far from home. They experienced racial injustice. They felt invisible. They worked to make Black Lives Matter, and to bring technology education to women living in some of the most dangerous places on earth. And what they have in common is that they all finally got to the point of understanding who they truly are.

To describe them as inspiring does not seem enough. Inspiring is an overused word. Their stories are often dark. But each woman triumphed in her own way. Their stories, though not widely known, represent women everywhere.

We don't talk much about dark times. We don't talk about where we failed or where things went wrong. We don't discuss it with ourselves or with our friends or family, let alone in a public way, like this. We have been trained to present the Hollywood ending, haven't we? We've been trained that we should only share the successes, the achievements, the awards, and the recognition. Happy, smiling pictures on Facebook are now our social achievement norm.

What does it take to get to that so-called happy ending? What's the price we pay? What are the sacrifices that we must make to have it? There is a sense of camaraderie, isn't there, in knowing that we are not alone in our pain? And relief that there are others out there who have struggled and suffered but have finally triumphed.

So let me tell you my final story.

I said at the start of this final chapter, I write this for cathartic reasons. It's also a damn good story. I know that there are many women with whom it will resonate. It's my final rebellious story.

It's a Saturday, and it's already been a hell of a day. I wanted to mention that it's a Saturday because I had PTSD for many Saturdays to follow.

Today it is my oldest son Jake's birthday. He is nine. He's had a birthday party. It's 2017 and we've recently moved back to England from the US. We "de-Trumped", as I liked to say.

The night Trump won the presidential election and even though my husband Robert, true to character, had been hopeful to the end, we decided that we would have a break from America and try living in England for a while. So, we had recently moved back to the UK.

In typical supermum style, I had created a birthday party of elaborate proportions for Jake in our new rental house and invited loads of kids that he didn't know but were all in his new class at school. I was feeling very pleased with myself - the new school year hadn't started, so the party would mean that he could make friends before it did.

We have all these strange new kids running around a strange new house. Parents have come along with them to check us out. I'm doing the right thing and creating a big birthday bash. Bouncy castle, all the sugar they could eat. Dozens of nine-year-old kids (mostly boys) are tearing up, down, and around the place.

When it came time for birthday cake. Jake put on his best brave face, got in front of the cake, and the kids started singing loudly. It was too much. He ran away in the middle of Happy Birthday, which trailed off and then faded into Jake's footsteps pounding upstairs, the candles flickering on the cake, and everybody looking awkwardly at each other. And that look when other parents feel sorry for you.

I didn't know what to do. I quickly blew out the candles and distributed cake while Robert checked on Jake.

Perhaps I was more concerned about the social stigma than Jake. I was focused on Jake's seemingly bad behavior, rather than the fact I had dumped my son in a room full of overstimulated prepubescent strangers. It felt damn stressful. I went to the cabinet, and poured whiskey into my coffee, something I had been doing increasingly often over the previous few months. It burned down my throat and I felt a little better. The party wound down, and the guests left.

I wasn't tired. Everyone else seemed exhausted. Robert put the kids to bed and went to sleep himself. A bit later, I went upstairs to check on the kids. The moon shone through the skylight above the stairs quite beautifully.

I said to myself, "If I die tonight, would I be happy?"

I wasn't sure of the answer. I felt confused. Why would I ask myself such a morbid question?

After I checked the kids, I started back downstairs. Suddenly I didn't feel well. I had a pounding headache. I was hungry. I scarfed down some of the party food and toasted a bagel. I took an ibuprofen and laid down.

I was feeling worse.

I sat up. My chest was in a vice. So strange. Breathe, breathe. Okay, Sam, take a moment, are you coming down with something? Yes, I felt like a cold was coming, but my heart was beating out of my chest. It wasn't stopping. It wasn't settling down. I could feel a panic starting to rise.

I went to get Robert and woke him up. He sat there with me and held my hand and softly told me to take deep breaths. I sat down cross-legged on the bed in my usual spot.

It was about 9:30pm now, and the chest pain was getting worse. We decided—Robert decided—to call the doctor. They asked their standard questions and abruptly, weirdly, unexpectedly, scarily stated that they were calling an ambulance right away. My panic level increased.

My first thought was, I should put a bra on. So, I struggled around hunting for a bra to be presentable at the hospital. I don't know why. To look the part? So as not to have my saggy boobs on show in the emergency room? I don't know. I couldn't work the bra clasp, so I left it and shoved on my baggy grey sweatshirt with FEMINIST emblazoned across the front.

Right. Saggy boobs and a statement.

We sat back down on the bed. I suggested Robert go next door to see if the neighbor we hardly knew would consider coming in and sitting in the living room while the kids slept, and Robert and I went to the emergency room. God bless her, she did. (Of course, she did, Annie has since become one of my best friends).

It was pitch black outside. I saw the flashing-colored lights of the ambulance through the front door window. Two young men in green paramedic uniforms came into the house, chirpy and calm, and all the things that you want when you think you might be having a heart attack. They moved me to the edge of the bed, took my temperature, checked my blood pressure, and asked me how I was doing.

It was too much. Too scary, too frightening. My body powered down. According to Robert, who was terrified by then, I started shaking uncontrollably and had a seizure. I fell off the bed and collapsed, unconscious, on the floor. I came round wondering why I was horizontal to the ground.

Why am I on the floor? Why is everything on its side?

I heard warped and warbled sci-fi voices saying, "Sam... Sam... Sam, you're okay. You collapsed." I felt nauseous and everything around me was moving strangely. The paramedics did an ECG to check my heart. They thought I'd had a seizure but weren't totally sure, and they wanted to get me to the hospital fast. They covered me with a blanket and carried me out to the ambulance buckled into a chair. The kids were fast asleep.

I was blue-lighted to the local hospital, Watford General. In the ambulance, I called my sister, Emma. I rambled to her something along the lines of, if I die tonight, would she look after the kids because Robert would need some help. She agreed and said that she was on her way from Poole, which was hours away. She also said that she would call Dad.

I arrived at Watford General Hospital, which is not your most attractive of places, especially late on a Saturday night. Normally people have a big wait on a Saturday night in an NHS hospital in the emergency room, but due to the severity of my episode, I was wheeled straight in and didn't have to wait. The triage nurse immediately took some blood to start running tests.

Robert stayed at my side. All the color washed out of his face. He was trying to appear calm as always, but his eyes told a different story. Panic, shock, disbelief. Could I muster some energy to try to calm him?

A doctor came in.

"The tests suggest that you have a blood clot," he said, with an Italian accent. "You're lucky you came in. You could have died tonight." He said they would give me blood thinning medication and do a scan to check whether the clot was traveling to my heart.

Done. Next patient.

Now, it's an interesting thing. Confronted with a medical emergency like this, there was a part of me that just got on with it. Okay, all right, what's next? Done. Now what? Next thing. And there was another part of me that was already planning my funeral and what would happen with the kids. There was a part of me that was in pure terror and another part of me, the rebellious part, ready for a fight.

I looked around me. Watford General. This is it? Of all the fucking places I've been around the world, all the things I've done, and I get to cash in my chips in Watford General? You're kidding me, right?

Watford General is an old, old, old building. A haunted building. A building full of overworked, understaffed NHS nurses and doctors who are trying their level best to do a lot with a little. They rush from one person to the next. Seeing sick people but also not really seeing them because they can't connect with every patient's emotion. How could they?

After a bit, they took me to a ward with six beds. I was in the middle bed on the left-hand side.

A nurse unceremoniously explained this was a ward for the people they didn't know what to do with while they were in transition from the emergency room to another ward, after they had—I suppose—a diagnosis or a death. I was officially on the ward of the dying.

It was now well after midnight. Robert had to go home to relieve Annie, our neighbor—she would have stayed all night. We couldn't have her do that. I was in a bed now, so I convinced Robert to go and be with the kids and send her home to rest.

I looked around at the other women in the ward. The woman opposite me was struggling with incontinence and the smell was bad. The woman to her right was probably in her nineties. Maybe she had dementia or maybe she was as angry as me. She was lying in her bed and wailing, "Fuck off! Fuck off!" She got louder, then quieter, back and forth, over, and over. "Fuck off!"

On the other side of the room was a young girl, maybe 16. She lay there quietly, asleep. What had brought her here on this Saturday night? The curtains were closed around her bed. I could barely see her. To my left was another young woman, also sleeping, with a feeding tube attached to her. The bed to my right was empty. They need to fill that one up, I thought.

"I'll be back," said the nurse cheerily, in a Jamaican accent. "For the blood thinner injection. Brace yourself, it will be a bit painful." She offered me some heavy-duty painkillers and encouraged me to lay down and try to get some sleep as everyone else was doing. I was about to do as I'd been told and lay down when suddenly I had a strong feeling that if I did so, I might never get up again.

I mustn't lay down, I mustn't sleep. I could see a dark brick wall out of the window. I was woozy now, my stomach felt like it had been stabbed with a knife. I had no energy, but I had to go to the bathroom. It was so close but it took me the longest time to get up and hobble there like it was the last yards of a marathon.

When I finally got back to bed, I was greeted by a cacophony of snoring, wailing, and swearing... and the smell. The thick odor of sickness and hospital. I sat up and took out my phone, luckily, fully charged. I opened Facebook and scrolled through photos, answered overdue messages, liked posts, basically anything not to lie down and sleep.

I will not die tonight. I will not die in Watford General. I will sit up and stay on Facebook until it's light outside, goddamn it. If I can make it through the night, I can make it through the rest of my life. I must make it. There's more left to do. To answer that question as I was going up the stairs:

No, I would not be happy if I died tonight.

I have so much more to do, thank you very much. Not to mention, I have three children. My mum died when I was 21. Do I want my kids to go through this when they're nine, eight, and seven? Not happening. Not tonight. Not any night. I will not lie down. I will stay awake. I will fight.

Maybe there's some grand plan? Maybe this is destiny or karma to enable my children to become better people and overcome their obstacles and be resilient and tell the story of how their mother died when they were nine. Bullshit. Not happening. Maybe that was a path, but it wasn't one I was going down willingly.

I do not see the light and I am not heading towards it, thank you very much!

The nurse came back and injected the blood thinner medication into my stomach. God, it burned. That's what's needed, that's what's needed. There was talk of a scan in the morning but nothing positive. It occurred to me that if a blood clot was traveling up to my heart, I probably should have a scan a little sooner than morning, but I had no control over that.

Eventually, dawn broke. I listened to the birds, watched the dark bricks outside my window get lighter, and the army of people coming in and out of the hospital. The women around me started waking up. I hadn't laid down the entire night. I forced myself to get up and move my body a little. All text, emails, and Facebook messages fully up to date. Empty inbox, thank you very much. I was also aware (thanks Google) of every possible fatal diagnosis coming my way.

As is always the case with the UK National Health Service, there was a shortage of beds. The job of the emergency room is to patch you up and get you out again. I did finally get the scan at 11am the next morning, and then waited for the results.

Robert came in and brought the kids with him. Oh, God! Their little faces. Boy, did they brighten up that ward. Even the elderly woman in the corner stopped swearing for a bit when she saw Jake, Charlie, and Grace bouncing in.

Dr. Sam Collins 315

They didn't know what was going on, of course. Kids have that amazing, beautiful energy, don't they? Everyone smiled. They were a little rambunctious, as usual. My sister came with her kids, too. My dad arrived. Everybody I loved was assembled before me. They all tried to look cheerful, but their eyes gave them away. I smiled, sank back into the pillows, and looked around. I had seen the night through.

After quite some time, a doctor arrived and said, "The scan is clear. You do not have a blood clot."

"What is it then?" Robert asked.

"We're not sure," he said, "But the fact that she is feeling a little better now is good. It's all right to go home. Follow up with your G.P. as soon as you can."

That was it. Discharged. I couldn't walk out. I thought it was over but little did I know what was to come. I got home and went to bed. I was exhausted. My stomach hurt badly; my head hurt badly. Every muscle in my body, every fiber of my being gave up.

I laid down in bed for nine weeks, unable to bring myself to move.

———————— >•< ————————

I hadn't been doing well for a while.

All the back and forth to Congo for Grace's adoption had taken an unforeseen toll. I've always tended to push myself, to do too much. I was on a never-ending merry go-round of work-kids-sleep-repeat. But inside, I was beginning to rebel against all of it - the cooking and the cleaning, the mothering, and the childcare, and the marriage. Against the interminable routine. And the boredom. The constant trade offs. The endless work-life conflicts. I was becoming more irritated, more often, by many more things. I was neglecting myself.

I wasn't happy.

Despite a seemingly perfect marriage, living in the perfect house, with a perfect family, I couldn't settle. I didn't seem able to be like other mums, other wives. I felt like an outsider. Like something was not right, like I was not right. I was trying my best to be something I wasn't, to conform when I didn't know the rules, to present a picture of perfect domestication.

Something was missing but I couldn't work out what it was. I was still traveling back and forth between England and the USA to conduct my Aspire workshops and conferences and events, which I loved. This was my purpose, my sense of excitement and adventure. I would go without Robert and the kids. I would stay in a hotel and have room service and sleep without being interrupted in the night, without needing to get up for something to do with the kids every single night.

On these trips I could escape from being someone's mum, from being someone's wife. And be me. I received positive affirmation, and praise. I was able to make a difference. I got to see transformation in people, and to dress up, and to eat out. To be me. I absolutely loved it.

But back at home, I wasn't anything like as happy. I ate a lot. I wasn't sleeping. I was drinking into the night, every night. Which brought me to that Saturday. Nobody said, "Enough, Sam. Time to stop." So, for 9 weeks, I couldn't get out of bed. I was burnt out.

I kept my work going as best I could. My stomach pain was intense, and constant. I started to see doctors who prescribed medications for me. Eventually they diagnosed that I had stomach ulcers. I needed to rest and watch my diet, not drink any alcohol, and not have stress, they said.

Dr. Sam Collins 317

Hilarious, isn't it? "Don't have stress." How is that ever going to be possible?

I developed hearing and vision problems. When I stood up I would hear buzzing in my head. I felt dizzy and everything bounced around before my eyes. My own house, a full time bouncy castle. Objects would vibrate. People changed shape in front of me.

The doctors called it Oscillopsia. They couldn't figure out why I had it. I was referred to a consultant neurologist for a suspected brain tumor.

His first question was, "What do you do, Mrs. Collins?"

To which I replied, "I work in women's empowerment and equality."

"Oh," he said, looking straight at Robert, who was with me. "How do you deal with that?"

Don't say anything, Sam, because you've got a brain tumor, and you need this sexist arsehole on your side.

He wanted to do an MRI immediately. You kind of know something bad is happening, don't you, when a neurologist says they want to do an MRI without any delay?

The MRI technician was very mean. He kept telling me I was moving my head. I was sure that I wasn't. I felt frightened and alone. I didn't share how scared I was with Robert because I didn't want to make him scared too.

After the MRI, I hurried to the bathroom and sat on the toilet and cried hard for my mum. I don't think I have ever sobbed like that. I wanted my mum so much. I'd heard that people often cry for their mum before they die, but I hadn't understood it before that point.

The MRI came back clear.

"No one can account for your symptoms, Mrs. Collins."

As if I'm making it up. As if I am an insane woman with random symptoms which are a figment of my imagination.

"It's probably anxiety," they said. "Maybe you are overdoing it."

"Oh, good," I said, "if it's anxiety..."

"No, no," they said, "anxiety can be a big problem."

For some reason, I thought that it was good to have anxiety because it was more of a mental health issue than a physical one. Little did I know. There then followed months of doctors visits, MRI's, gastrointestinal cameras, procedures, nutritionists, and so many other things that didn't make me feel any better.

Many, many Google searches. As they say when Googling medical problems, you're only two clicks away from dying. I can attest to that. Something was wrong with me and no one could work it out. Not even me.

Then perimenopause started. My periods became erratic, with extremely heavy bleeding. Then panic attacks started. I had stomach issues, brain issues, and eye issues, and now the sweats and panic attacks.

I wanted so badly to be healthy and well. I was lost and unhappy. I needed to focus on my health and looking after myself.

My Aspire events and conferences soothed me. My work enabled me to do what I love and to do it well. To help people. And to feel normal.

I really struggled with my vision. I had to sit down at book signings and look down at the book the whole time. If I looked up at the person in front of me they would start moving and changing shape before my eyes, which was terrifying. I needed frequent breaks when I was doing events. I could not operate normally. The room would pulse, the people would appear to move around. I wasn't coping.

I started doing all the physical things I needed to do to heal myself. I ate better. I stopped drinking. I was sleeping better. But I wasn't any better, not really. Robert suggested I speak to Luke, a friend in the US. Luke had explained to Robert that he knew an amazing coach who had helped him with his own life decisions. I spoke to Luke, and he introduced me to Rebecca in Australia, whom he thought might help me to channel spiritual advice. I had never heard of such a thing, but I had nothing to lose. I'd tried everything else.

By that point, I'd looked at everything from a scientific and practical perspective. Why not give spirituality a go?

Channeling spiritual advice sounded very "out there," but I was desperate. I got on a call with Rebecca, and when I saw her face I suddenly felt peaceful. She did a session with me where she channeled what she calls The Masters. Sounds odd, I know. One of the first things she said was that I have been reacting to my environment. I was in the wrong environment. England wasn't the place for me anymore. That I should not make decisions based on fear.

I had uprooted our family back to England because I was retreating in fear of Trump. As a result, I had gone backwards.

There were many things I loved about being home in England. Baked beans, marmite, and Mars bars from my childhood, the way people are, and living in a real village with a real pub. And the work. I was busier than ever with Aspire.

But I missed the wide open spaces of California. The mountains, the ocean, and the sun. Oh, the sun! The mess of it. The controversy of it. The politics of it. I missed it, and I knew I had to return.

That realization immediately made my body feel a little better. As if I had been trying to reverse back into a former life that I no longer fit. I had come up with good, objective reasons justifying the move to England in the first place. But it didn't make me happy. It hadn't made Robert or the kids happy either. We were not in the right place for us.

I started to meditate. I had done a little bit of meditation before, nothing serious. I went on a meditation weekend in London, and I meditated for an entire weekend. The. Entire. Weekend.

My stomach felt better. My body felt better. I felt better. I knew it was time to return to California. I was so excited about it and I couldn't wait to share with Robert, and to hear his reaction.

Of course, Robert is Robert, forever practical. His first reaction was, "We're just settled and got the kids into school." Then, "Really?" He looked at me the way that Robert always looks at me with a certain resolution that I am going to do it anyway so he may as well come onboard now.

The thing is, I'm the gas and he's the brakes. He'll always come with me. He's always there for me. Besides, he had lived in California for 40 years and he missed it too. So we made the decision to return to the US.

It felt so good and right to be back, despite Trump being President. I started seeing a new doctor. I worked on my diet, took supplements, and managed my stress levels. But I still didn't feel myself. I was still unwell.

Until one test showed I had some nasty looking stomach bacteria. Something picked up in Congo, perhaps. The kind that can lay dormant until it is activated by periods of stress.

Go figure.

By coincidence, I was prescribed a particularly strong antibiotic by my dentist at the same time I had the test showing the stomach bacteria. Nothing at all to do with my stomach, I had a tooth problem. Within three days of starting the medication, I felt different. My stomach, my eyes, my anxiety, and everything else was so much better.

Dr. Sam Collins 321

When I told my doctor, she explained that the antibiotics could have worked to eradicate the stomach bacteria as well as dealing with the tooth issue, which had perhaps inhabited my body since Congo in 2015.

All those years. All those doctors. All those tests. And nobody had given me a dose of antibiotics. Perhaps all I needed was a random tooth infection and a good dentist.

It is now 2021 and right before my fiftieth birthday. The big 5-0.

There's a lot of pressure, isn't there? Doing fun things on your fiftieth birthday. My very good friend Avril, in England, recommended that I have a week of birthday celebrations, so that I did!

On the actual day, Robert and I went out for breakfast. We sat outside our favorite breakfast restaurant in Santa Monica where we had originally brought Grace when she arrived in America, "Back on the Beach," where the tables are in the sand. As you sit down on the chairs, they sink into the sand, and there are umbrellas above you shading the sun. You can see out onto the wide open space of Santa Monica Beach, and the great Pacific Ocean beyond.

Think Baywatch. The Baywatch beach.

As we were having breakfast and planning out the birthday-day, I looked at Robert.

"You know," I said. "I think that since my mum died when I was twenty one, I have never given myself permission to be properly happy. I didn't realize I needed to give myself permission to be happy. To not do so much. To look after me. Today, I feel so happy."

This was a big statement for me. It was also a lightbulb, life-changing, thunderbolt type of moment. I expected Robert to be dumbstruck and in awe of my profoundness.

He looked at me and smiled and said, "Yeah, I have thought that many times about you too."

Wow! He knew me so well that he'd known this all along. He knew he had to wait patiently for me to work it out for myself, loving me until I did so.

These past few years have been difficult. I had taken myself down a path that caused me to damage my health. Do I wish I'd never done it? Sometimes. Would I be where I am today without it? No, I would not. Was it a necessary part of my journey? Absolutely.

I had thought that I had to struggle to be happy. That I had to overcome adversity to come out the other side. That I had to work hard all the time. Isn't that how most of us operate? Can we be happy without struggle?

I'm not interested in living in this kind of drama anymore. Isn't this true rebellion? To rebel against the idea that happiness only comes from struggle, sometime in the future, further down the road?

Can we be happy right now, here in the moment, even amid our struggles?

Gloria Steinem said women need to be less grateful and more rebellious. Perhaps we need to be more grateful and more rebellious?

As I reflect on my first book, Radio Heaven: One Woman's Journey to Grace, I realize I now have a deeper sense of what grace means. Grace is more than our adopted daughter. Grace is to be at peace with ourselves, despite our failings, despite our experiences. It is a state of being, a state of Grace. It is about happiness and wellness even when caught in the middle of a storm.

Grace means being transparent about our failures as well as our successes. Not overworking, overeating, or over drinking and thereby damaging health, relationships, and emotional well being, which sit at the root of so many mental health issues.

Dr. Sam Collins...323

I am grateful and I am learning how to be at peace with myself. I am ready to be happy like never before.

I am delighted to be happy. I am grateful for my life. I am 50 and I've made it.

Thank you, Robert, for your enduring love of a rebellious woman.

So, what is it time for you to let go of? What is rebellion for you?

Is your rebellion with the causes that are most important to you? Are you rebelling against systemic racism? Are you rebelling against inequality? Are you rebelling against the climate crisis? As you rebel, what do you stand for? For peace, equality, love, saving the planet?

Is your rebellion about the roles women are expected to play? Perfect wife, perfect mother, perfect body? It is time to change how society perceives women? How you perceive yourself?

Sometimes we must rebel against ourselves. Is it time to begin your own self-care rebellion, stop working so hard and put your health on the top of your "to do" list?

Learning to love and take care of yourself is not easy. And is totally rebellious. Moving on from our failures is hard. Yet, our mess ups, troubles, and mistakes always result in some learning and often help make us better people.

Declare, share, and shout about your rebellion. It will make it real and help you follow through with it.

Realize that you are not perfect. No one is. Life is for living. That's one thing that we have all learned in these last years. We each have our own unique path. We do not have to adhere to the social standards of what is or is not expected or get ourselves tied up worrying about what we should or should not be doing. We shouldn't be making decisions based on fear, which takes us to places we don't want to be, and then we suffer as we realize our mistake.

I stand before you now, a work in progress. I am who I am, and I love myself as I am. Warts and all.

That might be the ultimate rebellion.

The Rebellious Women

Sister Zeph, Teacher, Women's Activist and Philanthropist, Pakistan.

Sister Zeph is an educationist and a human rights activist from rural Pakistan. When she was thirteen her first article on Women's Rights appeared in Pakistan's leading newspaper the Daily Jung. She left school in grade seven, educated herself, and soon began teaching other girls. Over the last ten years she has provided free education to 200 children. Every year 300 women learn skills from her Skills Center. Sister Zeph's story has been told in an award-winning documentary about her life and that of three of her students, which highlights their struggle against child marriage, corporal punishment, and societal pressures.

Dr. Zareen Roohi Ahmed, Founder and CEO, Gift Wellness, UK.

Zareen is the Founder & CEO of Gift Wellness Ltd, which manufactures and distributes an award-winning range of natural feminine hygiene products. The GIFT range is currently the fastest growing brand of its kind in Europe and is a best seller in Holland & Barrett. Due to Zareen's commitment to helping women in crisis, over 5 million pads have been donated to homeless and refugee women as well as to food banks. This is all part of Zareen's vision to fulfil the dreams of her daughter who was tragically murdered in 2007.

Lilly Lewis, Women's Justice Advocate, UK.

Lilly Lewis, ex offender, survivor of domestic abuse, and victim turned perpetrator. She is a Woman's Justice advocate for Appeal London and the 2019 Center for Women Justice, and Emma Humphries Award winner for raising awareness of abuse of women and children by men. Having spent 4 years in prison of an 8-year sentence and losing her children to the care system, she decided to find her rainbow in the rain. Once released from prison, she realized she had to be the voice for women who had lost theirs.

armen Ward, Founder and Creator of "Becoming Carmen LLC, USA"

armen Ward serves as the Founder and Creator of BECOMINGCARMEN LLC. The sion for BECOMINGCARMEN came as she began to reflect on her own life. Carmen rovides motivational speaking engagements, spiritual coaching, and consulting services extraordinary people who are ready to share their authentic stories. Her fearless and edicated support, guidance, and resources help people take the next step to shake up eir traditional ways of thinking and become all they dreamed they could be.

Awah Francisca Mbuli, Founder and CEO of Survivors Network, Cameroon.

Awah Francisca Mbuli is a survivor of sex and labor trafficking, nearly a victim of organ trafficking, and the founding director of Survivors' Network, a female-led Cameroonian NGO comprised of trafficking survivors that raises awareness, helps victims escape their trafficking situations, and offers temporary housing, vocational training, and other essential services. As a survivor, she uses her experience to educate and prevent others in Cameroon from experiencing human trafficking.

Destiny Ayo Vaughan, Student, Ireland.

Destiny Ayo Vaughan is from Nigeria and is 22 years old. She now lives in Ireland and attends Waterford Institute of Technology where she is pursuing a Bachelors in Social Science. She is an advocate for child protection and sexual violence awareness. Over the years she's worked for different charities including Concern, Make a Wish, The Shona Project, Plan Ireland and Mind the Gap Ireland.

Pip Hare, Professional Sailor, Pip Hare Ocean Racing, UK.

At the age of 45, Pip Hare embarked on one of the toughest sporting events on c
planet when she raced a 60 ft yacht non-stop, single-handed, around the world in t
Vendee Globe Race. Pip launched her solo sailing career ten years ago with the expr
aim of entering the Vendee Globe Race and has progressed through the ranks
offshore sailing with steady determination. Pip has sailed fifteen times across t
Atlantic, seven times alone, and her achievements include setting one British saili
record and a world first in endurance sport.

Nasreen Sheikh, The Empowerment Collective, Nepal.

A 20 something year-old with resolute determination, Nasreen Sheikh does not know her birthday or exact age. In her native village bordering India and Nepal, girls' births are not officially recorded. Determined to empower disadvantaged women, she secured a loan and founded Local Women's Handicrafts in 2015 and went on to found Empowerment Collective. Nasreen is currently working on the ground in rural villages helping thousands of people obtain food and medicine, and empowering women with skills and education.

Dr. Ibtissam Al-Farah, Founder and Director, Lavender International Consultancy, UK.

Ibtissam grew up in Yemen. From arriving in England in 2004 as a single woman and refugee, she created a life with no family support, no recognized work experience, and no knowledge of the English language. She has since worked her way up to PhD level and is involved in projects for women asylum seekers and refugees. She has spoken at various academic conferences as a political analyst and delivered seminars for the United Nations Human Rights meeting in Geneva about women and children in war zones.

Jen Coken, CEO, Embrace the Ridiculousness of Life! USA.

Jen Coken is an executive coach for women who are ready to smash obstacles, jump over hurdles, and grab snarling dogs by the ears. For twenty years, she's been beating down BS with a velvet sledgehammer tasseled with humor. Jen is also a national speaker for leaders and their teams who crave actionable lessons from the heart, packed with a powerful punch. Her best-selling book, "When I Die, Take My Panties," is an inspiring, raw, and at times, funny memoir about coping with her mother's death from ovarian cancer and what it took to push on through.

Sarah Kitakule, Director, The Kitakule Foundation, Uganda.

An accomplished women's empowerment and private sector development specialist, Sara has been an active member of the women's movement in Uganda and globally. She ha extensive experience with leading international development organizations including th World Bank, International Finance Corporation, International Labor Organization, an the Commonwealth Secretariat. She is currently a trustee of the Cherie Blair Foundatio for Women and a Founder Director of the Kitakule Foundation.

Karen Sherman, President, Akilah Institute, USA.

Karen has spent her life advocating for women in war-torn and transitional countries. Throughout her 30-year career in global development, she has met and interviewed thousands of women. Their remarkable stories of strength, courage, resilience, and resourcefulness fuel what she believes to be true: championing women's education and economic participation has the power to transform the lives of women and the future of families, communities, societies, and, ultimately, the world.

Me at 16 yrs old!

Eileen Brewer, Accelerator Director, Takween Accelerator, Iraq.

Eileen is a global consultant, speaker, trainer, and mentor. She started her career as a program manager in Silicon Valley and worked on the US Tech Women program educating young women around the world about technology. Eileen works in start-up ecosystems across multiple countries. She can be found wearing many hats; as an accelerator director, a mentor, and a facilitator. Her focus is on advancing the status of entrepreneurship and start-ups across the globe. She is currently living in Kurdistan, Iraq to help build up the tech start up ecosystem there.

Dr. Sam Collins and Grace Collins Silverstone.

Women's equality advocate, social entrepreneur, coach, and author, Dr. Sam Collins has dedicated her life to empowering women all over the world through a powerful mix of speaking events, consulting, coaching, and mentoring. She is the founder of Aspire where she leads the team responsible for creating events and programming designed to promote individual, organizational, and social change. Today, Aspire has women attending events from over 80 countries and has positively influenced millions of women and girls from all walks of life. Her Majesty, The Queen recognized Dr. Collins for her contributions naming her "One of the Top 200 Women to Impact Business & Industry." Dr. Collins was also featured as one of the "Top 10 Coaches in the UK" by The Sunday Times. She currently resides in the US with her husband and 3 children, including Grace who is pictured above.

Printed in Great Britain
by Amazon